MAN'S WORLD,
WOMAN'S PLACE:

A Study in Social Mythology

by ELIZABETH JANEWAY

 A DELTA BOOK

A DELTA BOOK
Published by
DELL PUBLISHING CO., INC.
1 Dag Hammarskjold Plaza
New York, N.Y. 10017

Copyright © 1971 by Elizabeth Janeway

Chapter 17 of this book appeared, in different form, in
The Atlantic for February, 1970.

Grateful acknowledgment is made to Faber & Faber,
Ltd., and Random House, Inc., for permission to quote
three lines of W. H. Auden's "For the Time Being" from
The Collected Poetry of W. H. Auden, Random House,
New York, 1944, copyright 1944 by W. H. Auden; and
to J. M. Dent & Sons, Ltd., the Trustees for Copyrights
of the late Dylan Thomas, and New Directions Publishing
Corporation for permission to quote two lines from Dylan
Thomas's "Fern Hill" from *Collected Poems* by Dylan
Thomas, New Directions, New York, 1946, copyright
1945 by New Directions Publishing Corporation.

Delta ® TM 755118, Dell Publishing Co., Inc.
ISBN: 0-440-55163-3
Reprinted by arrangement with
William Morrow and Company, Inc.
Manufactured in the United States of America
Tenth printing—August 1978

"We live in a web of ideas, a fabric of our own making . . ."
Susanne K. Langer
"The Growing Center of Knowledge"

CHAPTER 1

It's a man's world. Woman's place is in the home.
Old sayings.

IF THERE'S NOTHING more powerful than an idea whose time has come, there is nothing more ubiquitously pervasive than an idea whose time won't go. The division of the world by sexes, challenged a century and more ago by the militants of the first wave of Feminism, still endures and, what's more, still prevails, in spite of new attacks upon it. "Man's world" and "woman's place" have confronted each other since Scylla first faced Charybdis. If the passage between is stormier today than it has ever been, the two old saws still rear above the flood, leaning together in logical intimacy, dividing the world in order to encompass it. For if women have only a place, clearly the rest of the world must belong to someone else and, therefore, in default of God, to men.

So old is this partition and so built into our minds and our cultural background that it still produces an illusion of inevitability and revealed truth. Outer space is reserved for men, inner place belongs to women. Even those who have risen to fight these ancient boundaries may find themselves trapped by the postulates prescribed by proverbial doctrine. I have heard the newest generation of radical women discussing whether or not they should "give sex" to men, and thus valuing their favors on the same basis as their grandmothers did. Every society has formed a set of conclusions and prescriptions for proper behavior on sex differences. Ours still does, and they are still far-reaching and deeply bound into the sense of identity carried by everyone. How this came to be, and what the effect of the division is on the structure of our society, is the subject of this book. For my purpose is to look at the ideas we hold about women and their role *not* in order to

investigate women and determine their "proper place," but to
explore our society, its beliefs and its dynamics.

Formulated no later than the days when ancient Chinese sages
first conceived the male and female principles of *yang* and *yin*,
the idea of innate sexual separatism still echoes in such psychological formulations as those of our contemporary sage and psychoanalyst, Erik Erikson. According to this formula, men are
active, women intuitive; men are interested in things and ideas,
women in people and feelings. Stand in the sun and experience
the bright, hot, active, positive male yang. Move under cover and
feel the dark, moist, cold, passive force of female yin. Little boys,
says Dr. Erikson in reporting a famous experiment,[1] * use their
toys and blocks to construct outdoor scenes of action and confrontation where wild animals threaten and automobiles collide.
Little girls prefer interiors, where their dolls serve each other tea
or play the piano. Man's world, woman's place, yang and yin,
make an all-inclusive pattern, and patterns are pleasing. There
is a powerful reason for them to endure in a chaotic and confusing
world, for they suggest control over life because they promise to
explain how the astonishing and menacing events we experience
fit together.

And indeed behind the pattern there does lie a system, inter-
linked, of thought and behavior. Ancient, mysterious, monstrous
is this system and all man-made. Who but we and our ancestors
before us have built the social system in which we live and
dreamed around it the culture that is its spirit and its expression?
Anthropologists, sociologists, theologians, prophets, seers, shamans
and witch doctors interpret the web of ideas we have woven in
an endless number of ways, but none is more central to the life of
the individual or more vital to society than the patterns of behavior constructed around the physical facts of sex differences.

When I began this study five years ago, the place and position
of women was a quiet sector among many other, quickened,
processes of social change. One might have concluded then that
the women of the suffragist movement had won the vote and proceeded to celebrate their victory by settling down to live happily
ever after in blameless domesticity. It's hardly necessary to say

* Source notes are gathered chapter by chapter on pages 308–314.

that what was latent and implicit at that time is now a matter of public debate. That may make my investigation easier to follow, but it changes nothing in the basic situation, for—as yet—*nothing much has happened.* Man's world, woman's place remain, and our society continues to ascribe different psychological attributes to each sex, and to assign different duties and ways of living to men and women because it is assumed that they have differing capabilities, moral, social and intellectual as well as physical. We may not talk so uncritically about woman's place in man's world, but (as we shall see) our society still takes for granted that one not only does, but should, exist. "Woman's place" is a shorthand phrase which sums up a whole set of traits and attitudes and ways of presenting themselves which we think proper to women, along with the obligations and restrictions that it implies.

Are these assumptions correct? Is it true that social and behavioral differences between the sexes, like physical differences, are ordained by nature? It is not only easy to think so (and restful to the brain as well), there is the most obvious sort of evidence all around us in daily life. Don't men and women behave, think and feel differently? They do indeed. And it is just because of these enormous and evident differences that the division of humanity by sexes offers a fascinating opportunity for investigation of the dynamics of society. For we can't assume that these differences are innate. This assumption is sometimes based on psychological tests, and the tests do show psychological differences that follow sex lines. But tests have to be made on people; and people, even young children, have already been affected at the time of testing by the attitudes our society takes toward the two sexes, and these attitudes are different. We cannot possibly tell how much they affect the way people (male or female) react on tests, but we can be certain that those tested have been affected (acculturated, the social scientists say) to at least some extent, which means that the tests are suspect to begin with.[2] Some psychologists believe that they have found reactions in babies which differ according to sex, but the conclusions they draw from these differences are not themselves subject to test, and some of them are farfetched indeed. If we limit ourselves to what we know for sure about innate psychological differences between the sexes we can go no further than to say that their existence is an unresolvable hypothesis. What we

can say besides is that there is little need to believe that men and
women are born with psychological differences built into their
brains because the workings of society and culture, by themselves,
are perfectly capable of producing all the differences we know so
well, and in my opinion they have.

I will not force my opinion on the reader. I came to it in the
course of my studies, and one need not share it, I hope, to follow
my exploration of the social circumstances which follow from the
existence of a special place for women in a world owned by men.
This is not a polemic but an inquiry; and what I am inquiring into
is a state of affairs that we can, I believe, all agree on: around
the core of difference between men and women, whether it is
merely physical or whether it is also psychological, a vast superstructure of myth has been built by emotion, by desire, need and
fear. Let us grant what I don't believe, that there are innate or
"genetically conditioned" differences in the psychological makeup
of the sexes. The result is much the same, for these differences
cannot be instinctive, they cannot lie just where we believe them
to be today, or why must they also be taught—and taught with
more sternness than goes into most present-day education? Why
do variations from them make us so uneasy—more uneasy than
the sight of physical crippling? If we are sure that sexual roles
are innate and inherited, why do we treat homosexuals as if they
had willfully chosen to be deviates? Above all, why do our standards of behavior for sex roles change from generation to generation and region to region? They exist in every society, but the
difference between them is always a little different. Woman's
place is always on the map, but it shifts about. Since the underlying physical arrangements don't shift, we have to assume that the
changes in what we think about them are just that—changes in
what we think. We have to posit a social mythology.

Josh Billings, the nineteenth-century humorist, used to say, "It
is better to know nothing than to know what ain't so," which is
practical nineteenth-century advice for how to run a railroad,
or conduct oneself in a going-business society. But we all know
"things that ain't so," and they are very often what we take most
for granted about ourselves and our world. They are the social
mythology our society depends on to cushion, to manipulate
and—above all—to explain the onrush of events, the demanding

present, the imminent and frightening future. But as gaps widen between what we expect to happen when we do things the regular way, by standard procedure, and what actually does happen, we may well find it wise to question both our expectation and the standard procedure which no longer works.

I intend to do just this with the customary attitudes, received ideas and mythic rituals that surround our vision of woman's role. There are no data more valuable for thinking about our social problems than the unconscious assumptions we bring to them, for they reveal not only where we are but where we want to go. The things we know that aren't so contain within themselves the seeds of what it is we want and hope for. The things we know that aren't true make clear the way we approach "truth," for they demonstrate the kind of explanation we can accept most easily and promptly as a map of the world. Let us look at that part of the map which includes the emotions we center on the old joined-and-divided symbol of yang and yin. We shall have to go back a bit and consider the making of this map, not in order "to learn from the past," which is always a rather doubtful undertaking (how do we know what it was like if we weren't there?), but rather to remind ourselves of the enormous scope and range of human potentiality. The present, taken by itself, is at the best of times a very small launching pad into the future, and these are not the best of times. We need the past, with its variety of human experience, to give us more room for takeoff. We need a sense of possibilities, including possible social patterns. We need a feeling for the way images and roles can change. Man's world and woman's place make up the human universe, and what we learn about the first two may help us deal with the last.

We had better begin our investigation with the yin side of the pattern, because it is the more specific: Woman's place is in the home. If we were to offer it for debate, it's easy to guess how the discussion would go. It would not center on whether the proposition is true, but on whether it ought to be true; not on how many women do, in fact, devote themselves to their homes, but on whether women in general should do so. Is home where they really belong, or do they have a right to range out into man's world and take part in its activities? Even if they have this right,

is it a good idea for them to use it? Doesn't working and acting in
man's world turn them away from woman's necessary tasks at
home? Don't they neglect their children, harden themselves and
destroy their femininity? Won't they be happier and the world
better off if they seek fulfillment where they have traditionally
found it, in nurturing and pleasing others, as mother, wife and
homemaker? Surely, in any case, such tasks come first, do they
not?

These are, in a special sense, unanswerable questions because
they appeal to opinions and not to facts. If one doesn't agree, one
can't disprove them but only disagree, or, more wisely, attempt
to change the ground of argument. Often such a response takes
a historical form, allowing that these opinions once did jibe with
the facts ("You are perfectly right") but that now we must look
again ("I am right too"). An advertisement in *The New York Times
Magazine* is typical: "Once upon a time," it begins, "woman's
place was in the home. But today's woman is interested in more
than diapers, dusting and planning dinner." [3]

This line is sound as far as it goes. Today there is less for women
to do at home than there used to be, and consequently some of
them get bored there. If they're bored, they're unhappy; and if
they are unhappy, that will in the end be bad for society and the
family. One must look facts in the face, and the increase of working women, who "vote with their feet" against staying home,
shows no signs of stopping. Beginning in the West, this tendency
has spread until it is now being felt even in the Arab world.

One way to deal with our shorthand scrawl, then, is to move it
out of the world of mythology and put it in historical context.
The trouble is that this doesn't seem to defuse it. The argument
goes on, adapting the old premises to the new ground. Indeed,
one development looks to the future and urges women to hasten
out of their old place and help men clear up the mess that their
world has got into. "One could make a good case for the fact that
the world is suffering from an overdose of masculine assertiveness
right now and needs above all a realization of the importance of
interdependence in all human affairs. Who could play a more effective part in creating this realization than the women for whom
such interests and skills come naturally?" So writes David Mc-
Clelland of the Department of Social Relations at Harvard. [4]

This is another effort to compromise the debate into a consensus that will please both sides: women have special natural skills which fit them for their traditional place in the home, but these can also be used from time to time in a larger area when they are needed there. The underlying assumption, however, remains that of a world divided in the old way into separate areas marked out by nature for the two sexes. Men are still the assertive innovators, women the healers. Feminine abilities complement masculine drives, but since they are different the former do not (read: should not) challenge the latter.

The point which emerges is that this new turn in the familiar debate over woman's place continues to take our adage as *prescription*, not simply as *description*. This is, I believe and shall try to show, a general characteristic of mythic statements, including the social mythology we take for granted today. We declare its tenets to be true because we feel they ought to be true and that we should therefore behave in ways that will make them true. But what happens if, for once, we take the statement "Woman's place is in the home" as if it were a simple description and ask how it meets the facts? The first thing we must do is consider the second term in this hypothesis, the word "home." To what reality does it correspond? Of course, this is one of the things we all know . . .

Or do we? Let me offer some remarks on the subject by the French social historian, Philippe Ariès, taken from his study on the development of family life in France from the late Middle Ages through the eighteenth century. "For a long time," writes Ariès, "it was believed that the family constituted the ancient basis of our society, and that, starting in the eighteenth century, the progress of liberal individualism had shaken and weakened it. The history of the family in the nineteenth and twentieth centuries was supposed to be that of a decadence; the frequency of divorces and the weakening of marital and paternal authority were seen as so many signs of its decline. The study of modern demographic phenomena led me to a completely contrary conclusion. It seemed to me (and qualified observers have come to share my conclusions) that on the contrary it had perhaps never before exercised so much influence over the human condition. I then went on to wonder, not whether it was on the decline, but whether it had ever been

1.e nuclear family

as strong before, and even whether it had been in existence for a long time." [5]

What Ariès' book suggests (and it is not the only one to do so) is that our idea of a "home" centered on one tightly knit group of parents and children denotes a way of living that did not last very long historically, or spread very wide geographically. His theme is the place and image of children, not women, in social history, but this naturally involves a study of the home during the centuries when children came to be treated as a separate class of beings, not just as non-adults whose status was very similar to that of other dependent members of society, such as servants, apprentices and slaves.

This shift in the way people thought about children, Ariès holds, was closely related to the rise of a new pattern of living. More and more the group that made up a household became the "nuclear family" of parents and children, living together in privacy and increasingly cut off from the wider community life of earlier times and regions other than northern Europe. Servants now formed a separate subordinate class, working within the house for the comfort of those living there instead of as apprentices or journeymen manufacturing goods for consumption or market. *House* was becoming *home* by separating itself from the world of work and turning into a stronghold of family living and leisure. This process, fairly swift for a social change of such magnitude, sprang up all over northwestern Europe during the sixteenth and seventeenth centuries and had become well established—in those classes it affected—by the eighteenth. The home had been born.

With it was born the picture of "woman's place" which we take to be traditional, age-old, time-honored and ordained by nature, a place isolated from the world of work and from the larger society, concentrated on home management, husband and children. From eternity to yesterday, we tend to assume, women dwelt in the bosom of their own families occupied by traditional domestic tasks, raising and ruling their children in the age-old role of mother-matriarch, devoted wife, skilled homemaker and mistress of the hearth, as ordained by nature. It is a charming picture, this, of our ancestresses spinning or sewing, with the little ones gathered around, the bread in the oven and the kettle singing on the hob.

It also appears to come straight out of a fairy tale. Not entirely, of course, for such families and such scenes certainly existed for a time at certain economic levels. But that home, that hearth, the gathered children were the exception, not the rule. Before 1700, except in very rare instances, it didn't exist at all—there were no homes in our sense for women to be in. It is fatally easy for most people to think of history, and particularly that barely illuminated area of woman's doing and being, as one continuous blur, a screen on which we project our assumptions. Our ideas of an old-fashioned home may be derived from memories of our grand-parents' style of living, or from nineteenth-century novels. We cherish the cozy warmth of such images. But the sort of home we "know" seems to have come into being as an ideal and an invention of the rising middle class, the people who ended the Middle Ages and ushered in modern times. Much of their mythology still sur-rounds us, and the home they created, as the middle-class revolu-tion spread across Europe, is the home we imagine to be the eternal, unchanging locus of women's activities. Note how this assumption strengthens the idea that woman's place is there and that there she should stay; for on the belief that she has always been there hangs the idea that, in moving away from home, she is acting to overthrow an eternal image and abandon relationships that have existed since time began.

Where were women, then, if they were not at home? If family-centered life is an invention of the middle class, how did people live in earlier times? There's no trouble in finding an answer. They lived in one or the other of two kinds of dwelling: the big house or the hovel. There was the castle on the hill, and there was the village clustered at its foot; there was the manor house and its cottages; and there was the bourgeois town mansion and the ram-shackle huts and tenements behind and around it.

In the big houses dwelt the elite, but not alone in their domestic circle, for the big houses were not merely places to live. They were fortresses, or economic centers, or both. Within their gates, the family was surrounded by servants, apprentices, employees of all levels, bailiffs and managers, clerks and clerics, and countless visitors and hangers-on. All told, about 20 percent of the popula-tion lived in such quarters, masters and servants cheek by jowl,

in rooms where tables might be set up at one time and beds at
another, rooms which opened into each other instead of onto a
corridor, rooms where no one was ever alone.

The rest of the population lived in the little houses, city or
country. They were, quite simply, slums. Sometimes they were
shared with livestock after the manner of Chaucer's peasant, "At
[whose] bed's feete feeden his stalled teme; His swine beneathe,
his pullen o'er the beame." The animal heat these creatures supplied was no doubt welcome in winter, for the little houses were
ill-built, damp and drafty, and firewood was not always easy to
come by. "Shelter rather than housing, and often inadequate at
that, was all that most of the population [of England] had ever
known," writes historian Carl Bridenbaugh of medieval and pre-
modern dwellings,[6] and he goes on to quote Thomas Nash on
typical seventeenth-century cottages which had "no other win-
dowes than to serve to let out the smoke, no other hangings, than
that the spider affords, no other bedsteads, or table-bords than
the bare earth, no other bedding than plaine straw."[7]

The poor were no better off in the cities. Crowded together
within the city walls which protected the merchants and markets
of the town, the little houses leaned on each other, opening on
narrow, smelly lanes and climbing over each other up hillsides.
If they were thatched, they were fire hazards—but who could
afford tiles? Even the growth of the towns often hurt the poor
instead of helping them, crowding them more densely together or
pushing them out from under any roof at all; urban renewal has
meant the removal of slum dwellers for a very long time. In seventeenth-century Coventry and Nottingham, it was noted that "a
great number of the inhabitants (especially the poorer sort) doe
dwell in vaults, holes, or caves, which are cut or digged out of (or
within) the Rocke."[8] For this "urban . . . proletariat of the starving
and the hopeless,"[9] the idea of a home and of family life was
unimaginable.

There is no need to wonder what it was like to live in such
dwellings then, for we have excellent descriptions of what it is
like to live so today. City and country, these little houses still
exist. In a town in southern Italy which she disguised as "Torregreca," an American woman, Ann Cornelisen, found "not real
houses, [but] caves that stair-stepped up the hill in such a way

that part of each roof was the alley-way on the level just above. Of course there could be no windows in such a house; the back went into the hillside and it was logical too that sewage dumped in the streets or even into [the] pipeless drains should filter down the walls of the houses below." That is the exterior. Inside, "conditions were medieval. There were a few houses with ceilings so low that I could not stand up straight. No one had water or toilets. They all lived on top of each other in one room, at the most two. One family of eleven people and two goats lived in a windowless room eight feet by ten." And family life? Miss Cornelisen goes on, "The old father [of this family], a young stepmother, a son and his wife and their two almost grown sons had bedded down in so many permutations that the five younger children might have been fathered by any one of the four men." [10]

City life in San Juan, Puerto Rico, under the American flag, is not so different. In *La Vida*, Oscar Lewis describes the "home" into which Fernanda, her man and her children had just moved. It opens on a paved alleyway about four feet wide and consists of two small, windowless rooms connected by an open doorway. The only source of ventilation and light is the outside door. The only water supply is a faucet in the alley. There is no toilet. Again, family life? Fernanda says, "Junior and I like to neck all the time and it looks bad in front of the children. Well, I'll just hang a curtain over the door and I won't let the kids in." It's clear she means the outside door, for she goes on, "I'll have to hang a curtain over the bedroom doorway too, but it won't do much good." [11] So any effort at privacy means that the children are excluded from the house.

In San Juan, progress has supplied Fernanda with a two-burner kerosene stove and an old-fashioned icebox. In Torregreca, there are gas burners and incessantly playing radios. But there are still chickens under the bed, a donkey at the back of the main room, and a pig, like that of Chaucer's peasant, "beneath." Unless the children are so small that they can't be expected to take a goat or a couple of sheep out to graze, the house is empty and locked all day. Women work in the fields around Torregreca, hoeing, weeding, or gathering twigs for firewood, just as they did in the Good Old Days when, for example, "at Lambourne, Essex, during the harvest of 1608, Grace Gage and her sister were employed by

Goodman Peacock to tread the haymowe," while in 1641 a York-
shire farmer reported that thatchers were usually provided with
"two women for helpes." Among their chores was "to temper the
morter and carry it up to the top of the howse." [12]

For the poor, then, woman's place was not at home and, considering the homes, one cannot be surprised. But what of the big
houses? Surely here the good housewife held her sway. And so,
of course, she did—but not over an establishment that we would
be likely to call a home. A noble lord, like the Earl of Pembroke,
might preside (as John Aubrey remembered from his boyhood)
over a "family" that consisted of "one hundred and twenty . . . up-
rising and downlying, whereof you may take out six or seven and
all the rest were servants and retainers." [13] That was semi-regal
living, but even the more ordinary big house was compared by
the economic historian, R. H. Tawney, to "a miniature coopera-
tive society, housed under one roof, dependent upon one industry,
and including not only man and wife and children, but servants
and labourers, ploughmen and threshers, cowherds and milk-
maids." [14] They lived together quite literally. Take a smallish
Tudor big house, like Barton's End, built in 1555 by Richard
Barton for his son John when he married. It had one separate
guest room, a great innovation, but for the rest, John and his wife
Mary slept in the main bedroom. Off it to one side opened rooms
for their sons and the male servants; off it to the other side, rooms
for their daughters and the maids. The only access was through
the master's bedroom.[15]

Everyone got up with the dawn, for daylight was precious,
candles expensive, and the ordinary rushlight too dim to do more
than help a weary maid to bed. There was, besides, a great deal of
work to do, for every house was in part a factory, producing not
only farm crops, but beer and bread and cloth and cheese and
often specialties for the market. And everyone had to be fed. On
August 1, 1413, it is recorded that Dame Alice de Bryene of
Suffolk, England, entertained a friend, sat down to all meals with
eight of her household and, since it was harvesttime, gave midday
dinner to seventeen more. All told, her pantry and kitchen supplied sixty loaves of bread, a quarter-side of beef, another of
bacon, a joint of mutton, twelve pigeons, and ale for all.[16]

We have to conclude on the evidence that, over the centuries when this way of living persisted, Dame Alice and those like her were not simply housewives, but managers of farms and workshops. Their organization of food supplies had to be based on planning which extended not from day to day, or even week to week, but over seasons and years. In addition they had to be familiar with methods of brewing and baking, know something about concocting medicines, tisanes and ointments, and supervise their application. Clothes had to be cleaned, linen washed, and fleas and other pests kept down as much as possible. Our ancestresses naturally didn't do all this themselves, but to the extent that they didn't they functioned as organizers of labor supplies, personnel managers, teachers and moral guides. When John Barton married Mary and moved into the new house which his father had built for him, it was Mary's duty to see that the maids, sleeping on one side of the master bedroom, were not seduced by the menservants sleeping on the other. Mary herself had lived eight years in John's father's house and had been trained in domestic economy by John's mother. During that period, John had been away living on the estate of an uncle, learning farming from him and manners from his wife. So the big houses were also academies.

When their husbands were absent, chatelaines like these might find themselves faced with even more demanding tasks. In the fifteenth century John Paston the Second, rich in the wool trade, went up to London from Norfolk to press important lawsuits. He left his wife Margaret in charge of his business affairs at home, and we know from the letters and diaries that the Paston family left that she proved a remarkably shrewd and able administrator. "She received her husband's instructions," notes H. S. Bennett, the English historian, "carried them out, reported action taken and warned him of his enemies' moves with great efficiency, and at the same time was not slow in taking things into her own hands when necessary. So she negotiated with farmers, threatened lawsuits and made distraints, endeavored to placate opponents and angry tenants, sent agents to buy and sell, to hold courts, to treat with justices and great lords—in short there was little that her husband could do that she did not attempt." [17] In her place at home Margaret Paston faced violence from neighbors who thought a woman easier to deal with than a man, and she fought back. Her running feud with the Duke of Suffolk reached a climax when she seized seventy-seven head of cattle and declared she wouldn't return them until their rightful owners paid rents to her, not the Duke. Hardly a feminine action, but by that time her house had been three times invaded by gangs of armed men. Throughout, her letters speak not only of her perils and exploits, but also of her love for her husband and her (rather dictatorial) concern for her children. In her life, woman's place had got thoroughly mixed up with man's world.

Meanwhile in the towns and cities of western Europe the house of the master craftsman or the merchant took on many of the functions of the country manor. Until quite late the shop or factory was part of it, and apprentices and laborers lived there and counted themselves lucky to doss down in outer rooms or shops, wherever they found space to sleep. At least in such circumstances they were fed—not always bounteously, for the master's wife might pinch pennies, but as a rule it cost more to supply their meals than to pay their wages. Dayworkers in the little houses roundabout often lacked the means of cooking a meal. For them, bread came from a bakeshop, not the housewife's oven, and on the rare occasions when meat came their way, they sent it to be roasted at an inn. Only as cities grew to maturity did the rich and great begin to live apart from their places of business. Even then the wives' knowledge of their affairs might prove very useful when husbands journeyed abroad to buy or sell or to set up a branch in another city, which could mean an absence of months or even years. Small shopkeepers went on living over their premises, and, as ever, their wives were partners in the business, and respected as such. "Your citizens' wives are like partridges," it was said, "the hens are better than the cocks." [18]

In a sense these women-managers were at home, in country manor or city mansion. But how do we describe the place and the status of the countless others who surrounded them, house serfs, maidservants, daughters of friends sent to be trained in house-wifery as Mrs. Barton trained Mary, wet nurses, kitchen maids, pious aunts and widowed dowagers? If woman's place is in some-one else's home, and the home in question is part factory, part workshop and part subsistence farm, the meaning of our maxim isn't what we thought it was. Nor was woman's work, in her place at home, confined to looking after her family. In fact, we must come in the end to agree with Philippe Ariès and conclude that our whole idea of a family as a group made up of parents and children plus an occasional relative and a few domestic servants isn't "age-old" at all, but has had a run of only a few hundred years. Originating in the fifteenth and sixteenth centuries (depending on the economic development of the region), it reached its full expression no earlier than the seventeenth century, and all the hoary traditions we surround it with can't be much more than three or four hundred years old, if that.

This is still, however, a startling conclusion, so startling that it is worth testing by means of other disciplines. Ariès himself calls in medieval law in support of his conclusions (it seems to support them), while I thought of enlisting literary criticism. This need not be very exhaustive or very scholarly criticism because we are looking for general assumptions, that is, for a common idea expressed in common speech. I took the word *home* as my clue, because "family" is still widely used in the old sense of "stock" or "line-of-descent," and I traced it through half a dozen good dictionaries of quotations in order to date its ordinary usage at different periods of time.

The derivation of "home" runs back through Old English "hām" to Gothic "heim," both of which can be found "in the primitive sense of village" (says the Oxford Etymological Dictionary) in place names like Birmingham or Mannheim. By the fourteenth century "home" could mean "native village," that is, birthplace; by the sixteenth, "one's own place or country." But when did the word begin to convey the sense that we now assign to it when we say that woman's place is there, the sense of family circle, or focus of family affection? If, as Ariès maintains, a whole new conception of home life came into being sometime around or after 1700, there should be a whole new usage of "home" that springs up after that date. Is there?

In fact there is. Before that date the feelings that centered about "home" might be warm with nostalgia for the place where one was born, or they might identify it with an ideal realm of innocence and honesty, a place of simple, unluxurious living, far

from corrupt courts and cities, a retreat from false hopes and ambitions. One might feel ancestral piety, as did Du Bellay's happy
man, returning like Ulysses to live out his days among his kinfolk
in the soft Angevin air. These were sincere, if stylized emotions,
but they reflect the individual reactions of busy, active men
dreaming of pastoral peace and relief from intrigue. The specifically domestic emotion that we know, the delight in the
Gemütlichkeit of family life, is completely absent—until the
eighteenth century.

Take an example or two. Vergil comes closest to our own domestic atmosphere when, in *The Georgics*, he bestows "darling
children [who] hang upon his knees" on the happy husbandman.
But they flash by so quickly in the text between a celebration of
harvesttime—grain, wine and olives—generously uddered cows
and playful kids butting and struggling on the turf that they appear rather as incidental addenda to the good life of the country
than as beings in themselves. The farmer entertains his friends
alfresco, "couched on the grass . . . while a fire leaps in the center,"
and if his "chaste home guards its modesty," this is a contrast to
the town, where pride, aggression and "insane mobs" are rampant.
It is not "home" in our sense, but rather an idealized life of unam-
bitious country virtue which Vergil is praising. And even the
classic restraint of this description seems less distant from our
ideas than does the Puritan vision of the family as a small con-
gregation to be preached at by "masters in their houses" (not
fathers), so that from "the highest to the lowest, they may obey
the will of God," as the Geneva Bible prescribes. This was not
merely a Calvinist view, for the famous Anglican divine, Richard
Hooker, declared that "to fathers within their private families
Nature hath given a supreme power; for which cause we see that
throughout the world even from the foundation thereof, all men
have ever been taken as lords and lawful kings in their own
houses." [19]

What a change occurs when we move across the dividing line
into the eighteenth century! In his "Lines to Dr. Blacklock,"
Robert Burns describes a very different paterfamilias. Far from
preaching continually to his subject-family, this good fellow believes that

>To make a happy fire-side clime
>To weans and wife,
>That's the true pathos and sublime
>Of human life.

In less than two centuries we have made our shift from the public
and the epic to the personal and the domestic, and with Cowper
we are already "at home" in our own sense of the word when (in
The Task) he offers this praise of winter:

>King of intimate delights,
>Fireside enjoyments, home-born happiness,
>And all the comforts that the lowly roof
>Of undisturb'd retirement, and the hours
>Of long uninterrupted ev'ning know.

Here is home, family life, woman's place. Familiar to us, it was
idealized in the eighteenth century and sentimentalized in the
nineteenth, but "age-old" it is not. Elizabethan and Jacobean
preachers, looking at home from the point of view of the commanding father, saw it as an arena for missionary work. Elizabethan and Jacobean poets and playwrights may well have been
reacting like the sons of such domineering dominies. *They* saw
home (at best) as a rural backdrop for the simple charms of pastoral life and at worst as a provincial backwater. "Men are merriest
away from home," wrote Shakespeare (perhaps he had been
preached at), and again, "Home-keeping youths have ever homely
wits." His younger contemporary, John Fletcher, enlarged an already familiar tag to read, "Charity *and beating* begin at home."
Perhaps he had not only been preached at, but had answered
back.

Thus the seventeenth century. But the cult of domesticity
trembled on the brink of birth. "In the eighteenth century," writes
Ariès, "the family began to hold society at a distance, to push it
back beyond a steadily expanding zone of private life." The writers
uphold him, as we have seen, and there is further evidence from
architecture. "The organization of the house," Ariès goes on, "altered in conformity with this new desire to keep the world at bay.
It became the modern type of house, with rooms which were inde-

pendent because they opened on to a corridor. . . . It has been said that comfort dates from this period; it was born at the same time as domesticity, privacy, and isolation." [20] And it was embodied in the home.

The astonishing thing is the rapidity with which this style of living spread. Obviously many social trends were working toward the same end: the actual and the proportionate growth of the middle class toward social dominance; the economic changes that culminated in the industrial revolution; and the loosening of older religious allegiances which had demanded that the deepest bonds of community should stretch beyond the family, these are the most apparent influences. The north European towns, with their comfortable burgher families and their relative freedom from the relics of feudal restraint, were early centers of such change. Women themselves, when they had the chance, were eager to see their families leave the backbreaking work and the isolation of life in the wilds for the growing cities, in spite of the squalor and the stinks to be found there.

If we look at a house like the one in Frankfurt am Main where Goethe was born in 1749, we find domesticity already in full flower. The house towers up over a little courtyard, with its back to the street, and touring housewives exclaim with delight over the kitchen gadgets, the ingenious furniture, and the great clock in the stair-hall with its suns and moons and planets and days of the week and the month and, encased on the front, the clockwork bear who grows tired just once a year and lies down; then it is time to wind the clock. A perfect example of the dream of family life, one feels, sprung complete from the golden days of its eighteenth-century beginnings.

It isn't so; or at least it isn't *precisely* so. For the Goethehaus, although some of the contents are authentic, is a replica. It was badly bombed during the Second World War and rebuilt almost in toto. Uneasily one becomes aware of something more than just a delightful example of early domesticity. The Goethehaus embodies not the past as it was, but the past as we want to remember it. We are in the presence of a modern urge to memorialize and celebrate domesticity not simply by preserving an example *of* it, but by building a monument *to* it. In the courtyard of the Goethehaus, looking up at this re-creation of an eighteenth-century

dream, we are not so much seeing history as we are stumbling on
the fringes of myth.

On the one hand, we have the statistics which show a steady
increase in married women who have gone to work outside their
homes. In West Germany, in the shadow of the Goethehaus, and
in England a third of them have done so, while in the United
States the figures have climbed to 40 percent overall, while just
about half the married women with school-age children are at
work.[21] Is the Goethehaus, then, simply a symbol of a way of life
that is over and gone, a "once upon a time" that need concern us
no more? Perhaps it is, but then why was it rebuilt? Why does
Philippe Ariès conclude that the family may have "never before
exercised so much influence over the human condition"? Why
does Kenneth Keniston enlarge on such views in *The Uncommitted*? "Americans increasingly think of the family as the center
of a man's or woman's deepest feelings and allegiances," he writes.
"In America the family is the primary area where feelings can be
fully expressed; and the emotional, tender, passionate sides of life
have become concentrated within our small family circles. Increasingly, the home is where the heart is." [22]

Indeed, the whole thrust of modern psychology, and of psychoanalysis in particular, emphasizes the unequaled effect of family
life on the child—including the binds and the traumas that family
relationships can produce. But such dangers only underline the
fierce vitality and need for mutual support which lonely humans
seek in the only truly intimate groups that exist today. "Some
families," writes Ronald Laing, the English analyst, "live in perpetual anxiety of what, to them, is an external persecuting world.
The members of the family live in a family ghetto, as it were . . .
[This family nexus] is . . . the 'entity' which has to be preserved
in each person and served by each person, which one lives and
dies for, and which in turn offers life for loyalty and death for
desertion." [23] From many other sources we can find dark and bitter
confirmation of the influence of the family today and the grip of
the home scene.

And all the time, in contrast, married women go back to work
outside the home—the increase in the labor force in one recent
year amounted to a million workers, and 63 percent of them were
married women. In March 1969 over half of all American families

depended on two incomes, and the "extra" working member was far more apt to be the wife than to be the son or daughter of the principal breadwinner.[24] What are we looking at in this apparent contradiction of fact and feeling? Is it merely that, or is it evidence of a profound ambiguity in our approach to life, an ambiguity that attempts to contain opposing drives by means of mythmaking?

For it is the nature of myth to be both true and false, false in fact, but true to human yearnings and human fears and thus, at all times, a powerful shaping force. Myth is born out of psychological drives. What we do not have, that is what we need; and that is what we present to ourselves as desirable and, finally, as "right." In this way does the statement "I want this!" become "I have a right to it!" We strengthen this mythic structure by projecting our fears out onto the world, whence they return as threats. So the fear that we may not get what we want, even if we have a right to it, becomes a threat to our desires and thus a justification for our acting against those we fear will deny our needs. Myth opposes belief to facts in order to change the facts, or at least to obscure them.

When we look at the facts around us, we observe that two-fifths of the married women in the United States hold jobs; more than half of them are mothers of children under eighteen and more than a fifth are mothers of children under six. These percentages offer no statistical basis for the statement that woman's place is in the home. Moreover, we have seen that a glance back at history turns up mighty little support: until quite recently, when women were at home, most men were too, and both sexes were working there. Home, then, was a workshop for artisans, apprentices, journeymen and many wives, or a trading center, or both; or it was a minimal shelter for overworked farm labor; or it was a great house which was both a center of economic activity and of general sociability that extended far beyond the family.

Over these facts, however, soars the superstructure of myth, sustained by desires, needs and fears, projecting its own air of plausibility and persuasion, capable of using facts as well as of ignoring or changing them. Let us explore this realm of social mythology.

CHAPTER 2

Whenever you begin, you will have to begin again twice over.
Erik Erikson
Childhood and Society [1]

EXPLORING SOCIAL mythology is easier said than done. The word *myth* itself, to most people, has come to mean only an archaic story, pretty, false, and totally unrelated to life. It is not, therefore, anything to take seriously. Others use it differently. Agreeing that the mythmaking urge did not die out with the Greeks or the Norsemen, they see the products of this process as simply false representations of life—the racial myths of Nazi Germany, for instance. The only reason for taking such myths seriously (this view of them supposes) is to disprove them and so put an end to superstitious nonsense.

I shall have to ask my readers to consider mythology and mythmaking from a quite different point of view. They are, in the first place, to be taken very seriously indeed, because they shape the way we look at the world. The urge to make, spread and believe in myths is as powerful today as it ever was. If we are going to understand the society we live in, we shall have to understand the way mythic forces arise, grow and operate. I do not believe we shall ever get rid of them and, in fact, I do not believe that we could get on without them: they are the product of profound emotional drives, drives that are basic to life. Sometimes these drives are able to act directly and effectively on the world of events. Sometimes they succeed in gaining their ends rationally and by logic. But sometimes (and particularly when they are thwarted) they substitute for action a will to believe that what they desire exists—or should exist. That is mythic thinking. It is illogical—or, at least, pre-logical; but from this very fact it gains a certain strength: logic may disprove it, but it will not kill it.

How do we think about it then? How do we manage the double vision that refuses to believe in myth but still takes it seriously? I have quoted Erik Erikson's advice on beginnings not only because his sibylline style makes him sound rather as if he had just come from a visit to the Oracle at Delphi, but because what he says makes great sense—as his words very often do. In investigating a psychological manifestation, he is telling us, don't try to proceed in a straight line, hand over logical hand. "A myth, old or modern, is not a lie," he points out in another passage from *Childhood and Society*. "It is useless to try to show that it has no basis in fact; nor to claim that its fiction is fake and nonsense. . . . To study a myth critically . . . means to analyze its images and themes." [2] When we think about myth, that is, we are to think about its purposes—its themes—and the material it snatches at to express, or clothe, those themes, for such material must have special, emotional significance.

In order to do that, we must think about myth analytically, but not logically—or rather, not *only* logically. Logic is an incomparable tool, once a problem has been isolated and the data that are relevant determined. But how do we decide the context of a myth? It doesn't come down to facts, as a scientific problem does, where logic helps us to form hypotheses and then test our hypotheses so that we arrive at demonstrable conclusions. Myth incorporates emotions, and against these logic will not automatically prevail. Facts can be disproved, and theories based on them will yield in time to rational arguments and proof that they don't work. But myth has its own, furious, inherent reason-to-be because it is tied to desire. Prove it false a hundred times, and it will still endure because it is true as an expression of feeling.

We have, for example, recently seen a number of books devoted to disproving the traditional myths about woman's role and place, some of them very effectively. But will they overthrow the myths? Only to the extent that they change the way people feel. It's certainly not impossible to do this, both by direct assault and indirectly, by changing larger circumstances in the world around us. Even feelings based on tradition are subject to change and sometimes with ease—when the traditions that upheld them are growing shaky. Changing emotions, however, is quite a different thing from disproving facts, and to confuse the two is, in its own way, a bit of mythic thinking.

We must, in short, tackle myth with different techniques and ask it different questions, questions that are anathema to scientific analysis and both useless and misleading for the criticism and evaluation of art, music and literature. Now, a number of people, if they think of myth at all, think of it as being some vague sort of art form. It isn't, and the difference will tell us quite a bit about what myth is. The questions we can ask of myth and shouldn't ask of art have to do with *motivation*. Our exploration of myth must take account of both what people believe, and why they believe it. In criticism this won't do at all. Even if an artist is able to give a reason for painting just this picture or writing just that book (and the more profound are his motives, the less likely he is to be able to explain them), he won't tell us a thing about the value of the book or picture. True, he may cast some illumination on the process of creation, but that's a different matter. Once the process is over, the thing created has acquired an existence of its own. It has become a thing in itself, a part of the world of reality. Whatever the inner impulse that set it going, the process has ended, and what matters is the impact the thing created has on the external world of events.

I must dwell on this point for a moment in order to disentangle thinking about myth from mythic thinking. People—and not only laymen—like to believe that sincerity and concentration and devotion affect the value of the work of art (or the scientific discovery) to which these efforts have been applied. In addition, analytic theory has sometimes suggested that art can be considered as the product of sublimated sexual desire, and even that scientific discoveries can be "explained" as a result of unsatisfied childhood curiosity about sex. Now, it's possible this is true. Perhaps the artist or the scientist did indeed take up his lifework because his desires and his curiosity were not satisfied in his formative years. But all that such an explanation gives us is his reason for beginning his work. It tells us nothing at all about the value that the work produces. To learn that (which is what we want to know) we have to ask other questions: Is the product good? Is it bad? Is it silly, useful, meretricious, ahead of its time? Where does it stand in the world of events, apart from its maker?

Motives matter to art and science only as *motors*, driving the producer to produce. If we ask about them, we find that we are dealing with the internal and psychological problems quite different from critical valuation. Why, for instance, do dedicated, hardworking individuals produce kitsch and nonsense more often than they do art? Why do curious investigators pore over mathematical formulas for years and predict the end of the world last Friday? Sometimes the same brain, operating the same way, turns out both sense and nonsense. During the years when Isaac Newton was working out his greatest discoveries, he was also conducting lengthy experiments in alchemy, seeking the philosopher's stone and the elixir of life with the same painstaking care that he devoted to the laws of motion. His motives were the same, his curiosity as intense, his labors as unremitting; what differed was the product. In the one case he brought forth the theoretical underpinnings of modern science, in the other, magical twaddle.

The point is that he did produce objective results and that these can be judged without regard to the motivation behind them. This gives us a clearer view of myth, in contrast to art and science. Myth does not detach itself from its creator and move into the world of reality on its own. It remains attached to the mythmaker, and when it affects the world of reality, it is because those who believe in it act to make it come true. If, for example, the Nazi myths had been scientifically accurate, the "superior" Aryans would hardly have found it necessary to wipe out the "inferior" Jews.

This brings us another step forward. If it is characteristic of mythic thinking to be wishful, it is characteristic of mythic action to be inappropriate to the end it desires to achieve. Killing the Jews did not produce a sound and buoyant Third Reich, fit to endure a thousand years. Let us assume that science, art and myth all begin with a sincere and dedicated desire to understand and act on the outside world. Scientific experiment is directly pinned down to fact, art completes itself in an emotional resolution which reflects some aspect of reality, but myth can do neither. Based on the same inner tension, its actions do not relieve the tension. The desire remains; the engine drives on, fueled by longing. The logic of the outer world may prove myth wrong, but it cannot reach the engine within and shut it off.

One more point. If we tend to overlook the distinction between art and myth, it is because we usually know the latter by means of the former: mythic themes inspire art, and art owes a great deal to the tension of mythic longing. But in art something happens to transmute the one into the other. *Oedipus Tyrannus* is not a myth, but a conscious finished drama by a great artist. In the process of art a theme, often a mythic theme, is taken out of the dark and placed in a context that jibes with the world as it is seen and understood by both artist and audience. The theme is tested as a scientific hypothesis is tested: by confronting it with reality. In the contemporary theater, for example, Harold Pinter is working with powerful, half-formulated mythic themes that frighten and attract us today without our yet understanding them. We feel the pressure of inexplicable emotions that we obscurely know are related to common situations in which we are all somehow involved. In a Pinter play, our involvements are worked out in action, they arrive at a climax and are resolved. The tragedy (or the comedy) which the mythic theme suggests becomes a separate entity. But myth *as* myth is unable to arrive at resolution and culmination, just as the formulas of neurosis cannot solve the crisis situation in the personality which has brought them about.

Then is myth just another form of neurosis? This, my last comparison, is the most crucial of all. Are myth and neurosis the same thing, the latter private, the former simply projected on a grander scale? There is much to make us think so, and certainly psychoanalysts have made great use of myth in exploring and explaining mental illness. Freud was the first, but only the first, to discover a correspondence between mythic formulations and the patterns and rhythms of unconscious processes as revealed by dream analysis and pathological behavior. Both the form and the content of myth have helped to light up the labyrinth of the unconscious mind. The opposite twins, the shape-changer, the cannibal lovers and the dark goddess present themselves as figures in both and represent efforts to deal with overwhelming emotions, efforts to identify them, and thus control them, by symbolization.

Fortune-tellers and analysts, in fact, make use of symbols in much the same way. The images on the cards of a tarot deck incorporate clusters and constellations of meaning; the images presented to the subject on Thematic Apperception Test cards, the inkblots of the Rorschach test, invite meanings to cluster about them. All of these serve as nuclei around which feelings can orbit and swirl, and so present an image of the relationship between an individual and the world he sees.

The figures and symbols of myth have built themselves up over millenniums as human situations have repeated themselves. They are abbreviations of emotional crisis, characters in an elementary calligraphy of feeling. No wonder that therapists find them useful for comprehending and interpreting the symbols which appear in neurotic formations. But can we reverse this process? Does an understanding of neurosis help us to comprehend myth?

Many, many analysts (beginning once more with Freud) have tried to do this, to explore the patterns of feeling that have crystallized into myths by means of the techniques worked out in their practice. If myth and neurosis are aspects of the same thing, one ought to be able to connect them backward and forward. When he named the child's attachment to his mother the Oedipus complex, Freud used myth—successfully—to identify the ground from which a neurotic formulation can spring. Then he tried it the other way around, in *Totem and Taboo* (to cite one obvious example), and the result was sadly different and thoroughly unconvincing. What Freud did was to imagine primitive society as being similar to a family in structure, and primitive people as being similar to children. The guilt of rebellious sons who killed their father was then declared to be the reason for the ban against incest which is found in all societies. From its publication in 1913 to today, anthropologists have vociferously disagreed with him.

This is not to say that they are always right and Freud always wrong. But his attempt to explain the myth which forbids incest runs into a problem that tells us a great deal about the difference between the two processes. Neurosis begins as internal and individual and in effect it remains so. If it uses mythic figures to express itself, it's because these exist already. But myths, in essence, are not simply common to a group of people reacting in the same way to the pressures of a given society, they are *public*: that is, they structure themselves for action in the real world instead of being merely defensive. They may start with private feelings, but they address themselves to public situations and they are understood by other members of the society in question. This can only mean that in myth there exists some reflection of, or correspondence with, reality as it affects whole groups of people who respond as a group. The distortions of a mad psyche are individual and private, and it is the business of analysis to deal with them

as private. The distortions of myth are comprehensible and persuasive to many. They must therefore represent something which
is going on in the external world that produces this particular kind
of skewness. Anthropology and sociology draw on psychology,
very rightly; but individual psychology won't serve to explain the
communal situation and shared emotions that give rise to myths.

One more point of difference between the proper approach to
neurosis and a useful effort to understand myth and the way it
works: analysts try to understand neuroses *because they want to
heal their patients.* But myth is not an illness, and society is not a
patient to be cured in any simple, primary sense. It's terribly easy
—and shatteringly wrong—to see myth and neurosis as similar
distortions of thought and set out to cure society of its ills by
getting rid of this kind of "sickness." But distortions within a
society have a basis that is more than psychological. They may be
so in part, but they are always bound up with social or economic
difficulties. What arrogance to imagine that changing minds will
remake the world! What a leap to conclusions! What—in fact—
an indulgence in mythic thinking, the sort of thinking that declares, "This is wrong, and I will cure it, because it is all in your
mind." Psychologists know better than that, in dealing with sick
minds; they understand that the sickness involves a relationship
with the outer world and that cure will come only as the relationship is adjusted. Social analysts would do well to realize that they
won't even be able to analyze a situation correctly if they begin by
prescribing a cure, for their own intentions will distort what they
see.

To sum up, the purpose of studying social mythology is not
therapy but simply and solely understanding. Any other approach
is touched with megalomania. If we begin by aiming at a cure, we
are clearly assuming that we know the rights and wrongs of an
enormously complex situation, that we know what needs curing,
and how to go about it. We don't. And we never shall, unless we
are willing to do nothing but listen and learn, to start without pre-
conceptions—including the basic preconception that the thing to
do about social problems is to "cure" them, to make them go
away and stop bothering us. This is the sort of misconception
which declares that revolutionaries are "sick" and (on the part of
the revolutionaries) that getting rid of The Establishment will set

the world aright. But, to go back for a moment to the Nazi example, what the Germans needed after the First World War was
not therapy, but economic opportunity and some change in the
social structure which would have made democratic political
processes at the local level more effective and more attractive.
The Nazi mythology spread through Germany because it appeared to take account of real problems. Its methods were false
and its answers disastrous, but it had its roots in actual needs and
desires, actual political and economic difficulties.

If this chapter is rich in digressions, it's because I have taken
Erik Erikson's advice and started again twice over. Let us see
where this has got us. Our aim is to explore the social myths that
surround us, shape and explain our world, and influence our behavior. They show up in the things we take for granted and the
attitudes we assume without bothering to decide why we assume
them. We must take the influence of myths seriously, at the same
time that we take their content with a grain of salt. We'll get
nowhere by simply disproving them in logical fashion, nor can
we cure them by psychotherapy. A neurotic individual has only
himself to please with his fantasies, but myths are plausible to
many. They gain strength from the connection that they supply
to their believers, the shared desires, the joint wishful thinking
that backs up one person's fantasies with another's, with those of
a like-minded group. They endure because they offer hope, because they justify resentments, but perhaps most of all because
they provide a bond of common feeling.
What all this suggests is that the way to study myth is through
a determinedly mixed approach. History, sociology and anthropology will give us data to check against the received ideas of
myth. Psychoanalysis will give us a very useful tool—as long as
we don't use it for the wrong purpose. Analytic techniques were
developed to study the inner workings of the mind, the curious
substitutions and connections and fantasies that shield us from
hurt and help us to hope. As we have seen, myths (unlike scientific
discoveries and works of art) remain attached to the emotions of
those who uphold them and take them as guides to behavior. As
long as we understand that any cure for mythic distortion lies in
the outside world, analytic techniques will help us to investigate

the emotional drives that power this distortion and keep it in being. The discipline of our familiar logic corresponds to conscious reasoning, but the techniques of psychoanalysis prepare the student to accept an emotional logic of feeling and its public constructions of myth.

In fact, I must now confess that Erikson's words on beginnings don't come from a discussion of myth at all. Instead, they form part of what he calls a "didactic formula" explaining the way in which an analyst works his way into a case of psychopathology, at the stage when he is seeking to know and not seeking to cure. "The relevance of a given item in a case history," Erikson continues, "is derived from the relevance of other items to which it contributed relevance and from which, by the very fact of this contribution, it derives additional meaning." Because the analyst is "unable to arrive at any simple sequence and causal chain with a clear location and circumscribed beginning" (that is, because formal logic is impossible), he proceeds by a kind of "triple bookkeeping or, if you wish, a systematic going around in circles." Wherever he begins, he begins again twice over.

This description is itself perfectly logical. Erikson is reminding his readers that a therapist deals with a mind, a body and a creature living in society. One must approach the problem freshly from each aspect, and yet one must connect what one knows already. In order to describe the way one approaches freshly and yet connects, Erikson reaches for a metaphor: "a systematic going around in circles," and it is a vivid and expressive one.

But what he has found is also, startlingly, a mythic symbol, and one which is as old and as widespread as any records of the human race we have. "A systematic going around in circles" is a very good description of a spiral. Now, from prehistoric cave paintings and engravings to the discovery of DNA, a spiral form has been associated with growth; and by extension, with the growth of understanding; therefore, with transition from one psychic, or social, state to another; with initiation to maturity and with other rites of passage, including the passage to death seen as a stage of life; and in exactly the way it is used by Erikson here, with the "conditional way" to the heart of a mystery. The spiral appears on the walls of Aurignacian caves and in Indian sand paintings. It shapes ritual dances and children's street games. The distin-

guished morphologist, D'Arcy Thompson, put a drawing of the
spiral shell of *Solarium perspectivum*, repeated three times, on the
jacket of his classic work *On Growth and Form*. To Anaximander,
the pupil and successor to Thales, who was Greece's first philosopher, spiral movement was eternal, assuring that "becoming shall
not fail." Vladimir Nabokov, in his memoir *Speak, Memory*, recalls
his "schoolboy discovery" that Hegel's triadic system of thesis,
antithesis and synthesis expressed "the essential spirality of all
things in their relation to time." [3]

The consistency of the metaphor is astonishing, but there is
nothing magical or eerie in it. Part of the complexity of myth is
that it contains psychic truth expressed symbolically. For thousands of years the symbol and the idea of the spiral have been
used to express the process of growth and becoming and the
intent which goes with becoming, the desire for initiation and
knowledge of emotional actuality. It is an axiom in a system of
thinking and feeling which does not oppose the linear reasoning
of logic, but complements it. The fact that Erikson found this
symbol to hand doesn't discredit his "didactic formula" but confirms it, by placing it against a background of millenniums of
human experience in which the same metaphor has been used
again and again for the same purpose, to express the exploration
of constellations of belief.

So, with our exploration of that commonplace, persistent tag
which declares that woman's place is in the home, let us begin,
knowing that we must expect to come around and begin again.
With this as our motto, we know that we must be patient, because
we can't expect to find everything out at the first try. But then
we are granted permission to form bold hypotheses, for we know
we shall have a chance to test them later. Our mythic proposition
will guide us by the emotional charge it carries, for argument
shows where the lines of force run and will offer us a center in our
systematic circling until, if we are lucky, we come down in a narrowing gyre and find a way in to the mystery.

CHAPTER 3

In earlier centuries most women in America worked, and they worked throughout the whole of their adult lives. In fact, whether a farm family was affluent or impoverished frequently hinged on the competence of the wife. . . . Exceptions were the small minority of families in middle- and upper-income classes who lived in urban centers. The major change in the pattern of women's lives occurred after the Civil War when accelerating industrialization and urbanization ushered in a rapid increase in the urban middle classes. . . . This isolation of women from work was a significant phenomenon in American life for only about eighty years—from the Civil War to World War II.

Eli Ginzberg
Life Styles of Educated Women [1]

LOGIC AND REASON deal with the relationship between facts. They tend, therefore, to speak in the indicative mood—as does Professor Ginzberg when he notes the long history of working women and the economic value of their labor. Myth, however, will not be argued down by facts. It may seem to be making straightforward statements, but actually these conceal another mood, the imperative. Myth exists in a state of tension. It is not really describing a situation, but trying by means of this description *to bring about* what it declares to exist. One might think that the hopeful, optative mood was more appropriate to wish fulfillment, but myth is more demanding than that. It doesn't merely wish, it wills; and when it speaks, it commands action.

Contrast a mythical statement with a factual one like Ginzberg's, and the difference in semantic value is clear. Here is Merle Miller, also talking about women at work: "They are almost always insecure and neurotic; they are out of place in the business world and ill at ease at home. . . . Eventually they nearly always fail at either their careers or their marriages, frequently at both.

. . . I am convinced that if at quitting time tomorrow all the married women in this country over thirty who have jobs were to resign, the republic would not only survive, it would be considerably better off." [2]

True, Miller was writing some years ago; but there is nothing in his words to indicate that he intended to confine their application to a particular time or place (this universality, as we shall see, is characteristic of myth). It is easy enough, moreover, to find equivalent assertions put forward today. Here are a few garnered from the stalwart and articulate Americans who reply to the questions put by The Inquiring Fotographer of the New York *Daily News:* "A woman's success in business has to be due to a man's help, either her husband or a male boss at work. She can't succeed in a big way without male help or encouragement." "Women are jealous of the success men have." "How many wives are successful outside the home? At what?" "Women have little practical common sense and even less native ability. They should remain what most of them are, housewives and mothers." [3] What Miller and the man in the street are giving us is clearly not a description of a situation, but a wish that something would happen. The wish gives rise to a demand, that women should go home.

But the trouble with mythic demands, as I suggested in the last chapter, is that either they don't work because the action they desire isn't appropriate to the end they seek, or the action doesn't take place at all. Women have not gone home, and they show less and less of a will to do so, even those who carry no banner of militancy. If the militants force a door open, there are women behind them waiting to surge forward into the gap, whether the jobs they are offered are as bank executives or telephone repairmen. The myth, however, pays no attention and continues to repeat its command: Women, go home to the place where you belong.

Why should this be? If we decide to question the myth rationally and ask *why* women should go home, we often get a perfectly rational and relevant answer: Women belong at home for the sake of the family, and particularly of the children. Within empirical limits, this is true. Children do indeed need to be brought up, and brought up in intimate, familiar surroundings. They need love, stability, consistent and unequivocal care and lasting relationships with people who are profoundly enough interested in them to look after them with warmth, gaiety and patience. They need sound human patterns on which to model themselves and guidance, as they grow, for the many possible experiences and ways of living which await them. Psychologists of every stamp agree that emotionally disturbed adults grow out of emotionally deprived children, emotionally swamped children, or children caught in circumstances which subject them to strain they can't cope with.

These are the prerequisites of child care. Mothering, within a secure family situation, is the obvious and the traditional way to supply a child with what he needs to grow to emotional maturity. Indeed, our current American pattern of family life depends on the mother for single-handed child-raising a good deal more than do other societies, where grandmothers, aunts and older sisters look after babies and children a fair amount of the time. The big houses where children swarmed in a swarm of adults have vanished, domestic servants have gone to work in commerce or industry, and the nursery schools and day-care centers that came into existence during the Second World War, when womanpower was badly needed, closed down at the end. In spite of recent demands, very few new ones have yet been set up, and those that have are not at all adequate. A government survey of the Aid to Dependent Children program made in 1969 found that nearly a sixth of women on welfare who were working or training to work left their children alone when they were away. Almost all the rest were lucky enough to have relatives who could help out, in the time-honored pattern. Day-care centers were used only by something between 5 and 10 percent, depending on the age of the child.[4]

Given this situation, isn't it sensible and logical to say that women belong at home? Of course it is, if the proposition is put sensibly, with regard to facts and not to the universals of myth. If we do this, we will set down a statement more or less like the following: "In American society as it is organized at present, the place for many married women during certain years of their lives is in the home, unless they are able to provide satisfactory substitute care. The time it is wise for them to spend at home can be figured as a function of the number and the ages of the children for whom they have accepted responsibility." Many men

and women have no difficulty at all in altering the mythic statement to conform with this limited proposition, or in living with
its requirements once they have done so.

It is when the proposition becomes a universal command that
we move into the realm of mythology. The imperative mood is
even more central to myth than is its emotional content. New
formulations of natural law, after all, may also produce emotional
reactions, as Galileo and Darwin both discovered; but neither
they nor their followers felt any need to *order* the laity to obey
the laws of gravity or of evolution. Their laws were provable and
testable in the real world. But mythic "laws" are based on longings, not on objective facts. The statements they make aren't
provable. Instead, they can be analyzed to yield an order or a
preaching. In psychological terms, they are not rational, but
rationalizations, ways of saying, "I want this and so it must be
right." In order to externalize and legitimize their wants, mythmakers insist that this is indeed a law, binding on all.

To deal with this problem, we need to change our question so
as to isolate the mythic element in the proposition we are considering. Let us ask, as we go around in circles, why women
belong at home if they are not married, or married but not raising
children, or alone for hours every day with children in school and
husbands at business; if home is no longer an economic center,
and the time and energy required for cleaning and cooking has
been drastically reduced by modern inventions?

The myth is quite ready to reply on its own terms. Here is a
recent formulation of an old, old answer. It comes from a popular
book by an intelligent and talented woman, and it is especially
useful for our investigation because it makes no pretense of
depending on logic or facts. "By and large . . . the world runs
better when men and women keep in their own spheres. I do not
say women are better off, but society in general is. And that is,
after all, the mysterious honor and obligation of women—to keep
this planet in orbit. We are the self-immolators, the sacrificers, the
givers, not the eaters-up of life. To say to us arbitrarily, as some
psychologists and propagandists do, that it is our *duty* to be busy
elsewhere than at home is pretentious nonsense. Few jobs are
worth disrupting family life for unless the family profits by it
rather than the housewife herself." [5]

This quotation from Phyllis McGinley's book, *Sixpence in Her*

Shoe, raises a number of interesting points. Clearly it envisages a world free of economic necessity, where a job is thought of in terms of emotional fulfillment, for it isn't take-home pay that Miss McGinley has in mind when she speaks of the profit from a job. This limits quite sharply the number of women Miss McGinley is talking about. Most women do, in fact, work for money, though as we shall see when we come to discuss women at work, "working for money" is by no means as simple a motivation as it sounds. Miss McGinley's view is certainly a far cry from that of the great-grandmothers of today's suburban housewives, the women Ginzberg cites, who expected to work "throughout the whole of their adult lives." They did it for money (or its equivalent), and saw little enough of it.

What is more important is that this approach to woman's place and woman's role transfers the whole question to a realm where emotion holds sway and factual data become irrelevant. Who, for instance, are these "psychologists and propagandists [who say] that it is our *duty* to be busy elsewhere than at home"? In a considerable body of reading on the subject I have not run into any. Even the militants (and Miss McGinley's book appeared in 1964, before the Women's Liberation Front was dreamed of) don't go around ringing other women's doorbells and telling them to get out of the house and go to work. They want to go to work themselves, to earn equal wages with men when they get there and be granted equal opportunities to compete for jobs at all levels. Why should this be felt as so menacing? It can only be on the grounds that this desire of theirs challenges the *universality* of myth. Otherwise, why should Miss McGinley, an excellent professional writer and a talented poet herself, *care* what they do?

But of course she is telling us why, and this is the most interesting implication of her words by far, for it ties our contemporary tag, Woman's place is in the home, into a far older and greater structure of mythology. Women belong at home, says Miss McGinley, because "the world runs better when men and women keep in their own spheres." The general good of society requires that each sex keep its place and play its proper role, or else . . . Or else what? Miss McGinley is joking when she declares that this keeps the planet in orbit, but the metaphor does imply that some kind of world order would be overthrown.

Now the preservation of the order of the world is the formally stated function and consciously held purpose of myth, and of the ritual behavior it demands, in all the societies where it is accepted as a living force. "Myth," wrote Malinowski, "fulfills in primitive culture an indispensable function: it expresses, enhances and codifies belief; it safeguards and enforces morality; it vouches for the efficiency of ritual and contains practical rules for the guidance of man . . . it is not an intellectual explanation or an artistic imagery, but a pragmatic charter of primitive faith and moral wisdom . . . a statement of a primeval, greater and more relevant reality, by which the present life, fates and activities of mankind are determined." [6] One does not challenge such beliefs without shaking the order which they impose and inviting the return of the primordial chaos out of which the world was made and from which it is preserved only by proper belief and behavior. This is why the myth must insist on its universality.

All of this Miss McGinley is hinting at: the reason for staying in one's own sphere is the preservation of the order of the universe. But she certainly knows, as well as anyone, that not all women are keeping to their sphere. The statistics of the Labor Department, let alone the slogans of the Women's Movement, make that clear. If women are indeed able to shift the orbit of the planet by their actions, *then they have already shifted it;* or, to return her metaphor to its place, they have appreciably changed the structure of society; and since society is better off if they don't (in this view), it must have been a change for the worse.

This takes us a step further forward. Not only is Miss McGinley writing in a context of myth, we can now make out which myth it is that her formulation accords with. As it happens, it is one of the rare myths which psychoanalysis has dealt with fruitfully and interpreted persuasively as being closely connected with woman's place in the family and her role as the nurturer of children. This is the myth of the Golden Age, the myth that tells us that society has indeed fallen from a happier state.

It is very widespread. Few cultures have not produced the idea that in some past era the world ran better than it does now. Eve had not left her proper sphere and shaken the order of the universe by eating the fruit of the tree of knowledge and tempting Adam to eat it too. Spring was everlasting then, wrote Ovid, food came of itself, and all were content. This was a green and golden time when the world was young and easy under the apple boughs, as it was for Dylan Thomas at Fern Hill: "So it must have been after the birth of the simple light, In the first spinning place." [7]

"This golden age out of the far-distant past is early infancy," wrote Bruno Bettelheim, summing up the judgment of psycho-analysis. "It was an age when nothing was asked of us and all that we wanted was given. This is the kernel of historic and psycho-logical truth in our dreams of a paradise lost." [8] And certainly, in the first weeks of our lives, each of us rested, a tiny ferocious ogre of greed, in the supporting arms of unquestioning love. Our time-less, overwhelming needs and desires were satisfied miraculously with no words spoken, for we had no words to speak. We were hungry and we were fed, we were thirsty and were given drink. When we roared with rage we were comforted by a ministering woman, whose place was nearby and whose role was our care. This Golden Age of beginnings is a universal, personal myth drawn from experience we all share.

The importance of these glinting, gilded memories varies with the individual. But within their ambience the statement, Woman's place is in the home, expresses a wish to go back to that Age of Gold when every desire was anticipated, to a land where fruit fell from the trees and roast duck flew through the air, a fairy-tale paradise which our earliest memories assure us once existed. Normally these memories form a kind of subsoil for later plea-sures: they have taught us how to enjoy experience and reach satisfaction. As we grow toward a mature control of our lives we grow away from them. But "normally" is a tricky word. Suppose that other people, or external circumstances, deny our right to control our lives? One way or another, there are many dwellers in this world who have never been, and can never be, satisfied *enough;* and there are times and situations which are so exacting that they "normally" increase the proportion of those who can't find satisfaction of their needs in the real world. None of us is ever satisfied on all counts, but there are degrees of want, and periods and situations when satisfaction seems impossible.

When this happens, myth wells up out of dream and memory, and if times are bad enough, memories of happiness once enjoyed refuse to stay put in the past. The glimmer of a lost paradise nourishes longing for a paradise regained. When what is real and actual becomes too hurtful and limiting to bear, the tatters of past contentment are rewoven into Utopian hopes and millennial strivings. If we were happy once, the logic of emotion asks, why can't we be happy again? And the Golden Age rises out of the past and flames across the future as an apocalyptic vision. Promises are on every tongue. "The World's great age begins anew." "We shall overcome." "Harvest time is here, so God himself has hired me for his harvest. I have sharpened my scythe, for my thoughts are most strongly fixed on the truth, and my lips, hands, skin, hair, soul, body, life curse the unbelievers." [9]

Sometimes these hopes produce collective action. Groups band together to prepare for the end of the world whether they see it as coming by revolution in which they take part or simply through a renewed gift of life, the arrival of the Messiah, or a Second Coming. When such dreams are brought to consciousness they can be used to construct ordered Utopias, beget new religions and shift political power. Left in the private dark, they run through the mind as veins of fantasy. But public or private, they share the universal quality we find in myth. The old order must pass for the new to be born, because it is exactly that, an *order* which is sought, a new system for all which will yet take account of individual yearnings. For mythmakers, the times are out of joint, not just their own unlucky lives; but they know this by the pain and disorder they feel on their nerve ends. Whether their plans for rebuilding the world are fantastic or not, this, the private ache, is real enough.

Now that we have set our proposition, Woman's place is in the home, in its mythic context of the lost Golden Age of early infancy, let us ask again what it means. In this relationship, we can see, it is a demand for the renewal of past happiness, which might be stated badly this way: "I want a woman of my own, whom I can command, and who will respond willingly, to comfort me in my lack and loneliness and frustration as my mother did long ago." With such a plea we can surely sympathize. This is the internal, remembered reality which corresponds with the external social reality, the emotion imprinted by the fact that children need mothering and get it most often and most easily from their mothers. Out of the need, however, grows the demanding mythic imperative, for our statement goes on to assert that a man does not just need a woman, he has a right to her and that right is a part of the order of the world. When she left her sphere she violated "the mysterious honor and obligation of women," the planet shook in its orbit, and the Age of Gold came to an end.

Phyllis McGinley's formulation of woman's obligation to her traditional role has brought us this far. Let us now look at another illustration of the emotional syntax of myth. In the summer of 1967 a study group of college students and young professionals was invited to stay for two weeks in the Bedford-Stuyvesant area of Brooklyn, visit local welfare and anti-poverty programs, and talk to a wide range of city officials and community workers. This Cornerstone Project, as it was known, had been set up the year before less as a frontal attack on the problems of the ghetto than as an effort to give young white middle-class men and women a feeling for what life there is like.

If myth rises out of deprivation and longing, out of the inability to control one's own life, if it clings to remembered happiness and dreams of its renewal in a new order of things, then we must surely expect the ghetto to breed such hopes. And indeed we find just such a mythic imagining reported by *The New York Times* in a story about a seminar held for the members of the Cornerstone Project. What is more interesting is the way in which it echoes Miss McGinley's words about woman's place and role. After all, in suburbia there are homes for women to be in and the pattern of life demands that they be kept up, that the children be clean and neatly dressed, ferried to dancing school and Cub Scouts, that meals be hot, cookies baked, husbands welcomed home and friends entertained. The real world, in other words, provides a plausible color to the idea that women belong at home.

For black women, the world is a different place. More black mothers work than do whites by a considerable margin, and some of those who are at home are there because they stand to lose their welfare money if they take a job. They are more often heads of families, and since Daniel Moynihan's well-known study appeared, the lack of a father figure in black families has become a sociologist's cliché. Any statement out of the ghetto, then, declar-

ing that women are properly subordinate to men must be a statement made out of need, not reality, a statement of myth, not fact.
Yet one was made.

"On a recent evening," runs the Times report on the Cornerstone Project, "the guest was Reginald Ecklestein, director of the
narcotics program for Youth in Action, the local anti-poverty
agency. 'The only way an addict can be cured,' began the bearded
young Negro, 'is through a woman.

" 'In my program I tell young girls they must be patient,' he
went on. 'The black man in Bedford-Stuyvesant is hostile and even
barbaric. Women have to understand that. Women were put here
to be hurt.' " (It is unclear whether by "here" he meant the world
or Bedford-Stuyvesant; but in that labyrinthine ghetto, perhaps it
hardly matters. The world beyond is very far away.)

"A girl in the audience slowly raised her hand. 'How do the
girls help the boys?' she asked. 'Do they talk to them, draw them
out, give them sex?'

" 'They have to listen,' Mr. Ecklestein replied. 'If she doesn't
listen, he has to turn to something else, like drugs. The only way a
man can be a man, is if a woman is a woman. A woman shouldn't
compete with a man, she should make him aware of what his
capabilities are.' " [10]

"Women are put here to be hurt," says Mr. Ecklestein to the ear-
nest young audience which has traveled into the hell of the ghetto
to learn and understand somewhat as Dante visited the Inferno.
Miss McGinley agrees: "We [women] are the self-immolators, the
sacrificers, the givers." The questioning girl in the audience who
thinks of sex as a gift from a woman to a man speaks in the same
key; of this, more later.

"A woman shouldn't compete with a man," says Mr. Ecklestein,
out of the dark and bitter slums. "If she doesn't listen, he has to
turn to something else, like drugs." And back from suburbia comes
the response, "The world runs better when men and women keep
to their own spheres. I do not say women are better off, but society
in general is."

What is it our speakers are telling us as their responses chime
and agree? On the face of it, they are demanding that women
subordinate themselves and their natural talents to men; not just

some women to some men in certain circumstances, but all women to all men always. Nor can they offer logical reasons for this, but instead invoke such misty concepts as the natural order of things, in which men are capable and women put here to be hurt. Here once again, played back more than a hundred years after the first feminists joined together to resist it, is the old myth of feminine weakness, of woman's incapacity and lack of value compared to the male. To the rational mind it is infuriating to hear it all again, with just as little basis as ever, just as little common sense; as if the natural order of things didn't produce capable women and silly men as frequently, repetitiously and monotonously as it breeds competent men and foolish women.

But let us remember that we are not talking about reasoned proposals, we are investigating myth. If we listen once more to these voices, perhaps we shall hear behind the demand for feminine subordination the statement of something quite different. "The mysterious honor and obligation of woman is to keep this planet in orbit." "The only way a man can be a man is if a woman is a woman." Is this really a description of weakness? Or does the myth mask another, older, more frightening and more fertile— the myth of female power?

CHAPTER 4

If a person continues to see only giants, it means he is still looking at the world through the eyes of a child. I have a feeling that man's fear of woman comes from having first seen her as the mother, creator of men.

Anais Nin
Diary, 1931–1934 [1]

"THE ONLY WAY a man can be a man is if a woman is a woman." We are still in the land of myth, but we are no longer talking about woman's weakness, limitations and incapacity. Instead we are being told that a man cannot fulfill his own nature and reach his full potential in life without a woman intervening to help. True, the form of this intervention is expected to be her withdrawal: "A woman shouldn't compete with a man, she should make him aware of what his capabilities are." But the fact that the action required of her is to stand back and let men act for her doesn't make the help she gives any less necessary or primary. She is being asked to withdraw by her own decision, of her own free will, to submit voluntarily. We can tell that it is important for her to *choose* submission, not just to submit willy-nilly, because she is offered something in return.

What she is offered is the knowledge that by her submission she does what the man cannot do alone: she bestows on him his full status. Her submission makes him a man. She and she alone has the power to create his mature strength, to show him his new, adult, face, to grant rebirth where once she gave birth. His dignity depends on her. Or so this contemporary iteration of an ancient belief declares.

This is the myth of female power and it is very old indeed, so old that we cannot trace its origin. The depths of pre-history allow much room for surmise, and perhaps Joseph Campbell goes rather far when he suggests (in his lengthy study of mythology, *The Masks of God*) that "In the very earliest ages of human history the magical force and wonder of the female was no less a marvel than the universe itself; and this gave to woman a prodigious power, which it has been one of the chief concerns of the masculine part of the population to break, control, and employ for its own ends." Campbell cites as evidence the "many primitive hunting races [who] have the legend of a still more primitive age than their own, in which women were the sole possessors of the magic art." [2] Certainly where shamanism, the religion of the archaic hunters across the northern hemisphere, survived into recorded time, women are often found as sorceresses and shamanesses and in some areas special powers are reserved to them.

Was the Golden Age, then, the Age of Matriarchy? My own feeling is that both concepts belong equally to the realm of myth; but whether or not a system of matriarchy ever actually existed, there is no doubt that women were seen, in the dim past, as supreme guardians and givers of fertility. Everywhere in ancient cave painting, engraving and sculpture we find evidence which confirms the profound significance that early man attributed to woman as sexual being. The very earliest art we know, which has been dated to the twenty- to thirty-thousand-year-old Aurignacian period of the Stone Age, includes the famous figurines of abundantly pregnant women, like the often reproduced "Venus of Willendorf." In these forms, small enough to fit in the hand but sometimes reflected in life-size wall engravings, an almost featureless head bends over swollen breasts and belly, and huge buttocks dwindle to narrow legs. More than a pregnant woman, this is the essence of pregnancy itself. Campbell believes that these "earliest examples of the 'graven image' . . . were the first objects of worship of the species Homo sapiens." [3]

These Venus-figures have been found over a huge range of territory, from western Europe past the Urals into Siberia, and everywhere they maintain a remarkable degree of similarity. Whatever they represent, it is an emotion that was central to a way of life which endured for millenniums. "Undoubtedly," writes Paolo Graziosi, the well-known Italian student of Paleolithic art, "the people of this ancient phase of the Upper Paleolithic were interested in the reproduction of the female form and emphasized the features specifically connected with sexuality and procreation; in every part of Europe and even outside it, this interest is . . . always displayed with the almost identical aesthetic canons, leading us to believe that so widespread a phenomenon must have had its roots in a deep reason, in a potent impulse, such as the diffusion of certain magical or religious beliefs." [4]

At the time when Stone Age artists were carving these representations of their beliefs, the power of the female to create life must have seemed awesome indeed for, let us remember, there can as yet have been no understanding of the part the father played. Anthropologists in recent times have found numerous primitive peoples who were unaware that the male seed was as necessary to procreation as the female ovum and womb. The myth of female magical power certainly had its origin in a period when the mother was the only parent, when her impregnation was as easily attributed to the wind, or the dew, or an ancestral spirit, as to the man she lived with. Kinship systems which reckon descent through the female line and assign power over children to their mother's brother instead of to the father also recall such an era even though the physical role of the father is now understood in the societies where they exist.

Indeed, the myth of female power may be fossilized in many other beliefs and rituals found among primitive people around the world. Initiation ceremonies, in which medicine men or secret societies or the elders of the tribe confer adult status on boys, have been interpreted as efforts by men to act out the rite of birth which nature denies them. The initiation ceremony can be seen as a statement that though women give birth to children in the ordinary course of events, men, by enacting the sacred rites of passage, turn these unfinished creatures into *men,* and that the latter act is as necessary as the former; without it, the children would never arrive at full adulthood. In token of this rebirth, the initiates often take new names and are always granted new dignities and privileges. The ceremonial social act thus becomes as significant as the process of natural birth and growth. It represents the acknowledgment by society of this growth, through the authority of the men in charge.

Now we find a young social worker facing the problem of how boys can grow to maturity today and be acknowledged by society as men. In our society no established ritual exists. Maturity, it has been assumed, comes automatically with age. Even in the Jewish community where the bar mitzvah ceremony is still honored and performed, this pleasant festival has no real effect on the life of the boy who goes through it. His schooling does not end, nor do his parents allow him one jot more of adult privilege than he enjoyed before. Western belief has held for centuries that the individual can be left to himself to grow into a place in a free, expanding world where power is easily available and adult status need not be conferred because it is there for the taking.

This era is over, Reginald Ecklestein is saying: "The black man in Bedford-Stuyvesant is hostile and barbaric. Women have to understand that [and] make him aware of what his capabilities are." Because society can no longer assure the transformation of barbaric children into responsible adults, women must be called in. Once more, metaphorically but unmistakably, we are witnessing an invocation of the ancient, magical force of the female who gives birth. Let her now put forth her power to aid in the rebirth of boys as men. The world of the ghetto, and not the world of the ghetto alone, has become so fragmented and disorganized that there are no longer social institutions or spiritual leaders who can effect the change of boy to man, irresponsibility to authority, dreaming to action. Where reality offers no hope, the world of myth is called in.

So the myth of female weakness which preaches subordination of woman to man can, it seems, mask its contrary, the myth of female power. This is a step forward in our exploration, but not of course a final resolution, for the myth of female power is as much a projection of need and a focus for fears as is its twin. We may find in this connection, however, an answer to an old puzzle: why have women so often and so persistently acquiesced in declaring themselves subordinate to men? Why have so many, as the suffragists indignantly phrased it, "hugged their chains"? Why have women preached to women that their role calls for abnegation, withdrawal from a direct confrontation with the world of action, and submission to the male—father, brother, husband, son, lover—who will mediate between them and events? These injunctions go far beyond the ordinary agreement that the world is divided between men and women, each with a different sort of job to do, but each job respected. They order women to give up not only activity, but dignity as well.

The immediate, pragmatic answer is that many women prefer to be subordinate because they have been brought up to be. We can't dismiss the obvious fact that habit, timidity and conditioning keep many people in uncomfortable places, whatever their sex. Laziness and greed are powerful persuaders too, for why should one want to change one's position if one is looked after and cosseted where one is? Rightly or wrongly, many women are persuaded that submission, frivolity and charm will get them more out of life than any other strategy. Some of them are right. Moreover, the traditional feminine role (which we will analyze in detail later) pushes women toward this pattern of behavior and also idealizes it: women are praised for being "feminine," which is another example of mythic illogic. Why should anyone be praised for being what she is supposed to be by nature?

But this is only to say that any status quo tends to keep itself in being, as a top tends to keep itself spinning. Of course, its myths will uphold orthodoxy, but a shrewd recognition of which side one's bread is buttered on is not enough to explain some of the sermons on the need to submit to the male which women have preached to women over the years. "There is something unfeminine in independence. It is contrary to Nature and so it offends." [5] This warning comes from a pre-Victorian adviser on female behavior, but it was echoed over a century later when Marynia Farnham, in *Modern Woman: The Lost Sex*, counseled her readers not only to give up the idea of competing with men, but actively to encourage them in their wishes for domination.[6] What can explain this more-than-acceptance of female passivity, this lust for immolation?

There is a school of psychoanalysts who reply to the question, Why do women act like masochists? with simple grandeur: Women *are* masochists. If we accept that this is a reply, we can go no further; but our look at mythology should now have got us to the point where we are willing to consider that this is not a reply at all, but simply a restatement of our original problem in mythic form. Women's behavior in putting up with exploitation willingly and accepting a role which subjects them to the will of others is so odd that the phenomenon can't be explained by ordinary psychological rules. So instead of an explanation, a name is given the situation which sets it off from the normal rest of life; that is, a *handle* is provided to pick up this queer condition and put it somewhere out of the way. In other ages we might well recognize such a reply as a signal that we are encroaching on an area of taboo, where questioning is not permitted. It is just this kind of explanation-that-is-not-explanation, and of refusal to go further, that tells us we are touching a sensitive point and therefore a significant one.

So let us persist in our belief that there must be some better explanation for women's acquiescence in the myth of female weakness than the response that that's the way they are made. Surely one reason can be found in the myth of female power which lies behind the myth of weakness. As Anaïs Nin intuitively guessed, in the quotation at the head of this chapter, the source of the myth of female power lies just where the myth of the Golden Age takes its rise: in the mother-child relationship. But now this relationship is being seen the other way around.

What we are looking at is the effective memory of the mother's power over the child which is *in reality* as complete as the child *imagines* its power over the mother to be. The grown child remembers the mother as slave, as loving nurturer who tends and watches and serves. But the mother is also the master. Having created the child as a living entity (and except for one not-unique act by the father she has created it. I am speaking of psychological, not scientific, truth), she now has the power to create it as a social being, a member of the community; and without her this creation will not take place, whatever ritual initiation the men like to indulge themselves in acting out. The child will not grow into an adult without her care, and the kind of adult it grows into will depend on her. Of course she is circumscribed by custom, responsible to her husband and his family for the baby; but the process of nurturing is hers and its rewards are hers. Every day she undertakes anew to love and to care for the child she has borne. It is this continued repeated choosing that authenticates her relationship with the child and sets up the psychological structure which is realized as the experience of motherhood.

Meanwhile, the child is in her power, is her toy. She can mold it and shape its habits, play with it, tease it, teach it and frustrate it, push it toward the fulfillment of her own desires and mock her husband's hopes, if she wishes to. *He* may assert his power over her and over the children, but she knows what she knows: that for a time *her* power is always greater. She can deceive him more easily than her children can deceive her, and she can manipulate them, frighten them and change them to a greater degree than she can be forced to change herself. This is real power; and to some women the fact that it is secret, where female weakness is apparent, makes it all the more attractive.

Indeed, the less control which a woman exercises over other areas of her life, the greater will be the satisfaction she derives from managing the lives of her children. A mother whose authority is limited to the nursery will attach much more emotional weight to what happens there than will another who works outside her home, or than did one who, in the past, directed servants and farm workers in productive processes that had an acknowledged economic value. The effect on the children of such a concentration of emotion we shall come to later. We are concerned now with the nature of this kind of intimate authority and the sort of psychological structure it creates. Elias Canetti includes some interesting speculations on this relationship in his study of rulers and ruled, *Crowds and Power*.

"There is no intenser form of power," he maintains. In the first place, the mother finds that she is no longer simply an isolated individual. Traditionally, bearing a child raises her social status. But beyond that, the weight of her authority increases because she now speaks for, and acts for, and can make demands for, more than one person. Of course this is most important in a small community; but what else is a family than that: a small community? In addition, her power over the child is absolute, and it is continuous. "She . . . feels a very strong urge to exercise this power all the time"; and the baby is there all the time, her intimate subject. Then there is the effect of their relative size. Physically weaker than her father, husband and brothers she may be, but there is no doubt that, compared to the infant, she is infinitely strong: "The concentration of the appetite for domination on such a small organism gives rise to a feeling of superiority greater than that obtaining in any other habitual relationship between human beings." This is guiltless power too. If she keeps the little creature prisoner, it is for the child's own advantage. Over it she enjoys sovereign rights. This is her reward: her care of the child "removes from her part of the long-standing burden of commands which weighs so heavily upon every civilized being." [7]

It is this bargain of power as a reward for submission which validates the familiar statement that women can best fulfill themselves as wives and mothers. It lies behind Marynia Farnham's assertion that "child-bearing is women's central function, and the one from which stemmed their major sense of value." [8] Phyllis McGinley, whose words we found so useful in understanding the myth of female weakness, is equally clear on the satisfactions of female power which happy wives and mothers may look forward to: "From the raw materials of four walls and a roof, a shelter over our heads, we will have made a home by the force of our own personalities. We will have warmed, cheered, and sustained the head of that house, turned progeny into a family. We will have learned a dozen skills and enjoyed the fruits of those skills. For us the baby will have taken his first step, repeated his first word. We will have heard the schoolchild call 'Mommy' as soon as he puts a foot inside the door, not so much to have a reply as to be assured that he is safe, life is ordinary, and that We are there. We will have been raised to a dizzy eminence as final authority, dispenser of justice, necessary Presence. A husband, no matter how willingly he gives himself to the role of householder or parent, never approaches such triumphs." [9] What better description of female power, in Canetti's terms, could one hope to find!

Miss McGinley's criteria are American, but this sort of interior domestic dominance is not confined to the Western Hemisphere. Social psychologist Robert Jay Lifton's experience of Far Eastern patterns of living is extensive, and he finds the reality of female power behind the mask of weakness there as well. "It turns out," he writes, "that the Japanese woman has an actual authority in human relationships within the family, often over her husband as well as her children, in many ways far greater than that of her American counterpart. Within this realm her service to others— her nurturing function—is her means of rule; her influence is all pervasive." Lifton tells us that the Japanese wife tends to be handed her husband's paycheck, to control the purse strings and dole out an allowance to him. If this is so, she has more domestic economic dominance than most American wives, for whom this is not a usual pattern. Indeed, Lifton feels, "When Americans have become sufficiently intimate with Japanese life to observe these patterns, it has been their turn to look on with horror and fascination at the Japanese woman's way of treating her husband in public as uncontested lord and master, and in private as another child in need of maternal care." [10]

So when women cling to their traditional role, it is not primarily because they find masochistic pleasure in being dominated (though no doubt some do) but because this role offers them power too: private power in return for public submission. This is the regular, orthodox bargain by which men run the world and allow women to rule in their own place. Some times it is a better bargain than at others. When women's activities are publicly acknowledged to have social and economic value, when within their place they can control the work to be done and order its processes, when they do not feel themselves isolated and cut off from man's world by a barrier of incomprehension, then the bargain will be accepted unquestioningly by a great majority of women. Enough authority within their traditional place balances an external subordination that is not too wounding.

Let us not stop here, however, with a summing-up because there is more to be learned from this arrangement if we follow Erikson's advice and look at it from another angle. The balance of private power and public submission which women accept touches only the factual aspect of their position. It assumes that power and weakness are separate and opposite things, contraries that contradict and offset each other. But they are not, not in the realm of myth which grows out of the interior world of feeling.

In that inner world, opposites are two sides of the same coin, as Freud found in his dream analysis. Positive and negative show the same picture. Power and weakness flow into each other. They are not divided, but are aspects of the same inner emotional tension. In mythic identification of power and weakness, women immolate themselves as a sign of strength. They are the givers; but how can one give if one does not possess riches and substance?

The double myth of female weakness and female power is not a contradiction, or a mask over reality, but two streams of feeling which comingle and feed each other. Not only does one aspect support the other, so that the weak are able to dream they have power, and the powerful find they can retreat into irresponsibility. There is an ambiguity at the heart of the psychic situation producing both myths which links the two, so that one can become the other, so that each implies the other.

Both rise in the mother-child relationship. Let us look again at this duality, which is in fact a mutuality. It offers both members a supreme satisfaction, a field of force that influences everything moving within its reach. It has no single measure of feeling as the sexual relationship does in orgasm, but it offers a gradient of satisfaction which, taken overall, can compare with that. For the child, it represents the Golden Age of apparent omnipotence, when the world seemed to bend to his will simply because he wanted it to and his wishes were answered without any action on his part. For the mother, Canetti's description seems valid: "It gives rise to a feeling of superiority greater than that obtaining in any other habitual relationship between human beings." Yet for each participant, the enormous power enjoyed depends on the other's presence, the child to demand and receive, the mother to give and to dominate. Without the other, the power vanishes. Here is the paradox: women are weak because they can be strong only through giving. They are strong because what they give is needed, and the need assures that their dominance will continue.

The enormous emotional tension of the mother-child relationship can be illustrated in another way. Within the Christian religion, whose cultural patterns still influence contemporary ways of feeling and of seeing the world, if not our way of behaving, it stands at one pole (the other being the passion, death and resurrection of Christ). It is peculiar to Christianity, of all major religions, that the myth of female power presents women not as goddesses, or symbolized by the Great Goddess, but as typified by the Mother of God. Her divinity is no longer her own, but depends on her motherhood. It has become reflected and vicarious. The two myths, that is, are here connected and compounded. Power and weakness meet and the necessary mother is dependent for her sacredness on her son.

At this point we reach a place where our exploration of the nature of myth requires a further attempt at differentiation and definition. We have seen that mythic propositions differ from factual statements because they incorporate desires and demands. They differ from the process of art and invention because they give rise to no formed and finished works which exist autonomously, apart from their creator and his intentions. They differ from neurotic formations because they include an element of commonality, which corresponds to some pressure that exists in the world outside the individual and groups him with others instead of dividing him from them. It is time now to consider how myth differs from religion.

CHAPTER 5

Why do you look around to see what He delivers you from, when He delivers you from evil? There is no need to go far afield, there is no need to cast your mind in every direction. Return inwards, look within yourself; you yourself are still in this evil state. When, therefore, God delivers you from yourself, He delivers you from evil.

St. Augustine, in a sermon to a
Council of Bishops in Carthage, May 5, 418 [1]

AUGUSTINE'S POWERFUL yet simple rhetoric was addressed to a world as confused and shaken as our own. The Goths and Vandals were on the move, the old order was changing, and Rome itself had been sacked by Alaric in 410. The ancient myths had fallen to the ground long since. Augustine, brought up a Christian, had lapsed from his belief and reembraced it only in mature years. Out of this troubled history sprang some thinking fundamental to the later structure of Christian faith, but beyond this, Augustine's emotions had been profoundly involved in his struggle between doubt and faith. What he says here touches exactly on the line where religion differentiates itself from myth.

The religious and the mythic ways of thought both spring from longing, but what myth wants is satisfaction in the here and now. Whether it wishes to preserve the old order of the universe, or to sweep it away and establish a system closer to the desires of the lost and dispossessed, it is in this world that the myth must operate. Freedom Now; Peace, Bread and Land; the millennial kingdom the German Anabaptists hoped to establish in Münster, these are mythic concepts at work on the social order.

Religion, however, places its hopes in another sphere: faith drives a man to transcend his personal satisfactions. To be saved, he must be delivered from the boundaries of himself even if this involves his own sacrifice. A Buddhist, he hopes to achieve a final dissolution of the self. A Christian, he sees the self as a continuing instrument of transcendence. But in any case, personal desires lose their importance and are subordinated to the rule of higher law or to the good of others.

No religion, however, is free of myth. For one thing, mythic images provide a vivid way of interpreting and communicating the revealed truths of any religion to its more simple believers. Such images, close to emotional reality, have a life of their own. Even if a religion has passed into limbo, its God declared dead, and the law He established no longer relevant to a changed way of life, the images in which it expressed its creed may endure. Formed on the template of religious reasoning, promising an order which no longer exists, myth falls toward its primitive roots of passionate, unsatisfied desire. But just as it can attach itself to a few facts and enlarge on them, just as it can inspire art, just as it incorporates and expresses psychological truths felt by many, so it may also bear the marks of religious thought and feeling, and at times invoke the transcendence of self.

If the myth of female power reflects the individual's experience of an all-powerful but all-giving mother, it also bears the stamp of the ancient religious representation of such a mother in the figure of the Great Goddess. She was, as we have noted, the giver of fertility, and this was not only the fertility of the hunters themselves, but of the game on which they depended for food. A very early aspect of the Great Goddess was that of Mistress of the Animals, for the maintenance and increase of the animal food supply must have been at least as important to early man as the maintenance of the tribe of hunters itself. Men must have been counted as mouths-to-feed before they became hands-for-labor, in times of famine and ever-present peril. The Eskimos, who were Stone Age men till yesterday, did not hesitate at infanticide if the animal population could not support the human.

We can feel the importance of the animals to those early hunters in the emotional power of the Aurignacian and Magdalenian cave paintings of bison and lions, horses and deer, apparent across tens of thousands of years. They themselves, in fact, seem to have been thought of not only as prey to be magicked into existence, but as sacred beings. Though they could be killed, they had still

to be feared and revered. Again and again one finds suggestions
(repeated at a later date in the reverence shown to totem animals
in primitive societies everywhere) that these great beasts "gave
themselves" to the hunters, a concept which is already close to
the divine figure who dies for the people. To preserve the fertility
of the herds, then, became not only a practical necessity, but a
religious duty. What rites were practiced in the holy places and
sanctuaries of the deep caves no one can tell, but we do find
everywhere among the throngs of engraved and painted animals
on the walls and ceilings the female sign, the vulva, symbol of
the power of birth and rebirth.[2]

Nor did the Goddess die with the hunters. When, ten thousand
or so years ago, the gatherers and users of plants for food and fiber
began to cultivate them deliberately, when agriculture supple-
mented the hunters' game and set off the first population explosion
by providing a new and relatively secure food supply, the Goddess's ancient power of increase and of fertility was still granted
her. Here we begin to know her names: Demeter, Ceres, the Corn
Mother, whose influence was felt down to the last century when,
in rural England, the first sheaf of corn cut at harvest was still
woven into the "corn dolly" and kept over the winter to assure
that the fields would bear again the following year.

Probably it was pastoralists and herdsmen who brought the
Father God of the Sky down to do battle with the Mother Goddess, for it must have been they who first learned and controlled
the male part in procreation, the role of the bull and the ram. In
effect, this God and his priests were declaring that they too could
increase the herds and take over this duty from the Goddess. But
even then the myth of female weakness which saw the woman
as a mere vessel to nurture and give birth to the male seed did
not triumph quickly over the Goddess's divinity. In the Neolithic
town of Catal Hüyük on the Anatolian plain, wall reliefs have
been found depicting the Goddess giving birth to bulls and a ram,
and all this about three thousand years after the domestication
of sheep. Clearly the Goddess still retained her power to give
birth, even to the symbol of the challenging male principle.[3]

The shadow of the Goddess can still be discerned in the stubbornly surviving, secretly satisfying myth of female power. We
have seen it invoked to shore up the self-esteem of the suburban

housewife, and we have seen it called on to come into play as a social force in the Negro ghetto. In the latter case it shows most clearly its connection with religion. This is not because black people are closer to primitive creeds than are whites, but because in the ghetto men are caught in an extreme situation. All of us are aware that life is more uncertain and our social structure less coherent than it was; and a coherent social structure, whether it is just or unjust, at least has the merit of being predictable. For the young men in Bedford-Stuyvesant the social system is both unjust and unpredictable. When the future is unknown, and therefore by definition uncontrollable, men may hope, but they cannot hope rationally. Old myths form again. As men who are starving dream of food, men who have been forced to live with frustration and impotence can go on living only if they more or less deny the truth of their circumstances—or find other values which outweigh their condition. The first reaction is mythic, the second religious.

The quickest way out of the ghetto is by another way entirely—by drugs, which turn an unbearable life into a dream. But it is also a way out of the world. In order to stop his charges from taking that way, Ecklestein, the young social worker, was trying to bring to bear the ancient mystery of female power: "The only way an addict can be cured is through a woman." But he was asking something more as well: that the women who "are put here to be hurt" transcend themselves in an expression not of mythic, but of religious, feeling. We noted earlier that the women who are destined victims are being asked to choose their sacrifice. Now we see the significance of this choice: it is an act which transcends the self. Freely willing it, these women must decide to be patient, refuse to compete with men who cannot endure such a challenge, and without a word, by listening alone, reveal to a man what his capabilities are. Sacrifice is not enforced, it is beseeched, and behind the pleas we feel the presence of the Mother Goddess: who but she can be asked to give up her power out of love?

Of course these correspondences and echoes of the rites of religion are psychic analogies, no more. Like dream symbology, they are metaphors. But they are metaphors which repeat ancient patterns of religious thought and are capable of wakening the feelings that such images have always evoked. Thus the acceptance of the role of sacrifice is felt not just as a means of deliverance from the guilty self and its limitations, but as an opportunity for creation. By the abnegation of herself, the woman is given an opportunity to create a man, a whole and mature social creature. Such a creation is a metaphor for divine power, the old power of the Mother Goddess, who heals, renews, absolves and offers life.

So in exploring myth, we find not only the ambiguity of feeling, where weakness and power reflect each other, connect and mingle, but also ancient patterns of thought lying close beneath the surface of ordinary life. They have been stumbled on often enough before and deplored as superstitious survivals among ignorant, primitive folk. They have, on the other hand, been saluted as archetypes of a collective unconscious, mysterious and powerful, at work in the depths of individual minds. Sometimes these traces of the past compel belief and honor even today in those who are sensitive to their influence. For the fine poet Robert Graves, the special symbols and attributes of the Goddess are the only source of true poetry. Painting and sculpture as well as literature have often reworked mythic themes, but the psychological impact of modern art has been seen as similar at a deeper level. Mircea Eliade, the well-known student of myth, finds the obscurity and difficulty of some contemporary art cognate with the deliberate mystery of myth: "Such works," he writes, "represent closed worlds, hermetic universes that cannot be entered except by overcoming immense difficulties, *like the initiatory ordeal of the archaic and traditional societies.*" [4] Thus our commonplace tag, Woman's place is in the home, has led us to discover fossilized remains of sacred belief and ritual lurking beneath popular expositions of woman's role, and desperate efforts to salvage lives being wrecked by extremes of deprivation and depersonalization.

Similar remains can be traced in another field which seems at first totally unrelated: in pornographic writing. But pornography is also an area characterized by incoherent passion and outraged dispute, where reasoned discussion seems outlawed. If we are right in thinking that such reactions indicate lines of social strain, we may expect to find the mythic process at work here.

So we do—and something more as well. It is characteristic of pornography that women submit willingly to outrage and choose victimization. They are raped and fall in love with the rapist, demanding the same treatment again. They are flogged and show the marks of the whip with pride and pleasure. They are chained to walls, imprisoned in cells, immured in harems, dressed in odd costumes which represent them to themselves and to others in roles compelled from outside—to the degree that the human mind can contrive new insults to individual autonomy, they submit to them, indeed they ask for them.

The purpose of this choice of utter submission is to absolve the man who inflicts the outrages on them of his guilt. He is allowed to be outrageous, licensed to perform acts of cruelty which lose their consequences of punishment. His most exaggerated desires are legitimized. He may commit the sin of Adam or the sin of Lucifer, or any other sin, and go free, because his victims choose their fates.

But the ability to grant such a pardon is a strange one for a victim to possess. Are these really victims? Or are they, in the ambiguous realm of mythology, priestesses empowered to perform the rite of absolution? When, in pornographic literature, the sadistic hero turns masochist and subjects himself to the whip, it is a woman who wields it. Both the acceptance and infliction of pain-which-is-pleasure become ritual acts. In the first, the hero is absolved by the forgiveness of the victim. In the second, he finds absolution through penance, and so is once more permitted to perform the extremes of outrage which bring him satisfaction. In each case, the agent of absolution is the woman. In the fantasies of pornography we do not find what we might expect, sheer amorality, the freedom to commit any sin at all, but instead a queer distortion of the forms of religion. The all-powerful hero enjoys his license to sin because he has granted his victim the power to absolve him, which power is divine.

Let us look at how this pattern works itself out in an example of contemporary pornographic writing, *The Story of O*, a book which was widely reviewed when it appeared as a successful effort to raise pornography to a serious literary level.[5] The religious element is not only present here, it forms the climax of the tale. O, the heroine, is kidnapped, beaten and chained in the classic style. When she has submitted herself entirely to the two men who possess her, and indicated her acceptance of this submission by wearing a chain which is linked into her flesh, she becomes, if not a goddess, then a sacred monster. She is, at any rate, given the trappings of one of the animal-headed deities such as were worshiped by the Egyptians and presented, naked and masked, as a figure of awe which both terrifies and inspires the onlookers. By accepting and acting the role of submissive woman to its uttermost extreme, she ceases to be a woman at all, for she passes beyond the realm of the human. Whether she is goddess or sacrifice, she has become a sacred object through complete depersonalization. The ambiguity of her situation is intended by the author and it gives an eerie horror to the final pages of the book which convey the real psychic terror of the sacred and the taboo.

There is another connection between these priestesses of pornography and the Great Goddess of times past. Like her, and like the myth of a Golden Age in which all was permitted, they can be traced back to the primary mother-child relationship of early infancy. Steven Marcus, in his study of nineteenth-century sexuality and pornography, *The Other Victorians,* makes these linkages clear. "Pornotopia" is what he christens the sexual Utopia which the works he is examining describe, and he sees it as a version of the lost Age of Gold. "Pornotopia is literally a world of grace abounding to the chief of sinners," he writes, finding the language of religion appropriate to his scene. "All men in it are always and infinitely potent; all women fecundate with lust. . . . Everyone is always ready for everything. . . . It is always summertime in Pornotopia, and it is a summertime of the emotions as well. . . . All our aggressions are perfectly fused with our sexuality, and the only rage is the rage of lust, a happy fury indeed." [6]

But this is the surface, and these happy figures are only the shadows cast by the bonfire of longings which cannot be satisfied in reality. "Behind these representations of physiological abundance and sexual plentitude," Marcus continues, "one senses an anxiety that points in the opposite direction. Pornotopia could in fact only have been imagined by persons who suffered supreme deprivation, and I do not mean by this sexual deprivation alone. One gets the distinct impression, after reading a good deal of this literature, that it could only have been written by men who at some point in their lives had been starved. . . . Inside every pornographer there is an infant screaming for the breast from which he has been torn." [7]

The greed of the unsatisfied child, then, has lived on to become an insatiate lust in the man: insatiate because now the hungry child can never be fed. His pornographic dreams are efforts to re-create the time past when satisfaction was denied him, and force those who frustrated him to bow to his will. We know who it was who frustrated him: the mother who should have given him ease. We know it, for one thing, because "of the gigantic size of these figures" (who inhabit Pornotopia). As Marcus remarks, this can suggest to us "in what age of life the imagination of pornography has its grounds." Or, as Anais Nin put it, those who see giants are looking through the eyes of a child.

Thus, the pornographers are looking with rage at the women who denied them their earliest pleasures, and in their subjection of them they are seeking revenge. But, as we have seen, they do not dare take their revenge unless they can do so with the full agreement of the woman. So they are also looking at this terrifying figure with fearsome awe. She it was who tended them and who held the power to give and to take away, to loose and to bind. She was the mother they ruled and to whom they were subject. On her they project the overwhelming emotions of childhood; and unless she forgives them for what they do to her, they are lost indeed. This is the symbolic and ambiguous figure which survives in myth.

Survives, in part, because it *is* ambiguous. Our lives begin in ambiguity. Our earliest emotions know no limit, overreach themselves and are thwarted because they cannot receive all they ask. Frustration and desire grow up together because desire can only learn its real limits by frustration. In another knot of ambiguity, the child's dependence on his mother gives him magical power. His needs are satisfied without any effort on his part. So, at the opening of life, there is nothing to tell us that this kind of effortless satisfaction will not continue forever, and that as we grow, only actions can produce results. Our own first actions, indeed, do not produce results; they are merely expressive. At first the hungry child howls *not* to bring his mother to him and the satisfying breast to his lips, but simply because he is hungry and uncomfortable. Only with time do we learn that cause produces effect and that processes have a beginning, continuance and end. We learn the structure of reality as we learn to act in it and on it.

And we learn, of course, through the attendant female figure who comes and goes, feeds and comforts, turns away and denies. Not only does she mediate between the newborn and the world, she is his world as he first perceives it. Her giving and withholding polarize the child's first amorphous emotions. It is through her that we learn what we feel. No wonder that our ways of feeling, and of thinking too, bear traces of these first earthshaking experiences, and that we build them into the arching halls of symbol in which we live.

In analyzing the nature and workings of myth, one must be careful not to fall into mythic thinking and turn a hypothesis into a universal rule. Clearly, we all had mothers and all suffered varying frustrations, but we are not all pornographers. It seems to me that the myths which underlie our thinking are best understood as tendencies, limiting factors and unexpected rigidities of feeling. They are like creases in material that has been folded for a long time. They can be ironed out, but they are apt to show a little even so. To the extent that our earliest experiences of life are similar and that we resemble each other—and since we are human beings born dependent on others, there is a similarity—these first impingements of the world leave similar traces in our minds. For some, these traces are deep and painful and the scar tissue from them inhibits the mind's freedom of movement in later years. For others, they are lightly etched and overlaid by later experiences. One thing they do, deep or light, is enable us to understand each other.

There is no need to assume that the figures of myth, echoing each other around the world, are archetypes carried by a race-memory imprinted on the genes. They can be explained by the similarities in the original meetings with the world that all human beings share. Their attraction, and their menace too, springs from these early days and the aura imposed by the haze of emotion, unsatisfied, puzzled, questioning, with which we then saw the world. Our myths were the hypotheses by which we attempted to explain the reality assaulting our sense. They do indeed concern "the order of the universe," for they were our first cosmogonies, the first rules we dared find to shield ourselves against chaos and help us guess what might happen next. The figures which move through them tend toward the divine because, when we first knew them, we could not understand them. They seemed omnipotent and complete—and incomprehensible. We needed them and were frightened of them. Somewhere inside us all they are still alive. They may manifest themselves no longer as divine figures breaking through into the human world in miraculous epiphanies, but their injunctions still carry the force of myth, and the rules of behavior they lay down still influence the roles that society assigns us to play.

CHAPTER 6

A social system is a function of the common culture, which not only forms the basis of the intercommunication of its members, but which defines, and so in one sense determines, the relative statuses of its members. . . . In so far as these relative statuses are defined and regulated in terms of a common culture, the following apparently paradoxical statement holds true: what persons *are* can only be understood in terms of a set of beliefs and sentiments which define what they *ought to be.*

Talcott Parsons
"The Superego and the Theory of Social Systems" [1]

OUR DISCUSSION of mythology has shown us that history does not live by facts alone. Another sort of logic is loose in the world, and we shan't understand the way people act unless we allow for the dynamics of greed and desire and the inertia of complacent power. So far, however, we have been talking very generally, and it is time to begin looking at these ideas in the small rather than in the large. One good reason for changing focus is that, when we look at them in large terms, they are very discouraging: if this is the way the world works, what can we ever do about it? Such disillusion and despair have their own effect on the phenomenal world because they tempt us to draw back from action. In addition, loss of interest means loss of the intense attention with which we follow activities in which we can see ourselves intervening. Someone who's playing in a tennis tournament watches the other matches in a very different fashion from the ordinary spectator. If we see ourselves as mere audience to life, we let events slip by and the connection between them remains unseen.

The world looks very different if we feel we can act upon it. And when we consider how emotional tendencies operate *within*

individuals, it becomes possible to think that other individuals
may have some effect upon them. Then those who hope to change
the world will find "the way things work" operating to their advantage, even if the advantage is only knowing where one is. As
Lincoln remarked, knowing where we are is what we need in order
to move on.

The way myths affect individuals is through holding up roles
for them to play. Talcott Parsons, whom I have quoted above,
was one of the first sociologists to explore the concept of social
roles, with particular attention to family roles. We shall come to
his views on the importance of parental roles in child-raising very
shortly, but at the moment I want to point out the clear connection
with mythic thinking involved in the whole idea of roles: that
we understand who people are only in terms of what we think
they ought to be. This is basic to the entire experience of a human
being in his world. Unless he knows who else is living in that
world with him, he is a lost and frightened creature; but he will
not know who these strangers around him are unless he has some
idea of what they ought to be. He must tie his feelings about
them (and so about himself) into his experience of what he sees
them doing and hears them saying, how they behave toward him.

Parsons' definition of "role" is tied up in a rather daunting knot
of sociological prose, but I shall quote it here because it can be
untwined to yield a very useful basis of analysis. A role is "the
aspect of what the actor does in his relationship with others seen
in the context of its functional significance for the social system." [2]
There are three factors here. First, playing a role implies a *relationship* with someone else. It is not, that is to say, individual
fantasy or mere pretense. The role of "mother" demands the
existence of a child to be mothered, or (a little more complicated)
someone who is treated *as if* he were a child to be mothered. The
role of "doctor" assumes that there are sick people to be treated
and, at a secondary level, nurses to be instructed and a hospital
staff to carry through the actions which the doctor prescribes for
his patients' cure.

Next, a role is built around an *activity:* what the doctor does to
and for his patients in his professional capacity. Out of his actions
grow familiarity and then expectation. No single act is enough to
establish a role. It demands continuity. The continuity of expected

actions within a relationship has an effect on the other person involved. *He* begins to act reciprocally, in response to what the role-player is doing. Thus he becomes a bit more than audience, though he remains that too. The sociologists call him a "role-other." So the pattern of role-playing within a relationship works out to action, acceptance and reciprocal action.

If we take one more glance backwards at the world view of early man, we find on the wall of the cave of Les Trois Frères in the Pyrenees a painting of a half-human, half-animal figure, apparently engaged in a stamping dance. He has been named the Sorcerer, and he wears a mask, horns, tail and animal skins. This is the first representation we have of the performance of a ritual role. Those who watched him, and the artist who recalled the rite by his portrayal of it, must have been taught a mythic explanation of the Sorcerer's actions. The ritual was part of a significant pattern and the dancer acted a role which both explained the myth and sustained its dogmas by repeating the action it called for. His costume was not a random disguise. (In fact, it is almost exactly the one which eighteenth-century explorers and anthropologists depicted as worn by the Siberian and Lappish shaman-priests whom they encountered in their travels.) It represented his role: what he ought to be. The onlookers judged his performance by their expectations. If things went well, he was a good sorcerer. If they went badly, he was a poor one. Then, no doubt, they acted accordingly and looked about for someone else to play his role.[3]

We, of course, can only guess what his performance was supposed to accomplish, and our ignorance brings us to the third element involved in role-playing: the *social system* within which the activity takes place and the relationship between role-player and role-others exists. This underlies and is part of the "common culture" of shared belief which allows each member of the relationship to understand what is going on between them. Both parties, actor and participating audience, need to share an interpretation of the meaning of the role and the purpose of the activity proper to it. Doctor and patient, for example, agree that the first intends to cure the second, and anything the doctor does is satisfactory to the patient as long as the latter feels that it jibes with this intention.

It is the surround of awareness and agreement which permits the actor to act effectively and the other person in the relationship to go along with the actions of the first. Without this grammar of recognition, the meaning of the role vanishes and the status of the actor changes sharply. So dramatic is a shift like this that drama has treated it often: Oedipus on the road to Colonus has fallen from his high estate to become a blind old man; Lear, after renouncing his kingdom, is a mad old man, raving and nonsensical, his occupation gone. How many such old men has America seen, who left their native lands to find themselves mocked by newer generations! The role of "elder" recognized and respected by sons and daughters, which they had seen their fathers play, had been left behind in the old country.

A role, then, is both public and private. It is not just action, but action-plus-expressive gesture, action undertaken in a way that is understandable to others. The weight of such actions can be enormous. In Parsons' view, for instance, children learn about the world and the culture in which they live by growing up in the subsystem of that culture which we call the nuclear family. In this are included the four roles of father, mother, son and daughter or, from the point of view of the child, brother and sister. As he grows, he learns and incorporates within himself a comprehension of his relationship to each other member of the family, and with it an understanding of who and what each other member of the family is.

Later he also learns that the members of his family represent social situations and relationships that are common to the rest of the world he lives in. What his father does is generalized to "what fathers do." Eventually his own behavior as a father will hark back to what he learned as a son. It may echo his own father's actions, or it may go in quite the opposite direction, depending on how the son feels about his upbringing, but either way he has learned what a father *ought to be,* and his judgment on his own father derives from this. He is seeing (in Parsons' words), what his father was in terms of what he ought to have been.

Outside the family the expressive side of the role is even more important than within it, where members are so deeply familiar with each other. Appearance counts most, that is, where people are strangers to each other. Erving Goffman, a sociologist who has done a great deal of work on encounters between individuals and on the way they work together in groups, sums this up clearly: "In performing a role, the individual must see to it that the impressions of him that are conveyed in the situation are compatible with role-appropriate personal qualities effectively imputed to him," that is, with what people expect. "A judge is supposed to be deliberate and sober; a pilot in a cockpit to be cool; a bookkeeper to be accurate and neat in doing his work. These personal qualities . . . combine with a person's title, when there is one, to provide a basis of self-image for the incumbent and . . . for the image that . . . others will have of him." [4]

All this is obvious: we judge people by how they fit into what we expect of them. What is interesting is Goffman's view of the effect of this on the role-player. "A self," he goes on, "virtually awaits the individual entering a position; he need only conform to the pressures on him and he will find a *me* ready-made for him. In the language of Kenneth Burke, doing is being." [5] Now this equation of "role" with "ready-made me" touches a note which is disturbing to the lay reader. It suggests that a role has its own dynamism and that, if we enter upon it, we will be carried along by its demands willy-nilly, caught in the nightmare situation in which the mask takes over the individual face behind it, in which a life becomes only a meaningless series of gestures from which spontaneity and reality are absent.

Is such a fear justified? It is very much what Betty Friedan described, in *The Feminine Mystique,* as being a typical situation for middle-class women who feel themselves cut off from life, though it is certainly not a feeling confined to women alone. [6] In replying, we must, I think, recognize that we are not only pondering the difference between the private and public sides of role-playing, but also whether the two aspects are compatible with each other at all. This is a very large problem indeed. It involves social judgments on a vast scale, and it may well be that any society—particularly the one we know best in this very moment of time—is capable of forcing private, feeling individuals to play public roles that are grindingly unsympathetic, overdemanding and dehumanizing. When this is the case, such a society is conniving at its own breakdown, for the choice of a "ready-made me" that it offers the child who is growing into man or woman is too far away from his own natural self to be endurable.

The resolution of this huge problem is beyond the scope of my inquiry; but it may throw some light on it to consider the advantages which an identifiable role offers when the demands it makes are not too heavy; that is, when role-playing is functioning in a useful and healthy way. If one's public role is satisfying and comfortable to the private self, one profits by the fact that is has been molded by the expectations of others and is clear and satisfying to them. One has a place in the social system and there are prescribed actions which will win approval for the role-player if they are well done. Even more, there are pre-existing standards of judgment by which a verdict of "well-done" can be pronounced on him. He is not only presented with a self, he is given a map of the world and the heavens, and a moral compass to guide himself along its coordinates. One can hestitate to take on a new self, but it is harder to refuse a whole universe where one's activities are accepted as meaningful and valuable, in which it is clear from the start that *this* behavior is appropriate and *that* is out of place. Most of all, it is hard to refuse a set of values that can be trusted to avoid paralyzing moral dilemmas by indicating what is worthy of respect and esteem. In a world where the public and private aspects of roles are not too far apart, a young doctor feels he knows what a good doctor is and does. His ideas may not agree with those of his teachers, but he has a grip on them and they on him. He has his work and his work tells him who he is; knowing this, he knows how to approach his patients. This is the "ready-made me" that has been waiting for him, and though it may give him a mask, it also sets up bulwarks against chaos.

For some, the very anarchy of the modern world can make a role seem a haven—better a mask than no identity at all. Women are sometimes envied by men for having a role to play. Paul Goodman, in *Growing Up Absurd,* contrasts the uncertainty facing young men who are offered no worthwhile goals with the role of wife and mother which lies ahead for girls.[7] So we find that the ambiguity of role-playing extends to our own views of it: we both dislike the limitations of traditional, ascribed roles and find in them definitions for living which we feel to be deeply needed.

A multitude of social analysts have described the way in which modern technological society has leached away familiar and comfortable feelings of context, of community and of causality. In the process, old roles have been smashed to fragments or vanished entirely. Once the proper deportment, dress, amusements and ways of living appropriate to different classes were clearly marked, and this was true for age classes as well as social classes. A burgher did not dress or behave like a nobleman, nor a young man like an old one. Different occupations typed their practitioners, and different villages and regions wore different clothes. The baker's son looked forward to becoming a baker and to living within the terms of his inherited occupation. The rhythm of his days for his whole life long was set by the need to have fresh-baked bread ready every morning. His moral problems were tied up with the price of his goods just as much as was his economic success. Should he buy at starvation prices when crops were good and hoard grain in times of famine—which could mean facing social anger and the denunciation of the church? For him it was all one life, not a mosaic of bits and pieces. Even if he broke away from his origins, he would find himself apprenticed to another trade and learning its customs as well as its skills.

The American idea of freedom has traditionally emphasized the limits of these customary ways of life and the waste of human talent they imposed. America was the product of Renaissance, Reformation and Enlightenment, which together broke rigid class and occupation barriers and permitted the immense upswelling of talent and energy that ushered in the modern era. Today, however, there is more disposition to find good in the support which a close-knit community once offered the individual. Where we once boasted that we were free, we are now more inclined to fear that we are alienated. Building a new world once seemed an intoxicating opportunity. Now it is a terrible necessity, burdening our dreams. Increasingly we look back on our European past with nostalgia; could there be a better example than *Fiddler on the Roof,* that sentimental hymn to the segregated Jewish village in the time of the pogroms, wept over by the children and grandchildren of those who fled from its reality? In the face of history, we stubbornly mourn what the English demographer Peter Laslett has named "The World We Have Lost" and imagine it as a time when (to quote the book of this title) "the whole of life went forward in the family, in a circle of loved and familiar faces, known and fondled objects, all to human size." [8]

Remembering Philippe Ariès' researches, we may be a little dubious about how many such close-knit and loving families really existed. Indeed, when Laslett gets down to cases, his figures run very close to those Ariès arrived at: in 1676 a typical village in Kent held two hundred and seventy-seven souls in sixty-two households, plus four old people in the poorhouse. Just under the 20 percent that Ariès found to be the average ratio were servants in the gentry's establishments or on the farms of yeomen. The big house of the village held twenty-three folk, while the twenty-four cottages belonging to "poor men and laborers" averaged two or three inhabitants; it was the children from these huts who served the farmers and the gentlemen and they, at any rate, did not grow to maturity "in a circle of loved and familiar faces." [9] Even so, we feel we know what Laslett means when he speaks of a human-sized world, and at times we may even surmise that there was something more than the Babbittry of Main Street in American small towns a century ago. A sense of belonging, of involvement in a community, of being known, is a human need which is as great as its counterpart, the urge to free, individual action. No doubt each seems most precious when it is least in evidence.

The passing of small communities in which individuals know each other increases the need for understandable roles. Yet, as we get further away from such communities, we find it harder to understand each other. Our common culture is becoming less common. This affects both the other factors that underlie the usefulness of role-playing: the activity of the role-player is less meaningful to us "role-others," and we are also uncertain about the relationships that form its immediate context. All three things are tied up together. In the beginning, it was the existence of a community that led to the creation of a range of relationships and permitted specialized activities to appear. "When Adam delved and Eve span, Who was then the gentleman?" goes the old rhyme. And aside from class, who was the miller or the blacksmith or the horse coper or the merchant?

For the community shapes the role as well as explains it. The size of the group, its economic base and its stability will affect the crafts and trades practiced within it. One can even find roles being created today. Erving Goffman offers a contemporary example from the Shetland Islands "where almost every man can do a surprising range of mechanical, electrical and construction work." In spite of this general ability, "one may observe tacit agreements among islanders to support one of their number as a 'specialist' in a skill, allowing him payment for jobs they might have done themselves." [10] Here we see occupational roles being distilled from ordinary activities before our eyes. The Shetlanders, incidentally, regard such specialization as desirable for other than economic reasons: where we feel nostalgia for the past, they are eager to be up-to-date and are convinced that the existence of skilled craftsmen will make them seem more so. But whatever the impulse (and we shouldn't be surprised to find mythic illogic at work here), the Jack-of-all-trades has begun to give way to the knowledgeable craftsman. If the process continues and the community grows, roles will grow more diverse, and special role-behavior become more necessary.

Within a community, of course, there is also scope for psychological roles. Old popular drama is based on the confrontation of familiar types, and even within a group as small as a family there may be found the clown, the hero, the miser, the romantic lady, the jealous loser, the activist and the dreamer. By its very existence, a community allows an individual not to do, or to be, everything. Some of life can be trusted to others.

Our difficulty today is that we have moved into an organized system so huge that it has ceased to feel like a community at all. One result is that occupation roles have become amorphous. Most jobs have turned into a monotonous repetition of fragmented actions, tiny contributions to an anonymous finished product. Part of our current material-mindedness is certainly due to the fact that buying and owning things have become so common, and we have lost the emotional reward that goes with the process of making them. Pride and pleasure in workmanship are almost totally gone, a phenomenon unique to our society. Other jobs may have retained their significance but have become so specialized that they are mysterious and can barely be described to anyone not familiar with the immediate context. What, for example, does a computer programmer actually *do*? It's a job we'd all be willing to agree is skilled and significant. Its adepts are so much in demand that "Help Wanted" advertisements for computer programmers' services usually take up more than a page in *The New York Times* on Sundays. They must be prepared to speak to so-phisticated third-generation machines in the language of Bal or Cobol, but how they do this and what it is they say is, for laymen, occult knowledge. This is not a matter of well-preserved "craft mysteries" as it was in the past, but simply a result of the distance that exists today between one section of life and another. Even those who have one skill are ignorant of other technologies, and this lack of comprehension contributes to our sense of losing con-trol over our world which its sheer size inspires. Our connections with the world of events have ceased to be reciprocal. We don't know those people out there—except for the pseudo-personal images on the television screen who seem to speak to us, but do not hear our answers.

It is not surprising that the only roles that can still awake a re-sponsive emotion, and not a negative shying away from the men-ace of *Them,* the unknown strangers, are personal: society can still comprehend the relationship within which they exist. In his study of role behavior Goffman takes a surgeon as an example of one with a "splendid" role to perform, and television, movies and popular fiction back up this value judgment. Recently in popular sentiment, an elite of doctors and professors has played the role of healers and guides which once belonged to the priesthood. Even here, however, the roles are becoming a bit suspect as what doc-tors do becomes more mysterious, and as teachers react to up-heaval in the classroom and on the campus with very little of the wisdom that had been attributed to them. Their place is being taken over by an elite of artists, prophets and seers who are capable of projecting themselves, even across electronic barriers, as sentient, emotive individuals. Part of the violence we have been witnessing lately is, I believe, due to the need for acting out and making unmistakably clear the role one is playing, whether it is that of rebel or rightist. We have been looking at gestures which are larger than life because a good deal of our life, and almost all of our public connection with the community, has ceased to be (in Laslett's words) "to human size."

The result is that it's hard to be personal without becoming a "personality," without acting the role of oneself. In this situation, the ambiguity surrounding role-playing makes it easy to condemn its expressive side and to see all roles as false and all players as gesturing mimes, nothing more. Indeed, in a world as complex as ours, the *actions* which a role was created to explain become more and more difficult to undertake because we cannot see how they will come out or where the processes they set off will end. The *relationships* surrounding a role are more distant, too, and less intense and solid. The expressive side, the gesture, remains. So we find politicians concentrating on the image they present rather than the accomplishments they may achieve. Presidents are not active men, coping with events, but products to be made and commodities to be sold. More and more they are not "actors" in the real world, but "actors" in the theatrical sense, as appearances become more important than results, or become the equivalent of results.

This is all true, but it leaves a good deal out. For ideally and in its origins, a role is not false, nor does it oppose or misrepresent the activity which it surrounds. Rather, it is a way of communicating to other people the meaning of the activity. It makes actions or situations or attitudes public and communal by tying them into a known and recognizable pattern of events and emotions. Consequently, like all means of communication, it must use terms that are common and recognizable to the public. Of course, therefore, it will never be quite precise, and its margin of imprecision will always be untrue. But this is the case with language itself: as T. S. Eliot's Sweeny said unhappily, "I've gotta use words when I talk to you." Any word, any gesture, any way of behaving can *become* false to a damaging extent if it becomes inappropriate to what is being done in its name, and thus inexpressive of reality. Often this happens because change has been too quick for expression to keep up with it, and so new kinds of action are being accompanied by outworn modes of behavior. Whether or not a President is made and sold by others, he will need to use words, gestures and attitudes to communicate to the country the significance of what he is doing. He must use a role to convey to his constituents what it is that he is trying to accomplish. In general, President Kennedy's style is remembered as being "right"—not only attractive, but appropriate to what people understood him to be doing. On the other hand, President Johnson put people off by his style of behavior. It seemed inappropriate, and consequently insincere and overdone. President Nixon's style makes for uneasiness in his audience because it seems to be too conscious. He appears to be making an effort to put something across, and (as with Johnson, though for a different reason) the gap between action and expression invites the question, "What is he really up to?"

Any appearance of insincerity on the part of our rulers is, thus, a great detriment to them, for it undermines the trust we place in them. And yet, sincere or not, our society is too big for them to get on without an expressive image to carry the people along with them. What comes out as insincerity is more apt to be insensitivity, a bad ear for the needed adjustment of image to aim. This is serious enough, no doubt, but to condemn it is not to condemn role-playing as such. Any language, even that of mathematics, can be used to tell lies.

What should make us wary is the continuation of inappropriate images. If people in power keep making this kind of mistake, if we ourselves, in our daily lives, find that we can't really explain what we're doing or why, and that lying is easier than looking for the heart of a muddled truth, then we have landed ourselves in a situation where reality must certainly be very different from what we think it is. Role-playing loses its usefulness if it communicates nothing but falsehoods. A child who is told only lies will distrust language—which must certainly have happened to many school dropouts. As the black community begins to find an identity for itself, it is willing to use in public the private language it used to save for its own members; and the use of this language is a measure of its distrust and dislike of the white language. Such distrust, however, is not inherent in role-playing, but springs up whenever language, including the language of behavior, begins to seem false.

As long as we need to act within a group, however, we shall have to have some way of showing the others in the group what we are doing. To do that, we must resort to ways of behaving that can be understood because they are familiar: we must play roles. If we don't, our behavior becomes frightening because it is strange. It's apt to be classed as "deviant" or crazy. The rest of the group grow confused and then hostile. Thus, even for those who want to break new ground, playing a role can be very useful indeed. It offers the protection of familiar behavior. Behind this behavior, innovation can take place as long as what is done is not *inappropriate* to what the rest expect. If the role-player is trusted, he can act to meet new situations within an old role and, if he turns out to be right about them, he can even change the role to keep it in tune with reality. A role should not be only a mask. It can be a shield, and an instrument too. Playing a role allows an individual to avoid the hostility that greets strange behavior. Sometimes one plays a role out of fear, but its primary purpose is quite different— to get something done without kicking up a fuss.

Role behavior has another use: it is a device for learning. We have noted Talcott Parsons' theory that the family is a center for teaching children their own social roles and, beyond this, the place of such roles in the structure of society. School and community together continue the process, for a great deal of education is not factual, but emotional and behavioral. "This is what people do, this is the way they feel," the child of a traditional society is taught, "in this situation or that—when grandparents die, when you go to work, when you travel abroad—expect this, don't be surprised at that, respond in this way, go to a priest or a rabbi for help if you are puzzled." So every individual finds the world structured and explained by other people's experience. It has been imagined for him in the shape of his native culture by those who lived before him. He may disagree with these findings, but at least he has a body of knowledge to argue against and a place to begin.

So, in the past, did myth explain the order of the universe, while ritual actions spelled out the emotions proper to this order in ceremonies which were designed to illustrate and sustain it. Myth and behavior intermingled, and man moved in a world of order whose meaning he understood and which he supported by his actions, by the role he played. His performance, like that of the Stone Age sorcerer, connected his daily life with sacred myth. In Rome, small gods directed the sowing and the harvest and even the proper fertilization of the fields. In medieval Europe, every craft had its patron saint, while the world itself was seen as a paradigm here below of the divine and eternal order above.

But the world we have lost is lost indeed. We cannot bring it back and, though we may miss its support, we could not endure its rigidity. We are used to a reality that can change. We see change as needed, we hope for it. But when reality changes, traditional roles get out of kilter. The behavior they suggest doesn't suit the occasion and they encourage expectations that can't be met. No doubt new ways of behaving will eventually grow up around any activity that lasts: this is something to hope for. But in the meantime, old ways applied inappropriately cripple society by conveying false information and hurt the individual by forcing him to do things that are silly and don't turn out right. Gesture and action are at cross-purposes.

When this happens many intelligent and observant people, particularly young people with their lives before them, opt out of society or rebel against it. They can see that the world of events and the world of myth do not coincide. Others forgo the full use of their talents because outworn custom has grown so rigid that, though it needs to be reprogrammed creatively, it fears and opposes the creativity that will destroy it. Some are caught in Hamlet's dilemma: forced by conscience to forswear the role that waits to be played, but questioning not only this ready-made me but also the inner identity which refuses to accept the public role. Like Hamlet, they slide toward the madness which haunts the play because it haunts the situation of its hero. He can't trust his role, but he can't trust the identity which urges him to mistrust it either, for without the role he cannot act.

The value of a particular role, in a particular time, is quite a separate thing, then, from the value of role-playing in general. Role-playing is a complex activity necessary to society and useful in many ways to the individual. But the virtue of any special role depends on its closeness to the mental and emotional makeup of the performer and to its appropriateness to his situation. Does the behavior proper to this role fit with the action that needs to be taken in the external world, or does it oppose it? Does it fit the player comfortably and yet loosely enough for him to move about within its protection and adapt his posture to changing circumstances? Does it, on the other hand, clamp him so tightly that it denies him any feeling of choice, or opportunity for imaginative innovation, or pleasure in achievement? Does it belittle his hopes

and deny him full human status? If the nega....
great, the individual who has put on a role will ceas...
former and become a puppet, moved wholly by the dem...
his role and feeling that his fate has gone out of his control. ...
ciety can survive that for a while, for the puppet still acts and still
expresses the meaning of his actions. But the individual is no
longer a person, only a bundle of prescribed gestures with nothing
inside to tie them together; and too many of these robots a changing society cannot afford, for they do not adapt to change.

Now that we have some idea of the mechanics of role-playing
in general, let us take a look at woman's role. So far, we have not
talked about sex roles, and there are profound differences between
such roles and occupation roles which are based on activities and
the relationships that grow out of them. When sociologists slide
from one sort of role to the other without thinking these differences through, they distort the term and confuse their hypotheses.
"Being a woman" is not at all the same thing as "being a doctor."
Before we take up the question of whether the role traditionally
assigned to women is suited to the world today, or even whether
it is particularly suited to women, we had better ask what ideas
are locked up together in the familiar phrase, woman's role. What
does it mean, anyway? This is another "thing we all know," so we
must tread carefully and expect surprises.

"...................... another wife like her? I paid 4000 rupees for her. S......... r work very well, she is young, she is beautiful. And when...... mad at her and beat her with my shoe, she doesn't get mad at me. She goes ahead and cooks good stew for me, good bread for me, then comes and takes hold of my beard and says, 'By N.N. [the name of their eldest son], don't be angry with me. Eat your bread, eat your stew. Forgive me.'"

An elder of the Marri tribe of Baluchistan

"You know what rights a woman has among us Marris. She has the right to eat crap. That's all."

A Marri woman
Robert N. Pehrson
The Social Organization of the Marri Baluch [1]

SEX ROLES, it is clear from the Marri man and woman I have quoted here, look very different to the one on the inside and the one on the outside. There is more. than this, however, to interest us in their words. They show us unmistakably what an assigned role can mean: a role which is not chosen but handed to one by others, in which ordained tasks and relationships are tied to behavior. The behavior expected of Marri women expresses subordination and is most highly thought of when it expresses only that. (The elder's praise of his wife, we might note, was spoken when she was ill and he was afraid of losing her.) This assignment of role has an importance of its own for the role-player, which I shall come to later. First, however, we had better try to see what the content of the role is. The Marri elder is judging his wife quite properly (in sociological terms) by how well she lives up to what is expected of her: what she is in terms of what she ought to be. But what is expected of her? What goes into woman's role in this tribal society?

It is a circumscribed and limited role, for women among the Marri are un-persons in any public sense: they are property. Even so, it is oddly difficult to fit the word "woman" into Parsons' definition of role and get any sense out of it. To say that woman's role is "the aspect of what (she) does in (her) relationship with others seen in the context of its functional significance for the social system" adds nothing to our understanding, whereas we can perfectly well fit the word "doctor," or the title of any other occupation, into Parsons' description and see what he means. A doctor's activities in relation to his patients have a functional significance, but what are the expected activities of a woman as woman? To whom are they related? What is their social function? Even among the Marri, woman's role seems too diffuse to yield an answer.

The reason is that, in the sociological sense, woman's role isn't one but several. The Marri man is talking chiefly about his wife as a wife. In this role she cooks for him, cossets him, puts up with his temper and makes him the father of sons. But since she has children, another relationship with its proper activities exists: she is mother as well as wife, and she certainly must behave differently in this role and respond to other demands. In addition, says the elder, "She does her work very well." So beyond bringing up the children and attending to her husband, there is some kind of work expected of her. Her role, limited and antiquated as it is, is triple. She is mother, wife and, at the very least, some version of home-maker; in fact, Marri women undertake useful economic work for the benefit of their families and of the community.

If we separate woman's role this way, we find that each part does fit into Parsons' definition. A mother's activities in relation to her children have profound social significance. The child's very existence, as well as its growth to maturity, can be affected by her care and affection. Her marriage provides her with an equally definable relationship to her husband and, in some societies, to his family. She has obligations to him which are both sexual and generally supportive. Even if woman's work is conceived as being no more than housewifery, that too demands activities within a relationship to the family group. In short, we can see that what a woman does in each of these segments of her life hangs together and operates as a coherent role. But if we try to add the three together and call the result "woman's role," we don't arrive at a unity. They remain as distinct as they did.

So woman's role is not only assigned to her—brutally among the Marri Baluch, more subtly in other cultures—it is also not a unified role, but a pluralism. Naturally, this situation isn't confined to women, but it operates rather differently for men. The several roles which they play, as husbands, fathers and breadwinners, are seldom blurred together into an attempt to find a unity which doesn't really exist. The distinction between these roles is more clear-cut and, in our day and age, men's professional activities are usually separated from their lives at home and go on in a different area and at a different time. Men know where they are, and they are more or less one thing at a time. By contrast, women's traditional activities are usually carried on in the same place and often simultaneously. Sometimes different roles demand different responses at the same moment.

This is nothing to complain of particularly, but it is worth noting because it has a cumulative effect on women's overall character structure. The multiplicity of their roles puts a premium on flexibility and adaptability. Not only is woman's work never done, it is continually changing both from role to role and within each role. As children grow up, they make different demands and have to be treated differently. Husbands' expectations change. So do houses and friends and class status. Women are thus called on to have different talents and, beyond this, to be able to bring these talents to bear quickly on changing situations. They are expected to be amateur professionals at a number of different activities with a number of different skills at their command.

This diversity of living can be very enjoyable and stimulating in itself, but one difficulty haunts it. Women's skills are subject to call by other people and often at the convenience of other people. Sometimes a woman decides when to use a special talent, but quite often she can't. She must be ready to respond with the proper skill when it is needed by the other member or members of a relationship and so she stands by, waiting to be called on, but not the initiator of action. In this situation she doesn't make decisions, she accepts them from others. When we are told that women are, by nature, bad at making decisions, we might reflect that they have usually had little practice at choosing consciously to initiate overt action.

Even so it is pleasant to have skills and to use them well. But a further difficulty arises from the fact that very few women can be really good at everything they are expected to do. Some are good mothers and bad wives, while some devoted wives and loving mothers are perfectly terrible homemakers. Some women who can do all these things adequately find it hard to shift back and forth from one to the other as quickly as may be needed. As a result, there is almost always a little failure packaged in with any woman's success in playing her various roles.

Again, this isn't a disaster. It's as well for human nature to be aware that its performance is far from perfect. It keeps us humble to fail once in a while. But once more the element of choice, or rather the lack of it, comes in. Men are more free to walk away from failure than are women. Woman's traditional role demands that she go on doing certain things even if she knows she's not very good at them. So women more or less have to live with the knowledge that they are failures in certain areas of their lives and see themselves as disappointing creatures who have to act out their disappointments over and over.

The effect of the split in woman's traditional role, then, is to direct women toward flexibility rather than single-mindedness, toward responsiveness rather than decisiveness, and toward the acceptance of the selves they live with as a bit inadequate. This shows up very clearly in the character structure that psychologists describe as feminine. Women are said to be more docile and more passive than men, less ranging in their ambitions, more alert to personal relationships and to the emotional background of human situations. They are given credit for being intuitive and sympathetic. They are faulted for not being able to organize large-scale enterprises and carry them through to long-term conclusions. Some psychological tests indicate that women are less inclined to think and plan ahead than are men.

All this fits the mechanics of role-playing which we discussed in the last chapter. "Doing is being," Erving Goffman quotes Kenneth Burke in summing up the effects of role-playing on the individual. What women do in their familiar place produces the kind of "being" that we call feminine. Even though sex roles differ in various ways from occupational roles, there is no reason to suppose that what one does as mother, wife, or homemaker has less of an effect on the doer than what one does as doctor, lawyer, or merchant-chief. The "ready-made me" that is waiting for women is a character who needs to be aware of what is going on in the personal relationships around her and will do well to grasp intuitively the emotional background of any situation. The public part of her role is a presentation of the myth of female weakness, and if the strong can ignore what other people think, the weak cannot. The present is where they live, watchfully, and their inattention to the future is rather to be expected of people who are going to have little say about what happens on the way there.

The diversity of woman's role is not related only to weakness. Woman's strength is called on too, but as we might expect, the connection is clearer on the private side of her doing and being. Just because the demands made on women are various and often simultaneous, there are occasions when they have to choose between the roles they play. They must stand back from their own activities and weigh one relationship against another. These are decisions that are just as difficult and just as influential as men's more overt determinations, but since they are made in private they are easy to overlook. Man's world offers few guideposts to a woman who is agonizing over the question of whether to back a son who wants more autonomy against a husband who is shaken by a challenge to his authority, or how to help normal children live with one who is retarded, or give a plain elder daughter enough stamina to stand up to her beautiful younger sister. If women make such decisions in the dark, they don't make them without intellection, judgment and the will to see them through.

This kind of decision-making is the stuff of soap opera; and that is why soap opera has such an appeal and such emotional impact. Books and serials like *The Valley of the Dolls* and *Peyton Place* do actually confront serious problems of morality. They then go on to offer artificial and inappropriate solutions in language of extreme and painful banality, but to condemn the treatment doesn't mean at all that we should dismiss the problems. We find the same effort to come to grips with real emotional decisions in the "advice" columns and in the suggestions women's magazines like to publish on how to arrange one's living schedules: when to forget the cleaning and play with the baby; when to let the baby cry and make love to your husband; when to insist on some quiet time for self-renewal and go collect seashells à la Anne Lindbergh. The *problems* which plague the heroines of soap opera are no different in kind from those that confronted Anna Karenina, Natasha Rostova and Emma Bovary. They involve decisions about choice and priority of values, and they are intimately connected with the fact that what we casually refer to as woman's role has a multiplex structure. The sociologists have a phrase that covers this kind of interior friction—"role conflict." There is a considerable amount of conflict built into woman's traditional role; *the conflict may be the one thing that gives it unity.*

The idea that a fundamental factor in the role women play is its diversity has been put forward by a number of observers. Professor David McClelland of Harvard, for instance, remarks, "Most women by inclination and force of circumstances will do many more things [than men do] in the course of a lifetime. The phrase 'part-time' catches a lot of the essence of the feminine style of life in a very practical sense. Women will be part-time cooks, part-time intellectuals, part-time workers. They may spend part of their lives being wholly wives and mothers and another part being wholly intellectuals." [2]

Many women will agree that this is an excellent description of their lives. What should give us pause, however, is that McClelland does not stop with describing the part-timeness of women's activities, but goes on to trace it back to what he assumes to be an explanation: "But," he concludes, "[women's] psychology permits this degree of alternation more easily than for a man who will often blindly follow a single course."

Let us pause on this last sentence because it imports something new into the concept of role which we have not encountered before. McClelland is not a sociologist but a psychologist, so we shouldn't be surprised at his mention of female psychology. He did, however, succeed Talcott Parsons as head of the Department of Social Relations at Harvard, and we are justified, I think, in feeling that the interests of the two men are close enough for us to consider Parsons' ideas about roles in the light of McClelland's remarks.

What McClelland is saying is that there is something about women—their psychology—which predisposes them to fill the demands of the role they play. Up to now we have looked at the

dynamics of role as a process beginning *at the other end.* The activities of the role-player shape the role, interact with the expectations of other participants in the relationship, and have "a
functional significance" in terms of the overall social system.
Nothing about psychology here, we note. Another sociologist,
however, Erving Goffman, gets into it when he describes the role
these activities mold as being "a ready-made me" and cites critic
Kenneth Burke's aphorism, "Doing is being." This agrees with
Parsons' hypothesis that children learn their social and sexual
roles in life as members of the family they are born into, through
their relationships with mother, father, brothers and sisters. The
assumption is that the psychological structure peculiar to a role
does not exist by itself but grows out of the role.

McClelland, however, wants us to bring in the psychology
suitable to a role at the start of the process: women's psychological
makeup allows them to play woman's role. But the minute we
accept this tautology, we lose the useful concept of role as a way
of learning and teaching and as a means of social communication.
What we get instead has the ring of a mythic statement: women
behave like women because they are women, which of course
produces the familiar injunction, "Women, do not try to change
your role or leave the place where you belong."

How interesting it is to find the myth surfacing at the heart of
the social sciences! We should remember, of course, that myths
are never entirely false, for they incorporate what people are used
to believing and what they want to believe, and they are able to
enlist enough facts on their side to be plausible. The facts here
are that psychological differences between men and women certainly do exist and show up on tests as well as in ways of behaving.
Where we step over into the bogs and quagmires of myth is the
point at which we decide that these differences are inborn and
not learned.

The question this raises is double. Our first query, naturally, is
whether or not it is true that men and women differ psychologically
because of innate traits carried in the genes and phased into their
body rhythms by hormones. (The second question has to do with
the importance of such a belief, and indeed with the importance of
the question, but let us deal with one at a time.) Are men, for
instance, born more aggressive than women, and do they form
bonds with each other more easily because they hunted in bands

a hundred thousand years ago and the behavior proper to hunting packs has somehow got imprinted on the Y chromosome which produces maleness? Are they more imaginative and better at mathematics because nature makes them so? We have noted that men's decisions are more openly arrived at, and so more easily observed, than are the choices women make in their traditional role; but are men more single-minded, as McClelland suggests, or can some of this be laid to the difference between public and private action? Are they, as he also suggests, interested in things while women are interested in people? Is anatomy destiny, to recall the famous and often cited dictum of Sigmund Freud (who said a great many other things which don't especially point to this conclusion)?

The idea that men and women are born different psychologically as well as physiologically is of long standing. Almost always and almost everywhere it's been assumed that women are born to be loving mothers and men to fight, women to comfort and men to command; not simply that they *do* these things, but that their minds are patterned from birth to do them. Variations have been considered freakish in theory, though, as we noted in the first chapter, some women (like Margaret Paston) have always commanded, and many poor women have had little time to comfort their families because they have been hard at work in man's world.

Recently, however, some students have come to believe that a large part (at least) of these psychological differences between the sexes (things we all know) are the result of learned behavior, of social training and acculturation. Even McClelland agrees that social training is very important for the performance of sex roles, and Parsons (as we might expect) goes further. "Some of the principal facts," he writes, "which Freud interpreted as manifestations of constitutional bisexuality [that is, as inborn traits] can be explained by the fact that the categorization of human beings into two sexes is . . . biologically given but, in psychological significance, must be learned by the child." The facts of physical difference, in other words, are evident, but the meaning that is assigned to them is something that children are taught as they grow up. "It is fundamental," he goes on, "that children of both sexes start life with essentially the same relation to the mother, a fact on which Freud himself laid great stress. It may then be suggested that the process by which the boy learns to differentiate himself in terms of sex from the mother and in this sense 'identify' himself with the father, while the girl learns to identify with the mother, is a learning process." [3]

Parsons is saying that among the many things which children learn about themselves and their social roles as they grow within the family is what sex they are and how that sex is expected to behave: which parent to take as a pattern. McClelland is more inclined to feel that the differences in the reactions of men and women to various psychological tests indicate that the sexes are born different, but he agrees that a learning process is involved. What strikes him, however, is that men tend to learn one kind of pattern of feeling and action, and women another. Of course, he agrees, "women can learn the male patterns; men can fail to learn them. All anatomy does is to make some associative patterns more likely in one sex than the other if nature takes her course, and if nothing is done to change what would normally be learned."

What might strike us at this point is that McClelland is making some very large assumptions: that we know, for instance, how nature takes her course and what is or isn't normal. Another assumption is that the reason why men learn one pattern and women another is built in at the beginning of the learning process and directs it toward this result. But when we actually come to look at the tests made on adult males and females to see whether psychological differences show up (and of course they do), something else becomes clear. The results don't have to invoke anatomy for their existence, because they can pretty well be explained by the different goals which our society (not nature) sets up as normal for the two sexes. These norms are old friends: men are assertive, women care about people and want to enter occupations where "interdependence" (a key word for McClelland) is important. Boys are self-confident and like rough games. Girls have clever little fingers and are irritated by dirt. And so on. With due respect to McClelland's insight into *existing* patterns of thought and behavior (and he has a great deal), the only surprise to be found in his conclusions is the ease with which modern tests turn up the same old stereotypes.

Perhaps the stereotypes are true. Perhaps sex does affect the brain. So far, however, we have been given assertions instead of proofs. We might note that these assertions all direct us away from the area of what can be tested and judged analytically toward the area of what can't: of what must be accepted as given and unchangeable. But to say that woman's role differs from man's because women are born different destroys any value that can be derived from the notion of roles. It knocks to the ground the idea of a role as a means of learning, of getting things done, and of communicating by means of behavior. It seems a sad waste to throw away such a valuable concept simply to put women back in their place.

With psychoanalyst Erik Erikson, we find ourselves in very much the same situation: "the ground-plan of the body," he feels, has a considerable effect on the psychological attributes of male and female. Once again we are being told that anatomy is destiny. This is all the more remarkable because the main thrust of Erikson's highly perceptive work is toward the importance of what we confront in experience, and how these "life-crises" form the "ego-identity" of the individual. We are shaped by the demands made on us by growing up into a social system, beginning with the tiny subsystem of the family; which is to say that we learn how to be ourselves by finding out how to manage what happens to us. Erikson has applied his method not only to an impressive analysis of our society, but also to Martin Luther, a man of another age, and to Gandhi, the product of a very different culture. There is a limit to learning, however, in Erikson's view, and that limit is involved with the "ground-plan of the body" and is inescapable.

A great deal of Erikson's analytic work has been with children. In the famous experiment which I mentioned in the introduction to this book, he provided a number of girls and boys with blocks and small figures and invited them each to arrange "an exciting scene." The typical scene made by girls was of a domestic interior, with or without surrounding walls, in which people and animals stand or sit about. "These interiors . . . were for .the most part expressly peaceful. . . . [Even when] the interior was intruded [upon] by animals or dangerous men . . . the majority of these intrusions have an element of humor and of pleasurable excitement."

Boys' scenes are different. If they build houses, these have "elaborate walls or façades with protrusions . . . represent ornaments or cannons. There are high towers and there are exterior scenes . . . There are elaborate automotive accidents, but also traffic channeled or arrested by the policeman . . . There is also much play with the danger of collapse or downfall; ruins were exclusively boys' constructions."

From this data Erikson concluded that girls emphasize inner, and boys outer, space, and that this reflects the ground-plan of the body. Allowing that each sex can learn to imitate the "spatial mode" of the other, he feels that "the spatial phenomena observed here . . . express two principles of arranging space which correspond to the male and female principles in body construction," and that these are "relevant throughout life to the elaboration of sex-roles in cultural space-times." [4]

There is certainly no getting away from Erikson's major premise: the two sexes do have different body plans. One can also see that these differences in anatomy will be part of what we experience and learn about ourselves. But (as Talcott Parsons was careful to point out) what we learn isn't simply that these differences exist. We also learn their *significance*, and their significance can and does differ from common culture to common culture. Sometimes it is overshadowed by the caste into which one is born, or one's nationality, or condition of servitude, or half a dozen other possible social facts. Assume that we are aware very early of the ground-plan of the body. We must still learn how to behave properly in the social situation we occupy, with sex as one of the factors, but a factor of varying importance. The physical typing by sex is inescapable, but there is nothing ordained by heaven about any particular social typing that derives from it. That is affected by when and where we are born, by caste and class, wealth or poverty, just as our "ego-identity" (in Erikson's phrase) is influenced not only by sex but by such factors as the size of the family we're born to, our place within the family, the kind of schooling we get and, above all, the peculiar talents and abilities of the single human being in question.

We come now to our second question about sex differences. It had to do not with the existence of innate psychological maleness and femininity, but with the importance of the idea that they exist. Why is it insisted on? Why is the ground-plan of the body assumed to influence directly and inescapably the way one thinks, arrives at decisions and undertakes actions? Theories that connect body types with psychological structures crop up from time to time (the intellectual ectomorph, the determined, athletic mesomorph, etc.), but the only one that endures is that which derives from primary sex characteristics. Why? May we not suspect that the idea is attractive because it is mythic?

There are two reasons for thinking so. The first is that we really don't need it to explain the psychological differences which very evidently exist in men and women. In fact, it's a questionable basis for these differences, because the psychological and social differences assumed to be proper to males and females change from one period or place to another, and the physical differences don't. Every society, however, considers sexual differences to be socially important, and consequently children are treated as typed by their sex almost from the moment of birth. The difference in treatment may be slight at first when the child is an infant, but infants are prodigious learners. They take in all manner of other hints about the world from the unconscious attitudes and motivations of their parents; we must assume they pick up self-knowledge, which includes the interpretation of the particular body-plan they are born with, just as fast.

The difference in treatment increases rapidly as the child grows. It has been suggested that some male homosexuals may have grown up "abnormal" because something went wrong with the teaching, or the learning process, and they took in the wrong information about their body-plan. If training can do this, it is powerful indeed. When cultural norms are on the side of the pressure toward a sex role, it must be even more powerful than when they are not. The ground-plan of the body is there, but what gives it its meaning for an individual is surely the deep, unconscious assumptions that a culture makes about it. All we have learned about role-playing suggests that the "being" of a woman will follow the "doing" that is assigned to her as proper for someone born with her kind of body.

The second reason for believing that we are dealing with a mythic idea when we assume that psychological sex differences are inborn is of course that we find therein the familiar imperative of myth. If women are born to be women, they can't not be women, and any attempt on their part to come out of their inner space and mix in men's world is unnatural. Men are often apologetic about this. Erikson, for instance, doesn't want it thought that he is "using [his] definitions concerning the central importance of

woman's procreative task, in a renewed attempt to 'doom' every
woman to perpetual motherhood and to deny her the equivalence
of individuality and the equality of citizenship. But," he continues, "since a woman is never not-a-woman, she can see her
long-range goals only in those modes of activity which include and
integrate her natural dispositions." [5]

"Unnatural" and "abnormal" are very difficult words for members of our common culture to face. They are the equivalent for
our age of what "damned" meant to our ancestors in the Age of
Faith. Women are intuitive enough, whether they were born that
way or learned it, to be sensitive to these implications. When they
are told by sociologists and social anthropologists that they possess
"special female attributes which spring not only from the capacity
of motherhood but from all those traits of womanhood whose sum
total is the true 'feminine mystique,' " [6] some of them may be
flattered, but others will be inclined to reflect that fine words
butter no parsnips. There can be little doubt about the intention
behind an assertion (by another sociologist) that "Woman's role
can never change. There can only be a shift of emphasis. The
immutable role of the woman as mother shows that the home
must always play an important part in her life." [7] It doesn't take
much awareness of personal relationships to see what that means:
Stay where you are! If a woman is "never not-a-woman," she vio-
lates her nature when she moves outside the place reserved for
women. In mythic terms, she threatens the order of the universe
by resisting the demands of her "role."

"What persons *are*," wrote Talcott Parsons, "can only be understood in terms of a set of beliefs and sentiments which define what
they *ought to be*." The ideas of our society about what women
ought to be are, then, part and parcel of any opinion about any
individual woman. Like the Marri elder's wife, she will be judged
by a set of standards that have nothing to do with her particular
capabilities. The pattern exists, and the role is assigned to her.
She may, as she learns her way into it, find it very comfortable
indeed, but if she doesn't she can't do much about it. She may
turn, she may break the mold of the role for herself, she may
outgrow it, but the role will still exist and she will still be subject
to the judgments of those who expect a woman to be "never
not-a-woman."

CHAPTER 8

Do the schools make "sissies" out of boys? They do tend to be "feminine institutions," says Professor Patricia Cayo Sexton of New York University. Professor Sexton is worried about the over-feminizing influence of the schools . . . [which], she noted, seem particularly unsuited to the needs and temperament of the more masculine boys. . . . The problem, Dr. Sexton said recently, is that school is too much a woman's world, governed by women's rules and standards. "The school code is that of propriety, obedience, decorum, cleanliness, silence, physical and, too often, mental passivity."

From Bernard Bard's column, "The Blackboard,"
New York Post, August 17, 1968 [1]

"The difference between teaching an all-boys class and an all-girls class is that when you enter a class of boys and say 'Good morning,' half the hands shoot up demanding to know what you mean by 'good' and the other half what you mean by 'morning.' When you say 'Good morning' to a class of girls, they all write it down in their notebooks" . . . I found [this] advice true and illuminating.

Richard Freedman, "Lines from a Ladies' Seminary," in
Book World, August 18, 1968 [2]

THE TWO professors quoted above remind us that being born into a social situation that will shape the course of one's life is not peculiar to women. If girls are born female, boys are born male, and are expected to develop masculine attributes and behave in a masculine way, as these things are defined by our society. The standards of both sex roles are inescapable. We can't, however, quite leave it at that, and our professors don't leave it at that either. Not only do they offer examples of male and female characteristics, they give us a hint as to which sort is preferred in our society. It isn't very hard to figure out that masculine initiative and activity are valued more highly than feminine decorum and passivity.

In other words, there is a difference in the way the inescapability of a sex role is felt. For the sex which is regarded as superior, its ordained role bestows a privileged status. The inferior sex knows that it will always be limited by the role assigned to it. Masculinity challenges men—which isn't always pleasant. Living up to traditional standards of maleness can sometimes be a bore and sometimes a burden. It does not, however, impose the sort of hindrance and restriction that femininity demands of women. "Superior" and "inferior" are rather harsh words, and many people when speaking publicly about sex differences would rather describe the sexes as being separate but equal. (Richard Freedman concludes the article I quoted by doing just that.) If, however, we consider the difference in the effect which sex roles have on men and women, I think we must agree that we do in fact regard men as superior to women, if only because masculine goals urge men to do things, while femininity as an ideal attempts to *stop* women from doing them. This difference has a further effect: one runs into the limits of a restrictive role more often than into those of a wider and more diverse one. That is why the limits are there, to keep one in bounds. So women are more apt to be conscious of their role and its restrictions than men are to be aware of their role, with its manifold opportunities. The fence around woman's place is more apparent to the people who live inside it than to those outside in man's world.

Assigned roles other than sex roles exist in our world, but they are a good deal rarer than they were in more traditional societies. There one was almost inevitably born into a status: master or slave, lord or serf, noble or commoner. A bit of this still goes on. In a casual way we still make allowances for artistic temperament, and the very rich are even now regarded as at least a little different from you and me, if only because they are assumed to be less bribable when holding public office. We know very well that the elderly and the young won't act or react in the same fashion. Only a few roles, however, carry with them as large an aura of expectations-to-be-met and norms-to-be-compared-with as ascribed roles did in the past. Race roles did until recently and sex roles still do.

Woman's role, looked at from this point of view, is archaic. This is not necessarily a bad thing, but it does make woman's position rather peculiar: it is a survival. In the old world, where one was born into a class and a region and often into an occupation, the fact that one was also sex-typed simply added one more attribute to those which every child learned he or she possessed. Now to be told, in Erik Erikson's words, that one is "never not-a-woman" comes as rather more of a shock.

This is especially true for American women because of the way in which the American ethos has honored the ideas of liberty and individual choice. We can find, in fact, an excellent description of the psychological effect of these traditional American attitudes in Prof. Erikson's own classic study, *Childhood and Society*. "The process of American identity formation," he writes, "seems to support an individual's ego identity as long as he can preserve a certain element of deliberate tentativeness of autonomous choice. The individual must be able to convince himself that the next step is up to him."[3] Very well; but then what about the limiting restrictions of being "never not-a-woman"? To the extent that these restrictions are effective, they get in the way of a "deliberate tentativeness of autonomous choice": some choices are simply not open to women; they are barred from some "next steps."

If this is the case, woman's role puts her at odds not only with the American ethos, but with the whole long trend of Western civilization toward individual freedom and individual responsibility. This becomes something more than conflict within a role, more than the sort of ambivalence that plagues women because of the multiplicity of the roles they play. For, if we accept Erikson's conclusions about American patterns of living (and they are patterns which not only had roots in post-Renaissance Europe, but which now are growing there and elsewhere with social mobility), and put them side by side with his judgment of women's inescapable femininity, the comparison suggests that woman's traditional role *in itself* is opposed to a deeply significant aspect of our culture. It is more than restricting, because it involves women in the kind of conflict with their surroundings that no decision and no action open to them can be trusted to resolve.

Take this a step further. What is the psychological impact on those who are assigned a role which is somehow at odds with the ideals of the common culture around it? A role, by its nature, is a product of the social system within which it exists. It derives its function and meaning from this system. So if the demands of the role are felt (however obscurely) to be in conflict with those of the overall social ethos, the role-player is bound to feel himself caught in a painful contradiction. The more devoted he is to playing his role, the more successful his performance, the more isolating and divisive will be this contradiction. Or, to apply this generalization to the example at hand, the more feminine a woman is, the less can she be part of the major, ongoing trend of life in our society.

No wonder, then, that the "ready-made me" of woman's role is consistently found by social scientists to be more conservative than the average man. Many factors work toward this end. Women are limited in what they can do, so they have fewer opportunities to act than men do. They also *feel* themselves limited, and so distrust action. They may not particularly like the place assigned to them, but if they are dubious about their ability to change it, they will hesitate for a long time before they try. A role-player who has to forswear certain activities in the external world is apt to forswear the ambitious frame of mind that sets him wanting to undertake these activities. What's the good of hoping to do something one knows one won't be allowed to try? Better to settle for what one has; and if it's all one is likely to get, why, then one will value it highly and try to conserve it. Having let high hopes and ambitions go, one comes more readily to live by such a code as Patricia Sexton draws up as being typically feminine: by "propriety, obedience, decorum, cleanliness, silence, physical and, too often, mental passivity."

We saw in the last chapter that the packaged-in failure, which women run into because of the diversity of roles they play, contributes to the constellation of character traits that is described as feminine. So does their enforced isolation from the ideals which their society sets up. This is true no matter what these ideals may be, but it is more oppressive in a society that honors freedom, if only in the abstract, and praises the right to choose one's fate and future, even if there's more praise than practice. Women who have been trained to regard themselves as limited will be leery of choice and frightened of freedom. They will indeed tend to be passive, and in an activist society, this will make them conspicuous and isolate them even more from the overall norms of behavior.

Another step. Isolation from the ideals of a society and from its norms of behavior not only makes the individual less likely to act within that society, it turns these ideals against him. However subliminally, he must ask himself, Why am I excluded from them, and even forbidden to aspire to them? To the extent that he accepts these ideals as worthy—and it is very difficult to live in a society without accepting some of its ideals—he must conclude that he is unworthy, perhaps even evil. The isolation of women, particularly during times of social strain, has resulted from time to time in their being called both these things. The fathers of the early Church were ready to denounce them as actively evil, and so were the Puritan divines of the Reformation, each speaking with the awful authority of the sacred.

It is not the voice of authority itself, however, which produces psychological conditioning, it is the acceptance by the individual under attack of what the voice says. Once begun, such acceptance grows progressively easier. Women's inability to identify themselves with the highest ideals of their society and to imagine themselves as active participants in the operations of their society becomes a self-sustaining force. If they are unworthy because they are unable to act, the less they are able to act, the more they become unworthy, and so on. Isolation from active life breeds timidity, timidity increases isolation and a protective unwillingness to take any interest in goals that can't be attained. "Why should I bother to study this science or tackle that technical subject?" an intelligent girl may still ask herself. "I'll never get a chance to use it." She is encouraged by the very situation in which she finds herself to let inertia take hold and say, "I needn't bother learning that, I'm only a girl."

We can see very clearly how this works out in the area of science, and its companion, the technological application of scientific knowledge to the world of events. Each is a major concern of our society, whose whole structure—its productive ability, its distribution of goods, its ways of communicating, its hopes for the future—has for long been involved with the increase and the application of scientific knowledge. As we all know, women play a very small part indeed in scientific activities; and their absence from the field is taken as evidence that they are unfit to be there. In the accepted view, normal women are felt to be abnormally incapable of dealing with, or even understanding, the scientific and technical underpinnings of our way of life and thought.

A paradoxical result is that when a woman does understand or deal ably with scientific or technical matters, there is a tendency for her to be seen as abnormal as a woman. This is elegantly illustrated in James Watson's story of the discovery of DNA, *The Double Helix*. Watson, along with Maurice Wilkins and Francis Crick, received the 1962 Nobel Prize in Medicine and Physiology for his work on the subject. His lively and very human book about this highly competitive effort has been widely read. Watson obviously took great pleasure in writing outside the convention of stuffy dullness which shrouds and mummifies much semi-official reportage. He clearly intended to astound the scientific establishment and to be scandalously candid both about personalities and about the ambitions and superficialities which are as much present in scientific research as in any other field.

This being so, one should not make more of his frankness than is there by reading malice into it. We may, however, certainly take advantage of his candor to note Watson's idea of where women belong in science: outside it. On the one hand we have Rosalind Franklin, a capable (if sometimes mistaken) research scientist in the King's College (London) team headed by Maurice Wilkins, which was working on the structure of the DNA molecule in competition with the Cambridge team of Watson and Crick. Watson's description of "Rosy" is personal and cruel. He is, of course, personal about everyone, and everyone is first-named, but no one in the book is so constant a target for aggressive attack as Rosy. She dressed badly, was stubborn in her views, harried her boss, wore her hair unbecomingly—in every way she was unsatisfactory, save as being the villainess of the piece and as being a member of the other team. Introducing her, Watson writes, "The real problem was Rosy. The thought could not be avoided that the best home for a feminist was in another person's lab." [4] Clearly Rosy, a normally good scientist, is abnormal as a woman.

By the same token, normal women are abnormally, indeed farcically, indifferent to science. Odile, the charming French wife of Watson's colleague, Francis Crick, is typical. Watson's presentation of her, at a time when he and Crick were struggling with an early and incorrect hypothesis, will recall his style: "Though

Odile could not follow what we were saying, she was obv
cheered by the fact that Francis was about to bring off his sec
triumph within the month. If this course of events went on, the)
would soon be rich and could own a car. At no moment did
Francis see any point in trying to simplify the matter [of their
scientific endeavor] for Odile's benefit. Ever since she had told
him that gravity went only three miles into the sky, this aspect of
their relationship was set. Not only did she not know any science,
but any attempt to put some in her head would be a losing fight
against the years of her convent upbringing. The most to hope for
was an appreciation of the linear way in which money was measured." [5]

Now Watson's views are Watson's views. Several scientific re-
viewers of his book, who knew the cast of characters presented
therein, were sincerely distressed by such thumbnail sketches,
and particularily by his treatment of Rosalind Franklin. Indeed,
in a paragraph at the end of the book he himself expresses his
regret for not seeing in her at the time the honesty, generosity and
courage which he later came to feel were an essential part of her
character. No one, I'm sorry to say, seems to have protested in
print about his character sketch of Mrs. Crick. Perhaps his colleagues, too, find the ignorance and selfishness attributed to her
charmingly feminine.

The point, however, is not that Watson is being outrageous in
his method of telling his story; of course he is. But it is worth cit-
ing because of his purpose in being outrageous. He is saying to
the common reader, "Don't be misled by fairy tales about noble
and selfless men of science who join hands to push back the fron-
tiers of darkness. We're really no different from anyone else, as
mean and selfish and given to intrigue as you are. *This is what we
are really like.*" He may be wrong, but he is not unintelligent. This
is the picture which his view of the scientific community from the
inside offers of the part women have played in that community,
and the part an attractive woman (Mrs. Crick) is seen as playing in
the world. If we allow for the unpleasant edge to his portraits
(since his book is intentionally unpleasant in order to abrade the
fuzz of clichés from the scientific hero), we find that he comes
very close to setting out typical beliefs and customary attitudes. In
its simplest form, the customary attitude toward women in our

ented world is this: if they are normal women,
~~al people~~; while if they are normal people, with
~~al interests and capabilities, they are abnormal~~
n't be both. It's a kind of double bind.

Another sort of double bind has operated against homosexuals:
abnormal men are regarded as abnormal people. The customary
attitude toward open homosexuality, which sees it as combining
two sorts of abnormality, has often been crueler by far than the
jesting and sometimes affectionate approach to the incompetence
attributed to women. This double bind can create an atmosphere
so lethal that homosexuals can live only by concealing their sexual
status. (Female homosexuals are spared the worst of this special
pressure simply because they are women and thus defined as in-
ferior/abnormal to begin with.)

In spite of recent breakthroughs, reminiscent of the early feminist successes, social pressure against seeing homosexuals as
ordinary human beings in their public, social lives is still very
strong. Like women, they are forced to accept one aspect of
themselves as isolating and opposed to the norms of society. In
order to be regarded as normal people, allowed to go about their
business in peace, they have had to agree that their sexual status
types them as abnormal men, and they have consequently con-
cealed their sexual characteristics. They may not, of course, have
accepted this enforced compromise morally or mentally, but the
fact of their concealment means that they have accepted it in
social (role-playing) terms.

This is the mirror image of the situation in which "normal"
women find themselves. They can act out their sexual status
openly, but the customary attitude toward them has caused them
to veer away from participation in the most advanced and progressive side of our activist, scientific culture and even to deny
that they are interested in it or likely to be competent at it. When
they do enter the fields of science and technology, they find that
their sexuality is apt to become suspect. Newspaper stories report
that women engineering graduates are beginning to move up on
the pay scale toward equality with men. Whether they will
achieve social and professional acceptance, however, is another
question.

"Normal people," in short, are normal men. What happens in man's world is the stuff we go by in judging the past, coping with the present, and planning for the future. Century after century of experience in running the world has persuaded men not only that they know a way to do it, but that the way they do it is right. In times of social strain they may begin to wonder about their achievements and suspect that something may have gone wrong, but they continue to believe that they will solve the problems which have cropped up, solve them alone and by the old methods, because they are the members of the human race who know how to do this. Even in bad times women are seldom welcome in man's world. On occasion they have been seen as scapegoats, responsible for the decline and fall of the normal male command of the situation, and firmly exiled from the arena of action. What recognition they receive in such eras is usually like that of Reginald Ecklestein or of Professor McClelland: an appeal to put their female skills to work at supporting activist men. It is not often a request to come out of the kitchen and lend a hand with running the show. In abnormal times, the idea of normality becomes very precious. It is not actual help in running the real world which men want from women, but the enactment of their mythic, traditional role, for this offers a magical reinforcement of confidence, an assurance that things are still all right, still more or less the same. Then men can deal with them by the old patterns, and women can help indirectly by offering emotional support.

But suppose things are not the same? This, of course, is the crux of the difficulty. If man's world can be purged of its difficulties and cured of its ills by men alone, perhaps the old division of roles is the right one. Perhaps effective action in the world by men has become difficult but not impossible; difficult, however, to the point where any single individual needs the support of others in order to act. If this is the case, a simple way to divide the human race into doers on the one hand and their supporters on the other is by sexes. Then if one sex is to be active and the other subordinate to the direction of the activists, the case that women would be subordinate to men is certainly arguable and indeed quite persuasive.

Should we, however, divide the world in two? It may be simple, but is it wise? How much talent do we lose by barring half the human race from acting directly on the ills we face? How much more do we tie up unproductively if the other half must spend part of its energies in keeping women in their subordinate place? Perhaps the male habit of command may, in the end, hamper social creativity as much as the feminine habit of withdrawal does just because it is a habit, and habits breed a fear of trying new ways to deal with changing situations. When the old ways don't work, power itself becomes a burden. The ruling caste, too, begins to find that failure is packaged in to its necessary activities. Self-pity is never far to seek in an emotional situation like that, and it is particularly corrosive for activists who feel themselves acting sacrificially for others but receiving no gratitude or comprehension in return. Their will to act suffers by such isolation. Power, said Lord Acton, tends to corrupt; and part of the corruption the powerful suffer from in bad times is a paranoid dislike of their own power, a petulant envy of the weak, and a sudden taste for frivolity. No one, in the end, profits by too clear-cut a division into rulers and ruled, for power is too important to be left to the powerful.

CHAPTER 9

All weakness tends to corrupt, and impotence corrupts absolutely.
Edgar Z. Friedenberg
Coming of Age in America [1]

FRIEDENBERG'S APHORISM does not contradict Acton's words, but simply states the corollary. It invites us to consider the effects of subordination everywhere, for weakness and power are opposite sides of the same coin in more situations than the myths. which sustain and explain woman's place in the world. If the powerful are corruptible by self-pity in bad times, they risk corruption by willfulness when they are confirmed and content in their role. Consistently they go too far and demand too much. Good or bad times matter less in the attitudes of their subjects, who always risk corruption by collusion with their masters. *Their* fault lies in bowing too easily to the irrational willfulness of the powerful when things are going well and remaining passive too long when burdensome power invites irresponsibility in the ruling caste. For them, it is a continual temptation to accede to the kind of immorality which, in our day, has been exemplified by Hitler and Stalin and then, in a kind of nightmare reciprocity, has begun to infect what once seemed to be American innocence.

Weakness and power work together both in myth and in reality. Historically we can see that the very existence of groups destined to lifelong submission invites arrogance and blindness in the dominant. Barriers to power which are held to be innate and thus uncrossable remove the check on the ruling group which alone can keep it in touch with the demands of actual events and situations. Unless they are subject to pressure from outside their caste, the powerful come to think themselves hallmarked for rule with a mythic symbol conferred by sex or race, secure in their magical dominance, and thus open to actual failure.

When the weak accept this magical difference, they condemn themselves to corruption. To the extent that an individual agrees that he is subordinate and barred from the highest ambitions of the society in which he lives, he will project this attitude into the roles he plays and build it into the internal structure of his own psychology. "Otherness," as Simone de Beauvoir saw very clearly, implies alienation from power. Women are *The Second Sex* because they are experienced by men as "others," that is, as essentially and inescapably different. It is not possible to be separate and equal, because being separate prevents one from acting in the one real world, man's world.[2]

This withdrawal from the possibility of action affects the behavior of all subordinate groups and, interestingly though not surprisingly, it affects them the same way. Those who have accepted subordination for whatever reason display attitudes and conduct which are typically and traditionally described as feminine. In history, song and story, the Negro Uncle Tom acts in orthodox "female" fashion: he is pliable, undemanding, trained to please and satisfied (on the surface, which is the only place it matters to his master) to live his master's life vicariously. He appears to want what his master wants, to find pleasure in his master's successes, to accept a place in the world that denies him a chance of independent action and judgment, and to do so without resentment. Since he cannot act autonomously, any plans he lays must find their consummation by means of tricks and indirection. If these tricks are discovered, he will be accused of such feminine faults as slyness and untrustworthiness.

The same thing holds true for another subordinate group, the poor, who exist outside the regular bulwarks of social recognition. Remembering his youth in a Brooklyn slum, Norman Podhoretz wrote in his escape story, *Making It,* "It is hard for the poor to make demands, for they know the demands will not be met and they learn to avoid the added bitterness of unnecessary disappointment by settling for whatever the world in its arbitrary way pleases to let them have."[3] That world, of course, is the world of economically normal men, and the observation could as well define the chronic avoidance of high ambitions which still plagues and inhibits women, even those of privileged class.

What it was like at the turn of the century for a talented girl appears very clearly in the memoir, *Period Piece*, which Charles Darwin's granddaughter, Gwen Raverat, wrote long afterward when she too had made her escape from the restrictions of her youth. She was an aspirant artist, untaught but always scribbling sketches, and of course she found herself reacting strongly to the work of various artists of the past. The reaction took a curious turn: she could not imagine actually being a famous painter; the most she could dream of was *marrying* one.

Thus, her admiration for the work of Thomas Bewick, an engraver and illustrator of some note, awoke within her a passionate wish to have been Mrs. Bewick. "Of course," she went on, "I should have liked still more to be Mrs. Rembrandt, but that seemed too tremendous even to imagine; whereas it did not seem impossibly outrageous to think of myself as Mrs. Bewick. . . . Surely, I thought, if I cooked his roast beef beautifully and mended his clothes and minded the children—surely he would, just sometimes, let me draw and engrave a little tailpiece for him. I wouldn't want to be known, I wouldn't sign it. Only just to be allowed to invent a little picture sometimes. . . . Of course I wanted still more, more than anything in the world, to be a man. Then I might be a really good painter. A woman had not much chance of that. I wanted so much to be a boy that I did not dare to think about it at all, for it made me feel quite desperate to know that it was impossible for me to be one." [4]

Actually, things were ceasing to be quite as desperate as that. Gwen Darwin did marry a painter, Jacques Raverat, but she did so after she had managed, all on her own, to get herself out of the world of well-brought-up, marriageable young girls and into the Slade School of Art. Of course it wasn't easy. She did it partly by positive persistence in going after what she wanted, but also by absolute refusal to act the expected role of charming young lady. This condemned her to live the formative years of her youth crosswise to custom and approval, odd-girl-out in all the usual social circumstances. One must want something very much to go through that.

Times have changed, but talented women still find themselves at cross-purposes with the norms of our society. Many feel that they must make a choice between working at their full capacity in pursuit of their ambitions and achieving success that is approved by others as being appropriately feminine. In comparing his mother's generation with college women of the sixties, David Reisman observed a kind of throttling down of aspiration at work in bright girls. They did not want to be dilettantes, but they felt that deep intellectual involvement in a discipline could be a threat to their happiness. Would not their choice of a demanding career put men off and prevent them from marrying? Fearing this, Reisman noted, "exceedingly bright and gifted students decline to extend themselves to the fullest lest they fall in love with a career that might restrict their choices in marriage." [5]

Since the mid-sixties when Reisman wrote, two forces have been working to change this pullback. First, of course, is the resurgence of active feminism, and second is the increasing cohesion of youth into a separate social group which turns its face against the traditional attitudes of the past. Whether both trends will continue to pull in the same direction is an open question. How influential they will be is another. For most women even now, success in the world should include success in woman's role. A career is not felt to be enough. And this ambivalence is a temptation to turn away from the possibility of high achievement as a human being and settle for second best, so that (like Podhoretz' poor) one will "avoid the added bitterness of unnecessary disappointment."

As we already remarked, homosexuals make up another group which differs from the norms of the powerful in our society, and they also pay for it by being separated from the use of power. Here too we find psychological traits which we think of as being feminine. It is easy—but I believe wrong—to assume that this occurs because male homosexuals naturally have a feminine character structure. Such an analysis is superficial even leaving aside questions of causality. Homosexuals vary greatly in their attitudes toward life. Some may really wish they were women. Some may simply not want to play the usual man's sex role. They are lumped together by the large and simplistic assumption that if they don't act entirely as men, there's only one other thing they can be: some sort of sham woman. This happens in other social contexts when a man wants to depart from the normal male role. Among some Siberian and American Indian tribes, for example, a man who wished to become a shaman-priest was required to wear feminine dress and, sometimes, to live entirely as a woman. The social system had no room for someone who wasn't either, just as some other systems have (or had) no room for twins, and consequently killed one or both so as not to raise puzzling and anomalous questions.

In fact, however, as I suggested in the last chapter, the double bind that distorts the homosexual's approach to life is not the same as that which shapes woman's role, but is its cross-cousin. Where women are allowed to act out their sexual impulses and constrained from pursuing their ambitions, it is the opposite for homosexual men. They can aspire as high as they wish as long as they pay the price of denying themselves the open expression of their sexual desires. The moment a whiff of doubt about these is felt, the suspect's grip on power can be challenged.

It is not their similar natures which produce similar characteristics in women and homosexual men, but their similar social situations. In societies where known homosexuality does not bar men from positions of power, these similarities are not found. They occur where members of each group are forced to deny part of themselves and accept a kind of abnormality as part of their nature. Locked out of the larger community of man's world, women and homosexuals develop profoundly ambiguous feelings about any sort of community they may set up themselves. Both groups are notorious for tight but short-lived cliques and bitter personal rivalries. Cattiness and disloyalty are expected, and cattiness and disloyalty are found, as they are found among all those who regard part of themselves as unacceptable. If society stamps you as a second-class citizen, how can you trust or value yourself highly? Then, *a fortiori*, how can you trust others who suffer from the same disabilities? Surely this, and not the genetic memory of prehistoric hunts, is the reason that men form bonds and women have tended not to. In fact, women do form bonds when they are able to see themselves as insubordinate potential activists; they have done so in both periods of feminist action.

Let us not forget, in cataloguing the traits which subordination tends to produce, to include the useful and valuable ones. Patience and endurance are true virtues, while there is great social value in the imaginative awareness of emotional atmosphere and personal relationships which is so often cited as being typically feminine. "If men in most societies play the instrumental assertive role," writes David McClelland, "they could not possibly succeed unless women were managing the interpersonal and emotional relationships which hold society together." [6]

This is flattering and partly true, but there is no reason to credit such a gift to women alone. It comes naturally to anyone in a subordinate position. One cannot live comfortably as a subordinate (in some extreme situations one cannot live at all) without developing a powerful sense of interpersonal relationships and social atmospherics. One lives around the edges of events, watching them and their instigators, profiting from them when one can, and always alert to avoid any threat they may carry. One cannot plan; one lives in the present and so, again, concentrates on the immediate surroundings of life. To cause anything to happen directly is difficult, if not impossible. One must, therefore, "manage emotional relationships" in order to get anything done; that is, one must work on the needs and desires of more powerful individuals and groups until they can be persuaded to do what the subordinate cannot do for himself. Again, this calls for a greater awareness of the human context within which one lives than is strictly necessary to an active, autonomous individual.

Nonetheless a larger awareness of the human context would profit us all in a world where the human context grows more important every day, where individual action becomes harder and harder, and where we desperately need to agree on how to work together toward common ends. To declare that this kind of awareness is sex-linked is both unnecessary and defeatist. Many men already possess this kind of intuitive insight, and surely more could learn it. It comes down, in the end, to an act of imagination: recognition of the reality of other people's needs. The subordinate learn it because they have to, but the powerful are not barred from this knowledge. With it, their power will be more lasting and their deeds more effective.

There is another characteristic which often accompanies insight into emotional situations and is all too easily taken as a virtue: the ability to please. This grace is not, of course, thought to exist in all women, but it is certainly a part of the feminine ideal. Indeed, real virtues like patience and loving-kindness are often praised in women not as admirable in themselves, but as admirable because they please men.

The whole question of pleasing is central to an analysis of woman's role, and we had better take time to consider its implications. I am talking, of course, about pleasing as a policy, and not about the natural desire to please those one loves and admires, or the spontaneous joy to be found in making one's intimates happy. This kind of pleasing is a part of loving and is to be found everywhere, in both sexes, among friends and lovers. Politeness is an attenuated social form of such pleasing, and an expression of general friendliness and trust. My subject here, however, is pleasingness as an attribute commonly expected of women and other subordinates by the powerful, and adopted by women and other subordinates both for defense and as a means of gaining ends they cannot achieve by their own direct actions.

On the face of it, the ability to please is an asset, though not a virtue, for any individual, whatever his sex. There are, however, circumstances in which this is not true for men. A Marine sergeant on Parris Island, for instance, is not at all anxious to please the men he commands. The emotions he first seeks to arouse in them (for patriotic ends, of course) are fear, awe and anger, shame and self-distrust. Unlike the sergeant, an executive may not actively wish to antagonize his aides; he may just find the job of pleasing them irrelevant to the matter at hand. Thus, when Robert McNamara retired as Secretary of Defense, a reporter recalled that the Secretary had combined great drive and decisiveness with an inability to exchange with his staff the ordinary commonplaces which a day-to-day working relationship usually calls forth. This lapse was pointed out to McNamara, and for some months he faithfully undertook to inquire about the health and well-being of the families of the men who worked for him. The effort ended when it proved to be more disconcerting to his aides than his normal disregard of personal ties.

Before him, Sherman Adams, President Eisenhower's aide-de-camp, was noted for his ability to create ill-will with no effort whatsoever. "It was a rare day," wrote Patrick Anderson in *The Presidents' Men*, "when a 'please' or a 'thank you' or a 'good morning' passed his lips. There was a grand egalitarianism about his rudeness; he bestowed it as casually upon secretaries and clerks as he did upon Senators and Cabinet members. Almost daily, his gruff demands would have one of his secretaries in tears, and one day, according to *Time* magazine, he managed the impressive feat of having all five of them in tears at once." [7]

The moral of this tale is obvious: the powerful need not please. It is subordinates who must do so—or at least it is subordinates who are blamed if they don't—and especially subordinates who live at close quarters with their superiors. The Negro Uncle Tom role was expected of body servants and those who worked in the big house, while field hands could be silent and sullen if only they submitted to the overseer's work demands. In the same way, woman's traditional role calls on her to please the wielders of power with whom she lives, as the Marri elder's wife pleased him, and as she was expected to please the other adult males of the family. If she did it out of love, well and good, but she had to do it out of duty, in any case. In most traditional societies the obligation to please extends to all adult males with whom a woman has social contacts. She need not please her children until her sons are grown, but this is her only sphere of autonomous power (extended, in the case of the mistress of a big house, to the servants) and, as we have seen, it is in this relationship of mother to young child that the myth of female power is born.

Socially, then, the need to please marks women as subordinates, though often they are petted subordinates, for pleasing is of course a delightful gift to receive. Success at anything is enjoyable, and a woman who knows how to please others may well be pleased with herself. There is, however, a problematic and generally adverse effect within a woman's psyche when pleasing becomes a political means to be used in any relationship at all, for any end: it is mentally and morally confusing. This brings a further fragmentation of effort into the already split entity of woman's role. One cannot dedicate oneself wholly to doing, and being, what is good if one must at the same time consider how to please, for the two sets of standards may well conflict. This ambivalence taints all virtues. It brings to their practice the consideration of how they appear to others. One can't simply be brave when bravery is called for; one must pause to ask oneself, "Am I being acceptably brave without being too hard and too stubborn?" One can't be generous out of a full heart without worrying over whether one is being too generous, at the risk of making a powerful intimate jealous. One hesitates before one speaks candidly lest one seem too outspoken, for that may mean that important confidences will not be offered in the future. Women's lives are molded by nuances like these. As we know, every role asks expressive behavior from the role-player, in order to explain the action he is taking. Woman's traditional role asks something more: that her behavior not only explain what she is doing, but indicate that she does it by the grace of her superiors. They are the watchers who hold power and in whose eyes one can so easily be shamed.

Shame, in fact, is an emotion which falls hard on subordinates. It is the penalty for not pleasing. One has misjudged the social situation in which one finds oneself, and failed at "managing interpersonal and emotional relationships." One is exposed. The powerful too may feel shame if they aspire too high and fail, but the emotion has a special edge for players of the feminine role because it is part of that role to be eternally aware of the potential judges who expect to be pleased. This is evidenced also by the fact that modesty, which is the sort of behavior that avoids public shame, is a feminine virtue, while boldness is highly thought of in men and poorly regarded in women.[8]

So to be pleasing turns out to mean that one must often conceal one's emotions behind the mask of the feminine role. Of course, this is another invitation to the slyness and indirection which men often find so baffling in women. Ideally, a woman will be discreet in public, but open and loving at home, in her own place. It upsets men to find that women sometimes continue to dissemble and disguise their feelings even there, even within the bounds of a known and intimate relationship. But trust, if forgone in public, is often hard to revive in private. "Managing interpersonal relationships," a feminine skill, is contradictory to acting out of a full heart. Changing back and forth between these approaches extends the split in woman's role deep into her own psyche. And always there is the chance that she may make a shaming mistake and overdo the expression of the feelings she has repressed in public. Then she runs the risk of finding that she is not praised for being warmly human, but condemned for being hysterical.

For once the idea that pleasingness is a proper part of the feminine ideal is accepted, it spreads everywhere and reinforces every limit which keeps women in their place. It can work in curious ways: Victorian women, for instance, were expected to be frigid. "I should say that the majority of women (happily for them)," wrote William Acton, a highly respected medical authority of the time, "are not very much troubled with sexual feeling of any kind. . . . As a general rule, a modest woman seldom desires any sexual gratification for herself. She submits to her husband, but only to please him." [9] To our generation, frigid submission may seem an odd method of pleasing a husband, but it removed the need for Victorian husbands to worry about pleasing their wives and reduced women to dolls whose demands could be ignored. It was, in its own way, a bulwark against female power, and the consistent repression of Victorian women must have increased the unconscious fear of their power among those dominant husbands and fathers.

Of course this mythic "fact" of women's frigidity was surely proved false by innumerable loving couples, but as a dogma it expressed an idea which still lingers on: that female passion can be too demanding to be pleasant. Labeling it abnormal is a familiar and handy way to deal with this problem. Then an unsatisfied woman has only herself to blame: she is a nymphomaniac. Even today, the typical player of woman's role may still feel it wise to hide her feelings until she is sure that showing them is safe.

The point is that failure to please, once pleasingness has been factored into a role, becomes a special disability. Any woman who acts persistently in an unpleasing way is not just committing a blunder which may, under certain circumstances (vide Secretary McNamara), be understandable and even forgivable. She is moving counter to her role and breaking its mold. Now a role-breaker, as we noted earlier, may begin by being simply funny or surprising, but if he persists he becomes frightening. To those around him, a role-breaker is a deviant, whose behavior is incomprehensible. It awakens hostility because no one knows where he will stop, or what he may be capable of doing. His behavior provides no clue to what can be predicted about his actions.

Recently we have been witnessing two excellent examples of the breaking of roles and molds and the frightened and hostile reaction to the changed behavior of the role-players in question, which occurred *even before* any overt threat to our social system was raised. Black people have broken their ancient silence and renounced their submissive (and traditionally pleasing) patterns of behavior. Young men and women increasingly refuse to play the old, and passive, role of learners in an adult world whose standards they now reject. Their use of dress and of hairstyles is a deliberate statement that they no longer care to please their elders, just as the wearing of African dress and hairstyles communicates the determination of the blacks to set up their own self-image, whether or not that pleases the white power structure. Long before violent elements had arisen in these groups, their simple presentation of themselves as they wished to be seen had provoked a startlingly intense reaction among those who still held—and hold—power firmly in their own hands. Growing a beard or wearing a dashiki confers no power on the defiant, it is merely a gesture. But the gesture challenges the *idea* of dominance as it is arranged in the present structure of society. It is a refusal to accept the norms of the past, and it declares a solidarity with others. All of them may be completely barred from actual power, but they no longer feel the need to please or appease it. Such gestures are mythic. They attack the order of the universe. The astonishing impact they produce is a measure of how deep is our sensitivity to mythic menace.

Women have been frightening in their time, and they may be again. The first reaction among men to the new resurgence of active feminism is, as we would expect, to find it funny. Other women react differently. What they have to say shows how deeply the idea of pleasing is twined into the traditional feminine role, for what good women tell their erring sisters the moment they challenge the order of the universe is that they are forfeiting their ability to please. "There's a certain look beloved women have, a look not apparent on the faces of those chosen to illustrate *The Second Feminist Wave*," a woman wrote *The New York Times Magazine* after it had published an article on a feminist group. "There is also a certain kind of envy that cannot be silent, but must attempt to bear down and destroy that which is envied—in this case the gift of love which some women attract, and others, alas, do not." [10] Like the old feminists, the new ones are being threatened with the most awful menace that can be mounted against them by a womanly woman: they will not be able to please men.

In the universe which woman's traditional role posits, this is indeed a terrible fate. Where men are seen as the only powerful actors and agents, a woman who cannot charm them has lost every chance of happiness and sees every road to fulfillment closed. Since, in this mythic world, she can do nothing for herself, her inability to persuade the dominant to take her part will doom her to being an old maid, a drudge, a beggar or hanger-on, an alien outsider at the feast of life. And her righteous, virtuous, pleasing sisters will tell her that it is her own fault. She has rejected the social contract which divides the world, by the mythic symbol of sex, into the mighty and the amiable. There is a rather repulsive *Schadenfreude* about such warnings by women to women rebels. One must remind oneself that they, and it, are born of insecurity and are a reflection of how widespread are the effects of the myth of feminine weakness, and how corrupting.

Indeed, such warnings have a use in the mysterious world which is structured by myth and patterned by role behavior. Role-breakers should be prepared to find themselves under attack, regarded as unattractive and frightening, running into hostility. Old, accepted roles throw shadows, and when the role-player steps away, he will find himself engulfed in the shadow role which is the reverse, or the negative role from the one he has left. The stereotype of the ideal, pleasing woman throws a shadow that we all know well: the negative role of the shrew. A consideration of this and of other negative roles will throw some light on the whole process of role-making and role-breaking.

CHAPTER 10

A whistling maid and a crowing hen
Are neither fit for gods nor men.

Old saying

It became the custom, when cows aborted, swine took fever, crops failed, floods rose and people perished, to look around for a witch. It has been a matter for much modern bewilderment that the guilt was almost always laid at the door of some lonely, poor and wretched old woman, hitherto submerged in humdrum insignificance. The explanation suggested by the witchcraft of West Africa is that the old woman voluntarily asserted and insisted upon her guilt. . . . In Africa . . . a witch spontaneously declares that it is she who killed every kinsman whose death she can recall, who ate all the dead infants, who blighted the dead cocoa-trees and engineered all the lorry-accidents.

M. J. Field
Search for Security [1]

THERE MUST HAVE been witches since time began. Shrewish wives and henpecked husbands appeared as soon as the institution of marriage did, and fairy tales tell us that ogres and evil stepmothers were haunting figures before history was written. Dr. Field and other anthropologists report that witch cults still flourish today. All these creatures are aberrant types, deviates from expected roles. No wonder they persist, for there are always people who can't fit the patterns prescribed by any society, no matter how lenient.

An interesting suggestion comes from Dr. Robert Jay Lifton, the social psychologist, whose knowledge of the Far East we have called on before. Lifton's study of China since the Second World War and the Communist take-over indicates "a sudden emergence in often exaggerated form of psychological tendencies previously suppressed by social custom." He believes that this "release phenomenon," producing a proliferation of deviant types, follows unexpected social upsets.[2] In other words, when aberrant roles are commonly seen, we may take it as a hint to look for profound social change. More and more individuals are finding it impossible to fit into the old sanctioned patterns.

Among women in China, says Lifton, the suppressed psychological tendencies which are now being acted out take the form of "displays of assertion and unwavering ideological aggressiveness." They are encountered not only among the female cadres of the Communist party, but also "in Chinese women who were still operating primarily within their families at a time when the society surrounding those families was literally falling apart." This outbreak of shrewishness was at least as startling in China as here, for the docile and pleasing woman was the expected, desired norm in the Orient as well as in the West.

It is Lifton's hypothesis that " 'the shrew,' whenever she appears in significant numbers, whether in China or Elizabethan England, is a specific product of social breakdown." We may add to these epochs that of our own stressful frontier society, which gave birth to such nineteenth-century militants as Carrie Nation, and we should not forget those vengeful *tricoteuses* of the French Terror, knitting away at the foot of the guillotine.

But the very fact that the shrew appears so promptly when shifting social circumstances call for changes in role behavior should warn us that she does not represent a true alternative to the old feminine role. As we have noted time and again, roles develop out of relationships, and it takes time for this to happen. Role behavior expressive of the action appropriate to a new relationship isn't understandable until it's been acted out, accepted and absorbed both by the role-player and the other people who are part of the changed situation. As these new styles of living appear, they combine character traits in new patterns, they open channels of expression here and they free frozen talents there. They are truly creative: one couldn't imagine them until the altered situation has called them forth.

Thus we can see how the growing strength of the new middle class at the end of the medieval era contributed to the blossoming of abilities which produced the Renaissance. Not only did the rising bourgeoisie channel economic vitality into the community, it also brought forth new men to challenge the old orthodoxies of thought and conduct, and a new mood of hope and daring very different from the endemic melancholia which Huizinga found so characteristic of the period he examined in *The Waning of the Middle Ages*.[3] No doubt the intimacy of personal connection which the new sort of home and the new small family produced had a part to play in this changed character structure.

We don't see this sort of new creation in the shrew. She is, rather, a negative caricature of the compliant, pleasing woman. As we know, there are two sides to a role: what the role-player does, and what the role-others understand him to be doing. *It is easier for each side to do the opposite of what was done before than to create something new.* Consider it first from the woman's side: overnight responsibility is thrust on someone who has been trained to leave action to others. The role she knows best will no longer serve her. With no one to please or beguile into acting for her, she must act for herself. In turning away from her old role, she reverses it in a total looking-glass shift to its opposite, with the idea that if the old ways won't work, she'll get as far from them as she can.

In the background is the long indoctrination she has had to assure her that women will lose their ability to please men if they act independently. Now she must act independently. What is more natural, then, than to assume that she will not please men and to let the whole exercise go by the board? Under the strain of making decisions and learning to manage for herself in man's world, it is likely that she will happily dispense with any social efforts that don't seem necessary, and that old methods of charming and persuading will be the first to go into the discard, for they have clearly lost their usefulness.

But this is a reversal and not a creation. The shrew's behavior expresses the same message as does that of the compliant woman: pleasing goes with dependence and subordination. Being no longer subordinate, being charged with responsibility and forced to act, the shrew accepts, and indeed may enjoy, the fact that she doesn't please her former superiors. As we all remember, Shakespeare's recipe for turning an Elizabethan shrew back into a pleasing woman was to reverse the reversal. He gave Kate a dominant male to take the possibility of action out of her hands, and she learned soon enough how to please him. If her role had really been a new creation, with its own vitality, it would not have been so easily overthrown.

As for the other participants involved in the relationship, we can understand their contribution to the negative role of shrew easily enough if we consider that what is happening is what they have always feared. The myth of female power is supplanting the myth of female weakness. The negative role of shrew is one they *expected* to surface, if that happened. Again, there is nothing for them to learn *de novo*, there is simply the opposite of what had been expected in the past.

The role of shrew, then, represents what happens when the ritual actor of the title part in the myth of female weakness takes the first step away from her traditional role, and it appears more forcefully when this step is sudden because external circumstances make it necessary. A forced change like this may call forth new energies as hitherto passive subordinates rise to the occasion, but it does not allow creativity to develop a new role. Negative roles are reactions, not actions. The unpleasing face of the shrew has had no time to learn a new expression, it merely reacts away from the mask of necessary pleasing it had worn for so long. If her behavior is rough and insensitive, it is because she has had to abandon the old virtues of the courtier which she knew so well: to please, to yield, to charm and to be docile. No one has taught her the prince's virtues of honor, generosity and panache. We know from Freud how close opposites lie to each other within our minds, and the shrew is the opposite counterpart of the feminine woman produced by the traditional role.

Of course throughout history there have been women who broke out of the feminine stereotype and got away with it, exceptional women who were allowed to be exceptional and were still admired. When we come to examine these cases, however, we find that one way or another these women who departed from the female role *took on another*. Their behavior was comprehensible because it could be identified with some other familiar pattern. The alternative role they made theirs did not have to be specifically feminine as long as it wasn't exclusively masculine. It was enough for the new role to be recognizable so that the player could be defined and some sort of prediction made about what behavior could be expected. Once this is possible, the player ceases to be a frightening deviate.

Thus Joan of Arc could be assigned to the role of saint, moved by God through the voices she heard, and so not herself responsible for donning armor and leading the French to victory on the battlefield. Her English enemies and captors did not dispute her supernatural powers. They simply claimed that these were evil, not holy, and burned her as a witch, assigning her, for political purposes, to a negative role. It was ineffective in the long run, and Joan figures in social consciousness today as saint and martyr. Elizabeth the First of England and Catherine the Great of Russia were queens, women who ruled. The role of ruler could be accepted as taking precedence over the role of woman in the public mind particularly because each woman was a successful ruler. Each of them, too, had a keen public relations sense and consciously played to the nation. Their much publicized favorites also let the public know that if they were unfeminine, they were not unfemale: though the queens did not play woman's submissive role, they did not overtly deviate from it as did Christina of Sweden, who suffered for it. Even so, the feminine Mary of Scotland, unsuccessful as a ruler, has always been more popular than her rival.

Victoria, of course, was the Queen as Wife. In her era, Florence Nightingale suppressed the open display of her considerable administrative talents and figured in the public mind as The Lady with the Lamp, nurse and healer. Madame Curie could also be seen in the role of nurturing woman whose work would contribute to healing the sick. What's more, she worked with her husband and not alone. And so on. Even Eleanor Roosevelt, who was hated and mocked at first view for the "unpleasing" qualities attributed to her, came in the end to be loved and esteemed when she had aged into the recognizable role of slightly eccentric great-aunt-to-the-world and lady of the manor with a concern for the poor.

These role-breakers make one thing clear: it is possible to move away from one stereotype with impunity, if there is shelter near another. If one doesn't find an alternative, the negative role which shadows the traditional role will take over. Sometimes, as with the shrew, the role-player may invite this to happen, but the other people involved will see that it does in any case. For these role-others expect to be guided by the role-player. If his behavior deviates from the expected pattern, they may find it simply funny at first, but if it persists they move from bewilderment to hostility. They cannot predict what this role-breaker is going to do, specifically what he is going to do *to them.* Bad enough; but beyond it there is a further complication: they do not know what is expected *of them.*

For roles are reciprocal. The principal player not only communicates the significance of what he is doing, he evokes the proper responses from the others involved with him. When the actions of the central figure become confusing, what are the other participants to do? Their first reaction, we have noted, is to laugh—if the deviation is minor and does not touch them too clearly. In fact, one of the great sources of humor is inappropriate action by a role-player. Probably humor has the specific social value of enabling this sort of minor deviation to be accepted and "laughed off," so that the tenor of life continues. To laugh at an action implies that it happened "in play" and needn't be taken seriously, and therefore that one isn't involved oneself. That saves the other members of the relationship from anxiety, and it also allows the entrance into the situation of "play" in another sense—flexibility and permissible deviation from a norm. This, in turn, permits a degree of change in the role which is acceptable because it isn't demanding and therefore isn't frightening. When a situation is only "funny ha-ha," as the children say, it isn't "funny peculiar." [4]

But if the inappropriate action becomes too strange or cuts too close to the bone, it ceases to be funny. Then the role-others feel themselves threatened from without by the possibilities of what the deviant may make happen. Worse, they feel threatened from within by the fear of falling into inappropriate actions themselves, for they have lost any certainty as to what their own behavior should be. This intimate difficulty is even more menacing than the threat of unpredictable conduct on the part of the mold-breaker. *That* might just possibly be ignored, but what one does oneself, one is responsible for and may be shamed for. One cannot ignore one's own inability to act properly, one's ignorance of what to do next. The role-breaker threatens the order of the universe not just by his own challenge to it, but by disturbing the accustomed connection with this order which is felt by other people. Suppose one becomes identified with this challenge? Strangeness becomes more than external. It invades one's own inner citadel, and it is this which is unforgivable.

Faced with this threat to their own inner stability, the confused participants in a relationship menaced by a role-breaker reach out for some explanation of his conduct, some guide to their own proper behavior in this unwarranted situation. What is he doing, and how are they to treat him? Being frightened, they want to separate themselves from the troublemaker and hold him at a distance. The means they find at hand is to call up the negative, shadow role, the opposite of the expected one. Thus, the pleasing woman, the public ideal of wife and lover, is shadowed by the shrew. Such a woman is seen not as trying to do something new, but as failing to do something old: so the feminists are told over and over that they are losing their ability to please.

The dominant male is also shadowed by a negative role. In his case it is not a reversal of the traditional pattern, but an exaggeration of it. What is feared in every negative role is willful, uninhibited, antisocial power, an ego on the loose and uncontained by social obligations to others. In the case of women, this means a reversal of behavior from docility to dominance. For men, it means the increase of the dominance they wield already until their power grows so great that they are answerable to no one. The shadow role of the dominant male is the ogre.

We have witnessed a near-perfect illustration of this shift from the traditional to the negative role in our own time. During his second term in office the public personality of President Lyndon Johnson underwent a remarkable transformation. Johnson had always been seen as a powerful and dominating character, but now his behavior became so obtrusive that it began to overshadow, in the eyes of the public, all that he had actually accomplished. His energy and his ambition had helped him to achieve a great deal, but now the "can-do" man began to do too much. He was breaking out of the relationship which must bind the President to the public, and he was ceasing to make what he was doing explicable. This came through as willfulness and insensitivity. The public began to feel that they could not safely predict his behavior. His actions seemed extreme. But not only did he appear unable to retreat from them, he did not even seem to recognize that they could be assessed as strange or unjustified.

Uneasily his constituents felt that he was leaving them behind, leaving them out of his calculations and moving past the proper activity of the dominant male into its negative role. Of course there were objective political reasons for the switch, but they do not explain the speed with which it took place. From being "Big Daddy," a figure of authority who could be understood though not loved, Johnson passed into being the shadow behind Big Daddy, which (as the fairy stories make clear) is the ogre who eats the young. No doubt Johnson himself changed very little, at least until he began to sense the change in the way people felt toward him. But public opinion changed quickly and profoundly because the expected role of President was violated and the ruler could no longer evoke the necessary reciprocity from those who were ruled. In their eyes all vestige of a father figure who respected their rights and their being had vanished. The result was an extraordinarily fast reversal from positive to negative in Johnson's image. This is evidence of the close tie between the negative image and the threat of unlimited power. Once Johnson announced that he would not run again for the Presidency, his popularity began to return; and when he was finally out of office, his aura of mythic menace disappeared entirely. Even some who had attacked him most bitterly grew rather nostalgic over the outsize gesture and rhetoric that had worried them before. Which should remind us that political factors are impossible to gauge except at the moment when the emotions they awake are actually in being. This is why the "science" of poll-taking founders so often on unexpected reefs.

The most familiar negative role of all is the witch. If the shrew is the opposite and shadow of the ideal pleasing woman, the witch is the shadow and opposite of the loving mother. Here too it is the power that is feared, but in this case it is magic power. It is easy to see why if we think again of the early mother-child relationship from the point of view of the child. The mother's power to give or to withhold comfort seems magical to the child, because he experiences it long before he can understand the whys and wherefores of the gift or the denial. It antedates language and logic. The child learns to trust and to love the huge creature who comes and goes, gives and denies, and changes the world around him before he and she have any words with which to communicate. Things happen magically, in mysterious ways. The witch retains the magical power of the woman who can effect these mysterious changes, but she has forfeited the trust of her partner-child. Joan of Arc thus was accused of witchcraft by the English because they couldn't deny her power, for she had beaten them in the field, but they couldn't permit themselves to think that such a defeat by a woman was normal. It had to be magical.

The witch, in short, is the bad mother—or, rather, the mother who seems to the child to be bad, for every child must be frustrated and left wailing by his mother at some point, since his desires begin by being total and what he really wants is omnipotence. Because the mother-child duality begins before any sort of behavior can be expected or any explanations offered, every thwarted child has had a glimpse of the witch behind the beloved face of his mother: this figure is really universal. She turns up everywhere, in any number of forms. The witch who caught Hansel and Gretel is (in psychological terms) the mother who might punish them for running away. The West African witch, cited by M. J. Field in the quotation at the head of this chapter, spoke of "eating all the dead infants." In Chicago only the other day (so to speak) Bruno Bettelheim found that one of the schizophrenic children he was treating "was convinced that her mother wanted to bake her in the oven and eat her," just as Hansel's witch was planning to bake him.[5] A nursing child, we might remember, "eats" its mother. Anger and fear of the mother, dating back to those early days, might well bring forth the idea that the guilty child may expect a reversal of the process: it will be eaten by the witch-mother. Among the Pueblo Indians, a cure for any disease which the patient believes to be caused by witchcraft is for the sick man or woman to be adopted into another clan. This effectively provides him with *a new mother* and breaks the link with the old one, now turned into a witch.

These negative roles are all associated with the abuse of power and, as Lifton suggests, with social change, for we often find that social change permits and increases this abuse: when traditional hierarchies break down, power is no longer bound by customary limits. The breakdown calls for new approaches—that is, for new roles—and at the same time it makes it harder for people to understand what the central role-player is trying to do: custom no longer helps to explain his actions. Lifton noted the appearance of the shrew in modern China and in Elizabethan England. The latter period was one in which we also find another deviant type, the witch, on the rise. Hugh Trevor-Roper, the English historian, has recently documented a recrudescence of the witch craze in the 1560s, at a time when religious wars were turning Europe upside down.[6] The witch hunts which became so frequent then lasted well into the seventeenth century and, as we all remember, reached as far as Salem, Massachusetts.

In India today social change continues to produce witches. There is a section of Mysore where irrigation has recently been introduced. With it has come a sudden prevalence of witches. The increase in the quantity and the variety of agricultural products has brought this backward region into a money economy and women have overnight become moneylenders. In the past, such few advances of credit as were made came from rich land-holders to their clients, were long-term, and were hedged about with traditional safeguards which prevented the ruin of the borrowers. The new women moneylenders, however, are not inhibited by such considerations, and they are often hard and demanding. Their driven clients tend to react by accusing them of witchcraft.

For these women are violating the role expected of them. The anthropologist who reports the case, Scarlett Epstein, remarks that they are not only being condemned for their greed, but that "such a condemnation is a reaffirmation of the traditional social structure in which women did not enter the field of money lending. . . . The ideal peasant woman . . . was a woman who worked hard on the lands of her husband and in the house, who bore many children, particularly many sons, and who was obedient to her husband . . . and generous to his kin." Summing up, Dr. Epstein adds, "A sociological function of witch beliefs widely recognized in anthropological literature is their tendency to support the system of values and thus to sustain the social structure."[7] In other words, negative roles work to support the order of the universe just as positive roles do. The latter are promises, the former threats.

Dr. Field's work in West Africa reveals another aspect of the witch role: the acceptance by the woman of the role. Social change has been endemic for a generation in this part of the world. Dr. Field is both an anthropologist and a practicing psychiatrist, who first went to Ghana in the 1930s and returned in 1955 to practice there. She is thus familiar both with the colonial period and with the effect of independence on the population. Aside from these political changes, both of which broke old tribal patterns, economic change has had repercussions.

In her practice, Dr. Field finds a regular tendency among women who are suffering from depression—that is, from an overwhelming sense of failure and weakness in their real lives—to accuse themselves of witchcraft, often including the murder of their children. They may fear this identification and struggle against it, and yet accept it because it seems to offer the only possible explanation for the course of their lives. Any identification, it seems, is better than the baffling confusion of not knowing where one is or what is to happen next. In addition, of course, the witch role permits the woman to imagine that she can exercise some sort of power, even if it is evil power; and no doubt it recalls the time when, as the mother of young children, she really did enjoy power. Thus, in her need for some understanding of, and control over, the world, she accepts and even courts (while still fearing) the dark role that shadows the mother role which once was hers.

The ease with which these negative roles appear suggests that roles have a cohesive internal strength. A questioned role doesn't simply disappear, it flips over into its opposite, with the character traits reversed but holding together in the same old way. It seems that even when the social context surrounding it begins to crack and to fade, a role will struggle to endure and to reproduce the same sort of relationship in which it was first conceived. The reciprocal action which the role commemorates and calls for worked once; perhaps it can be put to a new use.

What I am saying here is more than "habits are hard to break." So they are, and anyone who has learned a pattern of behavior will tend to persist in it, like Pavlov's dogs. But roles are, by definition, more than individual in their scope. They involve other people. They reflect the working of the social system and the influence of the cultural ambience. They express significance and invoke reaction: "If I do this, the right thing for you to do is that. If my attitude is thus and so, yours should respond in this fashion. This is a serious matter. That is a joke." Their persistence reaches beyond the role-player and affects those who are involved with him. Once these others have been taught what to expect from the player of a certain role, they will expect such behavior from other players of roles that are similar, and they will know how to behave in return. The self-sustaining momentum of a role, therefore, makes it a conservative force, but as long as it contains any social utility, it will also be a shaping force.

Thus, social upheavals are more apt to widen or narrow the utility of any role and to put it to work in new ways than they are to destroy it entirely. Woman's traditional triple role instructs girls in how to get on in the world by pleasing men, how to care for children and how to manage a household. How important each segment of the role is depends partly on the personality of each woman, partly on the people around her and partly on the current social situation. If we take an overall look at the situation today, we see that each segment of woman's role is affected differently. Pleasing men may be less important for more career women than it used to be, but it is still a valuable capability. Caring for young children is, in America, a larger part of a woman's life, for a limited time, than it is almost anywhere else. As we have noted, the two-generation family and the lack of servants put young mothers in sole charge of pre-school children more than 90 percent of the time, apparently a unique situation. Managing a household otherwise, however, has declined spectacularly as a socially useful skill, even with servants almost nonexistent. Nowadays one buys in a shop things that were made at home only a generation or two ago, and food is processed so completely that cooking has ceased to be a necessity and become a leisure art.

This decline in the economic value of woman's traditional role has, in fact, drawn a great deal of significance and reward out of it. When a household was in part a factory, women were in touch with society and its demands at home almost as much as their husbands were abroad, and more than many women with jobs in business are now. When Solomon described "the virtuous woman" in the last chapter of Proverbs, he set the limits of her activity very wide indeed. She was no housebound creature, but instead one who "seeketh wool and flax, and worketh willingly with her hands. She is like the merchants' ships; she bringeth her food from afar. She riseth while it is yet night, and giveth food to her household and a portion to her maidens. She considereth a field and buyeth it; with the fruit of her hands she planteth a vineyard. . . . She perceiveth that her merchandise is good; her candle goeth not out by night. She layeth her hands to the spindle and her hands hold the distaff. . . . She maketh herself coverings of tapestry. . . . She maketh fine linen and selleth it, and delivereth girdles unto the merchant. . . . She openeth her mouth in wisdom, and in her tongue is the law of kindness. . . . Give her of the fruit of her hands, and let her own works praise her in the gates."

Entrepreneur, trader, investor in land, manufacturer of many sorts of salable merchandise, capable of opening her mouth in wisdom and commanding respect for her opinions, here is the picture of a woman whose role made her an active member of the community, whose work had a fundamental objective value that was clear to all, and whose energies and talents could be used to the full. Nor was such activity thought to make her family suffer: "Her children rise up and call her blessed; her husband also, and he praiseth her." If this is woman's traditional role, it is being played today not by suburban housewives, but by the manager of a middle-sized business or the mayor of a small city. And yet the *idea* of a limiting traditional role is still piously invoked to keep women in their place "at home." It is a very different kind of home, however, from the busy community Solomon described, or even the reduced single-family unit of the nineteenth century which still possessed considerable economic utility.

What we have now is a discontinuity between the idea of what a role should include and involve and its actual contemporary content and usefulness. Getting rid of the role, however, is not the answer; or it is very, very seldom the answer, and getting rid of roles altogether is impossible. For human behavior is patterned by learning and playing roles, just as animal behavior is patterned by instinct. In fact, some ethologists are coming to believe that

animal behavior, too, is learned, in part at least, and not entirely
a matter of instinct. Even in the animal kingdom, that is, situations and relationships affect behavior. As for us, at any rate, to
recall Talcott Parsons' words once more, we do not know who we
are without roles, nor who other people are.

But if we don't we are lost in a world of strangers. The English
theoretical analyst, R. D. Laing, believes that it is just this sort of
confusion which induces schizophrenic splits: "Interpersonal action
which tends to confuse or mystify . . ." he writes, "makes it
difficult for the one person to know 'who' he is, 'who' the other is,
and what is the situation they are 'in.' He does not know 'where he
is' anymore." [8] Behavior, that is, has got to fit some accepted
pattern, or it will not communicate sensibly with those others with
whom we live from the day of our birth to the day of our death.
No single action means anything at all until it can be seen as part
of a language of conduct that is understood in a social system, just
as no single sound means anything until its hearers know what
language the speaker is using. By patterning behavior so that it is
comprehensible, roles keep society coherent.

This being so, the continuing concern of any society must be to
avoid freezing behavior into roles that were appropriate to past
situations, but have now lost so much of their utility that they
invite misunderstanding, both from the role-player who may find
himself forced into attitudes that don't suit him and from the other
members of the relationship. As Laing remarks, "Those who deceive themselves are obliged to deceive others. It is impossible for
me to maintain a false picture of myself unless I falsify your
picture of yourself and of me [that is, the picture of the relation-
ship]. I must disparage you if you are genuine, accuse you of
being a phoney when you comply with what I want, say you are
selfish if you go your own way, ridicule you for being immature
if you try to be unselfish, and so on. The person caught within
such a muddle doesn't know whether he is coming or going. In
these circumstances what we call psychosis may be a desperate
effort to hold on to something. It is not surprising that the something may be what we call 'delusions.'" [9]

A changing society tends to negate old roles, and so to falsify
them. Since we cannot make and unmake them quickly, we must
accept the necessity of changing them, or else our common lan-

guage of behavior will lose its relevance. The enormous advantage
that human beings have over the rest of the animal kingdom is
the flexibility which our command of languages—of words, but
also of behavior—gives us. We can keep in touch with new needs
and with each other. The conservatism of a going system tugs us
one way, the demands of new conditions tug us another. In order
to continue to speak to each other, we shall have to coin new
words and learn to accept and understand new ways of acting.

The position of women is one of the areas of contemporary life
in which new demands are being strongly felt. Woman's role as
conceived in the past was a means of channeling activities, some
of which have become outmoded, within relationships which are
changing their structures. The orthodox pattern is taking on an air
of absurdity and exaggeration: of falseness. Still revered by some,
it is bitterly attacked by others; Alexander Portnoy's view of the
mother role, for example, could hardly be more negative. His
mother's approach to the role was hated and feared. One reason is
that it doesn't work any longer. It is not what society needs.

But because some aspects of woman's role still incline women
to obsolescent behavior, we can see before our eyes the way that
social tradition and present social needs struggle together until
new life styles emerge. Woman's role is a good laboratory example
to examine, because it has been the scene of such a struggle long
enough for us to note effects and not simply beginnings. Here,
roles are changing and even some of the mythology surrounding
them has been shifted and replaced.

CHAPTER 11

Only a small part of reality, for a human being, is what is actually going on; the greater part is what he imagines in connection with the sights and sounds of the moment. . . . This is not to say that his world is a fantasy, his life a dream, or any such poetic pseudo-philosophical thing. It means that his world is bigger than the stimuli which surround him, and the measure of it is the reach of his coherent and steady imagination. An animal's environment consists of the things that act on his senses. . . . He does not live in a world of unbroken space and time, filled with events even when he is not present or when he is not interested; his "world" has a fragmentary, intermittent existence, arising and collapsing with his activities. A human being's world hangs together, its events fit into each other; no matter how devious their connections, there always are connections, in one big framework of time and space. . . . *The world* is something human.

Susanne K. Langer
"The Growing Center of Knowledge" [1]

CAN ONE CONSIDER controversy without falling into it? I said at the beginning of this book that any discussion of woman's place and woman's role was likely to start with the question of what it ought to be, not with a description of what it is or was. The closer we get to the present and to the immediate, the more likely we are to find ourselves taking sides on this or any other social question. Time and history give us perspective, room to ponder the processes of change and the imperatives of the past without being buffeted by the shock of immediate events. It is easier to accept the idea that any position, even the one we hold, is relative and that many ways of handling a recurrent situation have been found workable. But can we stick to this objectivity in the here and now?

Never entirely, I am sure; but least of all if we confine our discussion to woman's role and the changes taking place in it. Our chance of thinking impartially depends on our continuing to use "woman's place" as a landmark in a larger frame. As I said earlier, my intention is to explore the overall "set" of our society and the trends and processes at work within it, using the assigned position and role of women as a reference point. What does it mean for our society, for instance, that we have taken that "one big framework of time and space," which, as Susanne Langer says, is a unique, connected, human artifact, and split it up? What does it tell us about our ways of thinking and feeling?

We have already looked at the split in the human world between man's outer space and women's inner place in a general way. Now, as we move toward the situation today, we will find it useful, I think, to consider another sort of split. This is the unevenness that time raises in the way we look at the world. Why is it so much easier to deal with the past than with the present? The answer is obvious—something we all know; which means, as I suggested earlier, that it is worth pausing to look at it, instead of taking it for granted.

Certainly the fact that the present is controversial doesn't mean that the events of the past are established as true beyond dispute. Too many historians have assured us that the past is reinterpreted by each changing stage of "the present" for us to be deceived about that. But the very fact that the events and ideas of the past can be manipulated means that they can be separated from the framework of concepts surrounding them. We see that they are open to various interpretations. For the living, on the other hand, today's facts are embedded in today's situation. We accept them as being self-evidently true, as signifying what they are; or at least, we try to. We are unhappy with puzzles and ambiguities, uneasy with shifting roles and mysterious behavior. Why?

Because they demand something from us. Present events act on us and call for action by us. Since we can change them, not simply define or describe them, they acquire a moral presence. They pose a question of responsibility, and by doing so they change the way we look at them. The past can be described and debated, but it doesn't call for action—except, of course, as its effects continue into the present and so become the present. But of the true past, one can say: this condition existed, it resulted in these actions and reactions which produced these events and ways of looking at the world. Not so with the present. Here we say, this condition exists—in the same world as the observer. Therefore he is no longer merely an observer, because being present he is involved with the condition. Whether he evades direct involvement or not (and one can't, after all, become involved in every problem), the question arises: Do I approve of this situation? Is it right that it should exist? Can it be changed? And how?

So valuing invades description, moral judgment confounds analysis. The objectivity we found easy in looking at the past becomes a matter of degree when we deal with the present, not something we can achieve absolutely no matter how "scientific" our approach. Even the most dedicated social scientists find it difficult to get rid of the idea that some human situations are better than others, not perhaps in the way of an overall judgment of a total society, but at least in part. They may cling to an ideal of objective reporting, but it is hard not to form *some* conclusions about value, if only on the basis that the people being investigated seem happy and content with the way they live. An unspoken assumption hovers here that it is absolutely good to be happy, not simply that happiness is the measure of a viable society. Or, to put it another way, a viable society which contents its members is to be taken as a good society, while deviates, alienated fantasists and suffering neurotics denote a society approaching breakdown, which is a bad society. Even with this pragmatic approach, we have not avoided a value judgment.

So, in this sense at least, moral questions are bound to be raised when current social situations are under discussion. In fact, if they were not raised, a strange condition of separation between man and his world would exist, which would itself shift man's relation to life. No one can *not* care about the rights and wrongs of the human condition unless he has moved deep into alienation from humanity. The question is how to avoid being swamped by emotional reactions to pressing situations, in which analysis loses its saving distance of view and myth takes over. For myth, be it noted, exists entirely in the present tense: a continuous, demanding present, the mood imperative, the desire which powers it unappeasable. In his well-known analysis of myth, Mircea Eliade speaks of mythic events as taking place not in the sequential, historical time with which we are familiar, but *in illud tempore,* in another sort of time: sacred, eternal, ritual, and recurrent. The force of myth is due to the fact that we react to it *as if* it were present before our eyes, for it is indeed present in our taut nerves. In the past, says Eliade, ritual served to familiarize, and so to protect, the witness of this breakthrough of the other, sacred time into the everyday.[2] We have ceased, for the main part, to conceive of the sacred as underlying and shaping our everyday, secular world; but we have not got rid of mythic compulsions.

Our only defense is to be aware of them, to understand and allow for the fact that our view of the human world is apt to be adulterated by what we want to believe, by our unsatisfied emotions, our ambitions, desires and needs. These desires are a necessary part of our lives, for they give us the impetus to act, and so to attempt to control the future or change the present. The question is simply how best to use the drive of desires, how best to avoid being deceived by them, and above all, how to escape the fallacy which Freud christened "omnipotence of thought": the idea that the mind and the will can control the world without effective action, that to want something is enough.

A glance back into the recent past will show us how easy it is to believe our own moral imperatives, and how they can deceive us about our ability to change the world to match them. In America, both world wars gave birth to sincere moral aspirations which set out to meet real and continuing needs. They were sound reactions to real problems, easily forgotten in the negative era in which we live today, which is characterized by hostility between individuals and groups and by breakdowns in long-established social relations. Yet only a generation ago, W. H. Auden's description of our time as an "age of anxiety" was countered at popular level by Wendell Willkie's invocation of the "one world" that technology and statesmanship were already demanding. Throughout the political power structure, and in the mass media, Willkie's idea of global unity was extolled. President Roosevelt dispatched him around the world, during the critical days of the Second World War, to preach the gospel to our allies and their leaders, Stalin and Chiang Kai-shek. At home the concept was seized on as a noble war aim, but also as one that science and political necessity might, for once, bring into being in the real world: the logical next step.

Nothing happened. As so often occurs, the poet, Auden, turned out to be a better prophet than the statesman. Today the need to organize mankind into some sort of workable community is more pressing than ever—and further away. If we are more aware of those others who share the globe, the seas and the atmosphere with us, it is not in a spirit of brotherhood. They are frightening strangers, a pushing crowd of aliens and rivals. Instead of fusing us together, the pressures under which we live have opened the cracks in the social structure to let in ghosts: feared shadows, wrong choices, the children of the left hand who appear when our hopes have failed and turned to mistrust.

The trouble with Willkie's idea was not that it was wrong, or false, or foolish, but that it ignored the lengthy processes needed to implement it. It assumed that roles and social structures and ways of looking at the world which had emotion invested in them could be changed overnight by a plan that seemed logically self-evident. It ignored the inescapable truth which Susanne Langer states so simply: that we live in an imagined world, a world of intricately related concepts and causes, even as single individuals. Changes in the physical world, scientific advances, new forms of communication, access to new geographical areas will certainly change the way we think and feel and apprehend reality. But until our minds can take them in and fit them, somehow, into the pattern of reality with which we are familiar, they will not be a usable part of our world.

For it is not enough to experience events, not even enough to react to them. Our look at negative roles has told us that a reaction tends to continue the old situation, the old relationship, which by definition is failing. Far from bringing us closer to novelties and strangeness, unaccepted, unintegrated changes in our world are likely to make us step back in fear, angry and uneasy at the players of reversed roles that have taken the place of those we knew. We need time and effort for our imagination to find a place for these mysterious happenings in our old, familiar world, and an explanation of how they connect with us. We have got to think these events into juxtaposition with the old structure of experience, and the newer and more startling they are, the harder that is.

To say that it is necessary for human beings to accept change is true enough, but it is only the beginning. How does acceptance take place? It doesn't happen automatically. Necessity may be the mother of invention, but sometimes she turns out to be sterile. Acceptance of change involves a psychological process of recognition and placement and rearrangement of all that we construct upon the stimuli that reach us from the outer or the inner world. Individually, this is just what goes on during psychoanalysis, as the patient shifts his structure of belief and network of symbolization. His own desire for change can do a great deal to speed up the process, to the extent that it is a real desire and not simply a reaction to exterior pressure. Even so, there is always work to be done before an adjusted system of relationships feels so natural and habitual that we are free to think past it without being distracted by its novelty.

The psychological strain of meeting a continuing rush of experience and assembling it into some kind of order, some sort of structure that will hold together for the future and continue to explain the world, can't be measured, but obviously it's considerable. Challenging for some, it's certainly overwhelming for others. The effect of this kind of strain can be seen all around us, acutely in mental institutions and endemically in the distrust between social groups which we are coming almost to take for granted, as men for so long took for granted ague, malaria and leprosy.

For there is an evident corollary to Mrs. Langer's remarks. If the human world of the individual is an imagined world, the social world that we share with others is a world that we have imagined together and agreed with each other to believe in. We know its inhabitants by the roles they play, and its structure is expressed in our common mythology, as much for us as for the Brazilian Indians whom Claude Lévi-Strauss has examined so thoroughly. This mythology both explains the order of the universe—that is, it tells us how events are likely to follow each other in the external world and gives us some clue to the laws that govern them—and justifies our own actions. To act naturally and normally is good, in tune with the laws of the universe, and these repetitive, comfortable justified actions support the laws which sanction them.

So if the world of one individual takes time to change, social structures built of accepted ideas tend to be even more static. But, in a time like ours, they cannot be exempt from the effects of rapid change in the areas of technological methods and physical surroundings. Whole fields of knowledge fall away overnight: a tiny scrap of time ago, our whole agriculture was dependent on the horse and the plowman and the expertise that bound them together. New problems, like pollution, appear even more suddenly and demand answers. This kind of change means that losses in the structure of our imagined thought shake our great communal world, while new challenges strain it to the utmost. Whole segments of it vanish, and the theorems that held it together lose their validity. Some comfortable, justified and justifying actions cease because they are obviously absurd, and the moral values they sustained begin to turn into superstitions. Here is one source of a gap between generations, for the old naturally cling to the moral values they once learned to call good, while the young, who can't see how they fit into the scheme of things at all, are contemptuous. It is time which has made the change, but because the structure of myth declares itself to be eternal and always present, the old call the young immoral, and the young reject the old as hypocrites.

A century ago, to take an obvious example—obvious enough, perhaps, to have lost a good deal of its emotional charge—it was an article of faith, subscribed to by most Americans and Europeans, that girls should be virgin when they married. Today, it's hardly necessary to point out, this is no longer the case. But once upon a time there was felt to be a real and valid connection between a bride's virginity and her ability to become a good and happy wife. Now the young have come to dismiss this link as an old-fashioned superstition. Change has been so rapid and the present is so demanding that very few can spare any concern to know what social pressures did, once, create this connection. The old pressures have vanished and the quotient of truth in the statement, "Young girls are virgin when they marry," is steadily decreasing, while the idea that they *should be* is behaving like a mathematical variable moving toward the terminal constant of superstition.

Social truths, in other words, are agreed-upon beliefs. When we say that they are right, or when we declare they are wrong—whether because they've lost their relevance and degenerated toward superstition, or because they appear unfamiliar and threaten to introduce immorality—we mean something quite different from the rightness or wrongness of objective truths about the physical world. The truths of the physical world stay the same. They can be proved by experiment (at least in theory), and they are referrable to physical data. They do not change with time, and they are universal in their application; or, if they do change with time and circumstance, these deviations themselves can be referred to physical data and explained in terms of physical laws. (Are there psychological truths which can be accepted as provable in the way that physical relations can be illustrated? There certainly seem to be some; but when they get more complicated than the reflexes which Pavlov and B. F. Skinner have demonstrated, they become so protean and so open to influence that they are best thought of as I have been treating them here: as tendencies and probabilities.)

All this is familiar ground. But as we begin to talk about our present situation, it is worth remembering that there are kinds of things we can say about the physical world which are both true and useful; but if we are talking about the imagined world of social relations, where meaning is as important as fact, these sorts of statement make no sense. In the physical world (at least at the level of technology, where we deal with materials and processes), things have definable characteristics proper to a whole class of objects and materials, so that we can say, "Iron always behaves this way, and copper that." Theses can be advanced, and disproved once and for all. But though one can define "a woman" in biological terms, in social terms one has to fall back on generalities. And, unlike general statements about the physical world, general statements about the social universe are never entirely true—unless, of course, they are tautologies. One can't define the properties or characteristics of "a woman" beyond the physical fact of body structure, sex chromosomes, et cetera, and have them apply to all women. There are always exceptions.

The simplest and most objective of social statements are statistical: more than half the women in America, including some 40 percent of married women, have paid jobs outside their homes, to take a straightforward statistic. Obviously this can be true overall without applying to any particular woman. The amount of truth it contains varies with the class, the age and the educational background of the woman in question, and it can't be extended to, let us say, the women of France or Mexico. Statistical data are true, but limited.

Nor do such statements mean very much if they are taken by themselves. We have to interpret them—judgment comes in. Our statement about the percentage of working women in America doesn't really tell us much unless we refer it to another statement, to the number working twenty years ago, perhaps, to the number working in Spain, to the different sort of educational background which distinguishes women working in Britain from women working in America, to the different kinds of occupations of women working in Russia, to the number of women holding executive positions in the communications industry compared to the number of men—and so on. A social statement demands a referrant. It takes its significance from the context of our social system of beliefs, or from the behavior that goes with these beliefs. It is always a link with the human world, draws on our understanding of that world, changes or increases it.

Which means that we ourselves, the observers and interpreters, are involved with every social statement. Any statement will gain, lose, or shift significance *depending upon the audience.* It is not true in itself, as physical data can be taken to be at the working level; it is true in accordance with the meaning that it carries to its hearers. A social statement can fall in with our general body of belief, it can run counter to it, or it can exist outside it, and its value will be affected by this relationship to the audience. In terms of any particular audience, the value of a social statement depends not only on its truth, but on its plausiblity. We may be forced to believe something we don't particularly like by the piling up of objective evidence, but our reaction will be deeply conditioned by what we believe already, by how well this new truth falls in with our old patterns of thinking.

Interestingly enough, the usual public reaction to social statements that bolster our general attitudes is not enthusiasm or pleasure as much as it is boredom, as if one were to say, "We know this already. Why bother to tell us about it again?" (Repeated *behavior,* however, takes on an aspect of ritual and can evoke profound emotional experiences.) At the other extreme, statements that fall totally outside our system of beliefs don't excite us either, beyond arousing amusement or a kind of pleasurable shock at the oddities and quirks possible to human behavior.

The most illuminating reaction occurs when a statement is made which runs counter to the customary attitudes of any given audience. Sometimes it is directly upsetting; that is, the audience takes in its significance and disagrees. But more often the meaning is separated from the fact of the statement. Then people say, "Oh, I suppose this absurd and disgusting thing you tell me is true enough, but it doesn't matter because it's just an aberration." It may be true, that is, in the particular instance cited, but it isn't true importantly, because it doesn't link up to the overall pattern. It can, and should, be ignored.

A good illustration of this attitude was the public reaction first to the Kinsey reports and later to the studies on human sexuality made by Masters and Johnson. All of these investigations, which attempted to be as objective and "scientific" as possible, suggested that a number of things most people believed (and many believe still) about sexual attitudes and practices are closer to superstition than is comfortable for those who hold them to admit. Some readers found the data interesting and this conclusion plausible. Those who did not still assumed that the actual, raw data which the interviews and experiments turned up were true, but they refused to accept the conclusions which questioned customary ideas. What they did was to go back to the premises and conditions of experiments and question these because they produced unexpected results. Thus, such reasoning ran, since we all know that normal people do not like to talk about their private sexual experiences, the people who were willing to talk to Kinsey's interviewers could not have been normal. No doubt they said these things, though they probably told some lies (normal people are apt to boast if they do talk about their sexual experiences), but it is impossible to arrive at any judgments about the behavior of the rest of the world from what these perverted creatures had to say.[3]

The first Masters-Johnson study, on sexual response, produced the same kind of reaction: that the men and women who took part in laboratory tests of sexual responsiveness must have been oversexed to begin with. The study's most famous finding—that women achieved orgasm as quickly as men and probably more intensely—was itself used to bring the experiment into doubt. Since women are traditionally more modest than men, any women who were willing to take part must have been even further from the norm than men, and so their heightened responses are even less to be trusted: thus ran the argument which accepted the laboratory results as true and then turned them aside as meaningless because they contradicted accepted attitudes and beliefs.[4]

Clearly, even apparently scientific and objective data do not operate in the social world in the same way that they operate in the physical world. A "fact" can't be pinned down simply by being correct in the sense that, Yes, it did happen. In the physical world, hypotheses that don't work have to be abandoned. In the social world, hypotheses will swallow up "facts" that challenge them over and over again. As long as the emotion invested in them can keep them plausible, they will "work" well enough to get by, even though that isn't in fact very well. When they are finally abandoned it is a complex process, not a simple one: not only don't they work anymore, they are *seen* not to work anymore.

In short, the significance of social facts, not their existence, is what gives them vitality, and their significance will be judged according to pre-existing patterns of what we believe we know, of how we expect people to behave, on what experience has taught us. I labor the point only to make clear that we cannot reason from social knowledge in the same way that we can reason from physical observations. Social facts are three-dimensional, to be assessed for their truth, for their importance, and for their fit with the pattern of the ongoing social process.

Thinking about woman's place in the world today, therefore, requires a kind of triple thinking which involves history, values and facts. We must continue to spiral around our subject. We can't get rid of the social mythology we began with just because it is time to talk about the present, nor can we ignore the conventions that encrust woman's various roles. On the contrary, these are very much what we have to think about, for they give us our continuing context. Once we begin to see that the structure of social mythology and the ritual behavior of role-playing are ways in which society maintains itself and directs its members, we can observe them at work today. Granted that both mythology and roles are partly false because they incorporate desires, function as means while being taken as ends, and never exactly fit any particular situation—that is not the point. They will always work this

way, though their content may change and change again, and we
cannot do without their way of working. But again, this is off the
point. *The importance of myths and role behavior is that they provide a means of knowing and understanding the structure we have
built to live in.* They reveal our imagined world, and so they offer
clues to the way we—this society—attempts to deal with the demands of life and, by so doing, creates itself.

In this sense, general attitudes and popular beliefs help us to
map the unconscious construction by which we adjust our hopes
to our situation and change our situation to match what we dream
of having, doing and being. If we now look at woman's traditional,
accepted role in the social conditions of today's world, we see that
the economic side of it has split because economic activity has
moved outside the home. Women have followed it to an increasing extent, and their experiences in office and factory, where they
function as workers rather than as women, are reacting upon the
other segments of their role. At the same time, the fact that economic activity outside the home has, as a by-product, drawn off
women workers from domestic service means that some women
(mothers with young children) are more tied to their homes than
ever before, more alone in their job of raising children and
probably, therefore, more emotionally involved with them.
Woman's third role as wife and sexual partner is changing too.
She meets men in new ways as she works with them and as she
extends her education to match theirs. Science has given her the
pill and with it the opportunity to disconnect sex from pregnancy.
Meanwhile, our evaluation of sex itself has grown very ambivalent,
and the old pattern of "a good wife" is being blurred in many
ways. What we have to consider now is the significance of all
these facts.

There is no way to talk usefully about woman's role or to try to
describe her place in, and her impact on, man's (also changing)
world, except by talking about all three sides of her activities. In
doing so, I shall try, however, to keep the focus of my exploration
on one aspect of her role at a time. I propose to begin with her
role as mother, partly because its content has changed least with
the passage of time, partly because it is simplest (though not
simple) to compare it with the equivalent roles in other societies,
but also because it is still considered woman's prime duty, prime

glory, purpose and justification, even though for at least a generation it has been shadowed by the negative role of "Mom."

Clearly, the existence of this negative role indicates that there is
a division in our view of how successful women are in their job as
mothers; not, that is, as the physical bearers of children, but in the
social process by which the young are reared and civilized until,
as Talcott Parsons expressed it, "they can truly become members
of the society into which they were born." The work of mothering
doesn't end with birth; the social process begins there. "It is because the human personality is not 'born' but must be 'made'
through the socialization process," writes Parsons, "that . . . families are necessary. They are 'factories' which produce human personalities." [5]

Are the factories working well at present? A great many people
fear they are not. As we look at the role of the primary agents in
the socializing process—women as mothers—we shall find that
we are also discussing possible shifts in family structures and the
confusion in the whole social context which surrounds us today.

CHAPTER 12

The conflicts in women's role stem in large part from the isolation of the family. No longer integrally embedded in the community, the family has become specialized in the related tasks of managing feelings and bringing up children. As "guardians of the home," women are still expected to specialize in kitchen and kindergarten, home-making and child-rearing, tasks which contrast sharply with the cognitive, achievement-oriented, and independent world of work and public life. Trained and often motivated for working life as well, they are forced to suppress, sublimate, and displace their desires for "fulfillment." One common result is seen in the mothers of alienated students: women displace their own frustrated ambitions for achievement on their sons, expect their sons to make up to them "the things they gave up for marriage," "overinvest" in their sons, and thus bind them in a special intimacy. The characteristics of the mothers of alienated subjects thus turn out to be not merely personal idiosyncrasies, but efforts to solve problems inherent in women's role in our society.

> Kenneth Keniston
> *The Uncommitted* [1]

THE DOMINANT, normative middle class of American society has spent the last fifty years or so in an increasingly acute state of self-doubt and, as the "Americanization" of Europe has proceeded since the end of the last war, this condition has spread with it. Whether it was originally triggered by the closing of the frontier, the decline of the Protestant Ethic, the shock of the First World War, or some equally large and amorphous cause or combination of causes, the process was clearly under way in the twenties, when young writers, artists and musicians mounted a challenge to orthodox thinking and traditional culture. Though such challenges had been posed before (as in the Romantic Movement of the late eighteenth century), this one reached a wider audience which was

able to respond readily to new ideas. This defiance was followed
by the economic shock of the thirties, and by the international
political and supra-political involvements of the war years. In
reaction from that demanding time, the fifties saw an exhausted
retreat into personal and political isolationism, and an attempt to
revitalize some of the values and virtues attributed to a past that
had receded far enough to be reinvoked under the mythic label
of a Golden Age. A father figure was in the White House, women's
magazines preached family togetherness, the birthrate climbed,
and women who had been praised for holding jobs during the war
found themselves being reminded that they had a place at home.

By the sixties, this mood of retreat had changed sharply and
the decade saw the unsettling start of new drives toward unknown
ends. The young were once again defying the world view of their
elders, even though their elders were not very sure just what that
view consisted of. Hostile attribution of unpleasant roles from
young to old and back again marked the advent of the seventies;
but whether the obvious schism in the West between groups of
young revolutionaries on the one hand and the conservative old
on the other will indeed end our self-questioning is open to doubt.
Negative roles (hippie versus pig) are not comfortable, functional,
or autonomous. They are unlikely to endure as they are because
they began as defiant reactions against the status quo. As the
status quo changes, so will the reaction to it. If today's reversed
roles evolve into new and useful patterns, they will increasingly
become more understandable to others and, consequently, less
likely to arouse anxiety.

It has been taken for granted throughout this period that
women have been less affected by the troubled times than men.
To the extent that they occupy a special place shut off from man's
world, their reactions to social changes are secondary, not direct.
This doesn't, however, mean that women have felt the challenges
of change less than men; they may have felt them as deeply but
more confusedly, because they react to the reactions of others.
But the role assigned to them has remained more constant than
that traditionally expected of men. This has a double effect: the
role is a possible refuge, but it requires continuing work to mediate between the role and the changing demands of society. In a
sense, women playing woman's role are caught between the role

and the world around them. As we shall see, this strain has significant psychological effects.

Let us for the moment keep our attention on the role itself. The
accepted division of labor between the sexes calls on men to
mediate the outside pressures of the world for their families,
while women provide the continuity of stable personal relationships in a home-haven. This is true even for working women, for
their homes are still a major interest and a possible retreat. Besides, the sort of jobs that women hold are, with few exceptions,
below those top echelons where decisions are made and where
alertness to change is not merely an asset but a necessity. Short
of a revolutionary breakdown in the social structure, women are
everywhere assumed to be doing a job and occupying a place
closer to that of their grandmothers than are men when compared
with previous generations. The feminine ideal of a charming
woman—Jacqueline Kennedy supplied a prime example for the
sixties—does not include an interest in the political or economic
events of the wide world as a necessary ingredient, even for a
woman whose position forces her into contact with them. In the
larger society (at least on the surface) a preference for the private
and personal world is still taken to be a positive virtue in women.
As for the counter-culture of the young, it is doubtful that female
activism is regarded as an absolute good here either. Certainly
homes have changed, have been swept bare of servants, reduced
in size, wired for appliances that have reduced drudgery but reduced along with it the value of knowing and practicing special
housewifely skills, but the personal attitudes and obligations of
the lady of the house are presumed to be pretty much what they
have always been, though the economic ties to the community
and the social connection with a larger cousinage have both
dwindled.

Mothering is the area where any questioning of woman's role
has made least impact. What the new feminists themselves seem
to be asking is not a dissolution of the tie between mother and
child, but rather an enlargement of the relationship, so that the
father gives more, and earlier, care than has been usual in our
society. In some cases where families have grouped themselves
into communes, small children will be cared for by several women
(and some of the men) together or separately. But this is, in fact,

a reversion to an old and still widespread pattern of child-raising in many small village-communities. It is nothing like as radical an innovation as the rearing of babies by professionals in age classes which some of the kibbutzim in Israel have practiced for decades.

Of course woman's role as mother has come under discussion, but the discussion has not led to a change in the fundamental social fact that women bring up children and that, in our world, these women are almost always their mothers. Another thing that has not changed is children's earliest needs. They learn about the world not merely *from* their mothers, but *through* them: through the emotional ties which show them what feeling is, what connection is, what response is. Babies learn love and trust and their place in the universe from the people who look after them first, and this learning is the foundation and the shaping plan for everything that happens after that. So it has been, and so it is.

What children need is pretty much the same thing always: a map of the world, and instructions on how to use it. But the information comes wrapped in different packages by different cultures, and the maps are different too, since the one human world Susanne Langer describes is illuminated and observed in different ways by different societies. Nonetheless the uniformity of an infant's needs in its earliest days affects the attendant mother with some uniformity. One learns (or learns to use) patience, intuitive insight and imagination, to enjoy the immediate moment in anticipation of change when it comes and the miracle of potentiality that it points at. One learns a good deal about time—that it passes, and yet remains solid as experience. One learns that life changes even if one sits still, when it's wise to sit still, and when it isn't. Most of all, one learns other people and one's own limits in terms of relationships with them. All this is important learning, but let us once again refrain from supposing that it is learned only by women and valuable only to them. It is the kind of knowledge that is learned on the way to maturity no matter how the path winds.

But in spite of Tolstoi, not all happy families are alike. This early uniformity of demand and response is soon affected by the overall patterns of behavior characteristic of any one society. In the Western world our conception of what a mother should do (once the first physical demands of the child have been provided for) has been shifting in the wake of social change. In part this is due to widespread, if rather mythically simplistic, knowledge of psychoanalytic theory with its emphasis on the importance of the child's relation to his parents in infancy and early childhood. In part it is due to the isolation of the family, which Kenneth Keniston remarks on in the quotation at the head of this chapter: women at home are very much at home and very much less a part of any larger social, church, or community group than they used to be. In part it is due to the semiconscious social salesmanship that arose in reaction to the first wave of feminism after it had reached its crescendo in the teens of this century.[2]

Two generations ago, we might remember, some women (and those well publicized) were more active as dissidents and more upsetting to the rest of society than the new movement for Women's Liberation has yet become. Because they were more shocking, they had to be more militant, more autonomous and more dedicated than the feminists of today, and they had served a longer apprenticeship. They marched, picketed and demanded their rights, broke up meetings, chained themselves to the White House fence, were sent to jail and went on hunger strike. It was all very unpleasant to the silent majority of those days, and as soon as the suffragists got the vote, some awakened antigen in society began putting out a soothing, healing flow of praise for femininity and its attendant qualities of pleasing charm, devotion and high-minded self-sacrifice.

Society, in fact, had been frightened by the woman militants, and it entered upon a somewhat self-defeating promotion campaign for Happy-Wife-and-Motherdom. The Freudian mythos was invoked to justify a repeated affirmation of the enormous importance of woman's natural role as mother. No social activity, women have been told ever since, can be more vital than this nurturing work; and as usual with mythic statements, this applies to all women. It is the mothers who will raise the next generation, who control the future, who do not have to look for creative careers because the very nature of their noblest and most significant task is creation. Their lives are self-justifying. Before their eyes the future is made manifest, and it is they who will shape it through their children. American women still hear this today, as they have in the past, at almost every level of intellectual discourse. They are firmly being instructed in how to do what is supposed to come naturally.

The result of these injunctions and assurances is interesting. Far from deflecting or damping the problem of adjusting to a changing world, the heightened emphasis on the mother role has been making women nervous. It was doing so long before the storm of youthful antagonism to the orthodoxies of their parents shook households across the country. In a cross-cultural study of how children are raised, made during the late fifties and early sixties by a group of social scientists under the direction of Leigh Minturn and William W. Lambert, a New England town was compared with villages in Mexico, the Philippines, India, Okinawa and Kenya. The women of New England, it was reported here, "worry much more than other mothers about the correctness of their own behavior and that of their children. Although most mothers were, unlike those in other samples, aware that the investigators were 'professionals' and anxious to make a good impression, they frequently expressed doubts about their ability to raise their children well. Their success in this maternal role was most important to them since children's character is believed to be shaped largely by their mothers." [3]

Confronted with their vital social function, these mothers doubted their ability to do it properly. Now, doubts about one's competence are always upsetting, whatever the job to be done may be, and the more important and complicated the job is, the greater and more distracting become the doubts. In simple rote jobs, routine skills are easily learned. Where crafts still exist, apprentices are trained on the job. Service jobs, from hairdressing to fund management, begin with training or can be studied, like accountancy, in schools and colleges. The arts and the professions, which require talent, are of course different. The most one can do is find out ahead of time, from practice and training, whether one has a gift or at least a knack for writing or doctoring or corporate law. The authority that goes with success comes later. But even as they begin, aspirant artists know they have a *choice*. They are not absolutely compelled to go on trying to write poetry or play the cello if they become convinced that they are not, after all, competent to carry on these activities professionally. It is different on all counts for mothers. The woman who fears she is not successful must still struggle with the task. The nannies who could have taken over for her mother or grandmother have all but ceased to exist.

Women are not trained to be mothers in our society, or indeed in any society. It is difficult to imagine how they could be on a large enough scale. But in other places around the world, the sort of apprenticeship in living which was part of our past continues. Little girls look after little children much more than they do with us. Besides, families are less isolated from the community within their homes, so that child-raising goes on in public a good deal of the time. In fact, it is in part carried on *by* the community as well as by the family, if only by the enforcement of community standards of behavior and attitudes. There is less tension to the whole business, too, because almost everywhere there is a larger agreement on how children should be raised and on the sort of adults they should be brought up to become than exists here today. So young women elsewhere are apt to know more about mothering and be more confident of their ability to do it.

The very fact that our society does train initiates formally for most jobs (though perhaps not very effectively) makes woman's role archaic and atypical in that women still learn by doing. They take on the vital, creative, important, central concern of their lives, which matters so much to everyone (they are assured), with very little advice or background. New mothers are expected to act by instinct; and this expectation in itself sets them apart from the rest of society, where people assume that they will be taught the basic rules of the jobs they have to do. The expectation that they will be able to act by instinct sets women apart, also, by suggesting that they operate on a more primitive level than is normal for the rest of our world.

If the first source of anxiety for young mothers is being told to do an important piece of work pretty much on their own, another and related uneasiness follows. Can the world really be run this inefficiently? one tends to ask oneself; and often a suspicion grows that, somehow, one has missed out on learning what other women must surely know. Such self-questioning is not too far removed from the puzzled, accepting guilt of Kafka's heroes. This doubt is strengthened by the isolation of young women, cut off from their own families and older relatives who elsewhere not only advise but reassure. Our own continuously and rapidly changing ways of living create, prolong and harden generation differences. As the social scientists studying child-raising need hardly tell us, "The New England mothers have very little help in caring for their children." To a certain extent they prefer it that way—or at least prefer it to other possible alternatives. For, our students point out, "Value conflicts may occur even within the family. Some mothers resent correction of their children by grandparents. The wisdom of the aged is not respected as much here as in other societies, and grandparents are not given the authority to reprimand their charges. When parents are present their word takes precedence over that of the grandparents." [4]

This attitude with its rejection of traditional wisdom is not, however, based on a firm and self-confident conviction that one knows best, but only on the assumption that one knows better than one's mother, aunts, or mother-in-law. An expression of the generation gap, it vitiates the value of advice from older members of the family and lessens the reassurance that can be gained from them. Doubt of the wisdom of the past joins doubt about one's own instinctual sense of what to do.

The normal American approach then takes over: ask the expert. When young mothers turn to Dr. Spock's manuals, they are asking for reassurance at least as often as for advice. But in the end they are still on their own, for Dr. Spock unfortunately is not there with them to say "Yea, yea" or "Nay, nay." He offers general rules and observations and is helpful about averages and norms, as was Dr. Gesell before him; but what a particular mother does about a particular child's behavior in a particular circumstance is still up to her. She consults the expert as if he were an oracle, and then goes on from there, uncertain as to whether she has interpreted the oracle correctly or even asked him the right question. It is in such doubtful situations that women worry about doing right.

That phrase can be emphasized two ways. Beyond the question of *doing* right is the problem of doing *right;* that is, of knowing what goals to aim at. What kind of adults should one's children grow up to be? It is not a question that can be settled by one woman or one family, for in large part it requires an external answer from society at large. In the past it has usually received one and, usually, parents have accepted the answer and brought up their children according to the standards and customs of their time and their class, caste, or tribe. Even when a child's potential was severely limited by these standards, when one had to know one's place and one's station, most parents passed on the training to their sons or daughters whether they were happy about it or not. External pressures, social, economic and physical, saw to that. The rise of the bourgeoisie which accompanied the technological and organizational changes of the industrial revolution worked to relax these pressures and to open the world of power to "rough diamonds" and "social climbers." Or, to accentuate the positive, ideals of liberty and equality of opportunity abrogated old, restrictive rules and cleared the way for the common man's ambitions.

Thus the economic and social revolution which ushered in the Age of Affluence in the West left us with at least a temporary remission of the old imperatives, but at the same time with a society that (no doubt also temporarily) has lost its ability to formulate models which parents or children can agree upon. Most of us have only general or abstract views about what we want our children to grow up to be, and if we do have clear ideas, our children often disagree violently. We suffer from a hesitancy about imagining the future which hinders us in engaging ourselves ardently with the present. To the children, confusion often looks like hypocrisy: why do we urge them to accept goals we don't seem to believe in ourselves? On the other hand, small goals of comfort and personal success smell stale, reek of complacence. Babbittry is dead, but its memory has inoculated our society with a distaste not only for conventional success, but for almost any approved success. When orthodoxy does try to sketch a hero-type for the young—the astronauts, for example—the emotional appeal is nil. Our real and compelling heroes are rebels. In the decade of the sixties, they were most heroic in death, when they became incorruptible and ended the fear that the fulfillment of their promises might disillusion us. So the Kennedy brothers achieved apotheosis, so Che Guevara succeeded Castro, so Martin Luther King became a saint instead of a liberal to be rivaled only by his fellow martyr, Malcolm X. The growing division in society as the seventies began raised live rebels to the Pantheon as the possibility of a counterculture began to seem more plausible.

For most of us, this only adds to the confusion and the doubt. Official heroes are put forward, strain unsuccessfully for charisma in the pages of *Life*, and fail to waken a spark of emulation. True heroes whom the young will accept end in exile or are shot. At the same time there has been no change in the assumption cited by our social scientists that "children's behavior is believed to be shaped largely by their mothers." But to what end? It is a difficult position. The traditional sources of wisdom are distrusted, or at least felt to be badly out of date both as to methods of raising children and as to the kind of adult who will be successful and happy in a puzzling future. One gropes in the dark for guidance. And yet there is no alternative; children must somehow be helped to grow up. The more the importance of the mother-child relationship is stressed by psychologists, the more the adult member of the pair feels the burden of her responsibility and the potential guilt of failing to live up to it.

Is it possible, one asks oneself, that the emphasis placed on the mother-child relationship may itself be aggravating the difficulty of the family task of bringing up children? It is instructive at this point to consider the famous methods of communal raising of children practiced in the kibbutzim of Israel, where children are normally separated from their parents when they are four days old. Babies are breast-fed by their mothers till they are six months old, and there are daily visits to the parents' living quarters, but all care and training is performed by nurses and teachers. Bruno Bettelheim, whose pioneering work in restoring disturbed children to health gives him special competence in this field, provides an absorbing account of these methods and the results they produce in a recent book, *The Children of the Dream*.[5]

To get the hang of the operation we must first understand why the pioneer generation of kibbutzniks opted for this dramatic departure from old ways. It was very much a question of goals, both positive and negative. The founders of these communities, socialist reformers who helped to lay the foundations for the State of Israel, were eager to remove their children from the ghetto atmosphere in which they themselves had been raised. They saw the old religious tradition of the Jews, responsive to the oppression of centuries, as producing a people who were overemotional, over-intellectual, and contemptuous of physical labor. The closeness of the Jewish family itself, which was a reaction to the hostility of the outside world, was unsuited to life in the nation they hoped to build, and in addition, it tended to bind children into the old attitudes. They felt that the intense mother-child tie not only weakened and softened the children, but kept women from taking their rightful place in the world as well. So they formulated a system in which children are raised by professionals, nurses, care-takers and teachers, with parents left at a remove—affectionate, in evidence, to be seen every day, but not in charge; or rather, not in charge specifically of their own children, for the whole grown-up community feels itself in the parents' position toward all the children.

The results, which can only be summarized very briefly here, were successful, depending on what sort or degree of success one is considering. The children of the kibbutzim grow up to be healthy and healthy minded, courageous and capable in the face of the demands of the life they know. There is a generation gap between the founders and their children, but though this is pain-ful at times, it is what the founders intended and expected. In its own way, it is a sign of their success. The character structure of kibbutz children is different from that of their parents, and that is what the parents wanted.

Different in what ways? This is the interesting question, not only because it involves value judgments, but because it throws much light on exactly what it is that the closeness of a small, nuclear family can ideally give its children. The answer seems to be, different in reach of imagination and depth of emotion. At least the kibbutz system, as now administered, appears to produce a kind of emotional flattening in the second and third generations. In place of close ties to the mother and later the father, the pri-mary emotional involvement of these children is with the other children they have been brought up with and who have been their constant companions from their fourth day of life.

I cannot attempt to reproduce Bettelheim's profound and per-ceptive discussion of how this life experience, this enforced in-timacy with its changed and lessened dependence on any one person but its great dependence on "the peer group," changes the internal abilities and structuring of the psyche. The whole argument deserves careful reading by anyone interested. I shall simply record his conclusions. These children, who have never been alone, find it difficult to achieve intimacy with any one or two others. They have lived a life of action and doing, a life which allows no time for introspection, in which they have not needed to imagine the interior life of others, because that life was being acted out around them all the time. Asked hypothetical questions, it is hard for them, in their answers, to imagine any change in their ways of thinking. Loyal, devoted comrades, their own individual selves are most present when they are most absorbed in the group.

The absence of the group is frightening to them, and rejection by it the worst imaginable danger. As one of them wrote after the June War of 1967, it was not merely the need to kill which he found so terrible, but the need to kill *alone,* by his own decisions. Their record in the fighting, however, is of great bravery. Their casualties were far out of proportion to their actual numbers. At the same time, there are higher officers who suggest that prudence is sometimes the better part of valor and that the young kibbutzniks who died so well might sometimes have lived to fight another day if they had been quicker to come to the complicated sort of decision which is at the heart of successful strategy.

What we have, then, is a picture of children whose unorthodox upbringing has socialized them well and successfully for one kind of living, and that a very useful kind and not too narrow. Moreover, it appears to prevent the waste and loss, the rejection of one's part in the world, which is becoming a chronic, frightening illness in the West. These children grow up in a secure and structured community, in which they know they have a place and are wanted. Even the mentally retarded or brain-damaged are kept in the same community, under normal conditions, and looked after with love. The price of this security has been, to put it crudely, creative imagination and individual decisiveness. The lows are gone, which is an enormous gain; but so are some of the highs.

Whether the price is worth paying or not is another sort of question. The kibbutz communities are largely agricultural, they

have never survived in an urban industrial setting; their population is a small percentage of the whole, and it is dependent on
the rest of the community and the economy for its continued life.
The kibbutzniks are strongly goal-oriented: they know what they
want their children to be, and those who find themselves unhappy
usually leave quite early to seek a different way of life, which is
of course available. Successful as communal child-raising has
proved itself to be, it is successful as part of a wider, pluralistic
and more complex society. How it will be affected by the continued strain of Arab pressure on the Israeli state cannot be fore-
seen. Certainly in the form practiced in Israel it would not suffice
to produce all the types and personalities needed in the huge and
changing world of today, though, of course, other forms could be
imagined and tried. Nonetheless, it shows the rest of the world
what can be done, and it underlines the tragic failures to which
our close, small-family child-raising methods are subject when
they don't operate ideally.

Bettelheim has documented some of these failures in other
books which relate the heartbreaking case histories of autistic
children, with whom he has worked for so long at the Orthogenic
School of the University of Chicago. These are extremes, however,
involving a good deal of personality distortion. We can perhaps
see more easily how one danger avoided by the kibbutzim operates if we look instead at Kenneth Keniston's study of alienated
young men, *The Uncommitted,* which is quoted at the head of
this chapter. If the kibbutz children found it hard to grow into
intimate personal relationships with other people, Keniston's
young alienates did too, but from an opposite cause. They were
overwhelmed too early by an excess of intimacy and not allowed
to grow out of it. All of them (and they differed in this from two
control groups who were also examined by Keniston and his colleagues at Harvard) remembered an early, strong and very special
relationship with their mothers, a relationship whose depth and
feeling tone were exceptional.

Now, unlike the kibbutzim, in a society like ours, where care of
babies is almost entirely in the hands of the mother, the profound
dependence of an infant on her is inevitable. The relationships of
Keniston's subjects to their mothers, however, lasted far longer

than the period of infancy. More important, they appear to have been reciprocal. The mothers, as Keniston puts it, "overinvested" in their sons. Rather like those who are deafened by too much noise, these boys were blasted by too much love, too concentrated an emotional concern.

In the nature of things, the mother-child relationship can't be as important to the mother as it is to the totally dependent child—unless, that is, the mother projects into this relationship emotions unsatisfied in the rest of her life, which may (as we have seen) include the desire to exercise control, or power, over some other individual. Normally a mother has a living, present husband, she is likely to have other children, above all she has an adult role in the world even if it is a small role in a small world. Her mother role is a partial one. It is a changing and, in essence, a temporary one; or perhaps one might better say it is open-ended. Its purpose is not simply to adjust a child to a family situation and to accustom him to personal relationships. This is where it begins, but it is equally important for the mother to see, with the father's aid, that the child moves out of the family orbit and into a wider world. From the point of view of society, this is the function of the family, and it is why a ban against incest has been emphasized again and again as *socially* necessary, quite apart from any emotional reason against it.

The mothers of the young men whom Keniston was studying failed at this second task. Instead they bound their sons into too great an intimacy for them to be able to move on easily. They evoked "a special sympathy . . . a special identification, a special regret at their mothers' unrealized potentials, a special suffering at their mothers' unhappiness." In the end their sons did make the break, but at considerable cost to themselves. The emotional effort of repudiating the lingering identification with their mothers left them fearful of close bonds with anyone else, disliking and distrusting themselves because they felt themselves guilty in their mothers' eyes of betrayal, and doubtful of their ability to cope with the world. Like the hardy young kibbutzniks but for different reasons, these young men had lost their ability to imagine other people or to grow into intimacy with them. The kibbutzniks had never learned to, but these boys were afraid to; and since they had no comrades to turn to, they were left alone in what seemed a remote and unaffecting world.

Keniston's judgment, quoted at the head of this chapter, was that the women whose attitudes crippled their sons in this way were not behaving in a manner that was atypical of our society, but merely exaggerating a tendency that exists fairly widely.[6] Women have always had the largest care of their children, but in the past and in many other cultures today, they had and have supplementary concerns as well, which absorb much of their time and energy—spinning, weaving, some of the farm work, growing special crops and selling them on market day, and so on. All these traditional activities for women are related to family duties, and often they are done with the help of the children.

But in doing them, mother and children are not simply being together, but *working* together for a functional end beyond, or outside, their own emotional relationship. Feeding and clothing the family and providing for some of its economic needs, as households still do all over the world, go beyond immediate child care and make a connection for both mother and children with the larger community. Today in the West, to quote Keniston again, these functions have atrophied and "the family has become specialized in the . . . tasks of managing feelings and bringing up children." [7] This obviously invites the sort of emotional concentration on personal relationships which can tie a child into a binding and hampering closeness with an adult whom his life will later require him to leave behind. It was just this tendency which the kibbutz founders consciously feared and which, men and women alike, they chose to prevent.

The social scientists who studied the emotional attitudes and the child-raising practices of mothers in different societies do not disagree with Keniston. The situation they found in the typical New England community which they named Orchard Town seems to predispose families to the relationships between mother and child on which Keniston reports. "The mothers of Orchard Town," they write, "are unusual in that they are relatively isolated and spend much of their time alone with their children and in exclusive charge of them. Their belief that they must guide their children's development along proper channels, their anxiety about conforming to ideal norms that are culturally unclear, and their conviction that no one else can adequately substitute for a mother makes them reject alternative caretakers even when they are available. The relatively high emotional instability of these mothers appears to be due, in part, to the large amounts of time they spend in charge of children." [8]

We must conclude that our society today is asking women to bring off something of an emotional *tour de force*. First, they are asked to regard the bearing and raising of children as at least a very large and significant concern of their lives and, perhaps, as the crown and center of their existence although, in the nature of things, this undertaking will demand their full efforts for something less than two decades out of a life that will run to seventy years. Second, they must fit their children for a society whose needs and aims are at best uncertain, and which may in fact seem to the mothers as well as the children morally unjustified and emotionally unsatisfying. At the same time, the most admired goals of society are pretty well closed to these women themselves. Third, they are expected to do all this *only* by means of an emotional relationship, instead of (as in the past) with the help of economic activities and social processes that relate to the larger world. The sanctions of the community seldom join directly with parental injunctions inside the home circle, but instead are conveyed to the children through their parents. Fourth, having called forth this relationship, mothers are aware that they should maintain it in such a delicate balance that the child can grow out of it without harm to his own psychic strength. This program they are supposed to carry through with little training and little support from society itself, in the belief that any failure will justly be laid at their door.

In view of these expectations, it does not seem odd that the mothers of Orchard Town are rated as having "relatively high emotional instability."

CHAPTER 13

Women [can be designated] as labor market workers or home market workers. Home market work differs from labor market work in several important respects. First, there are no monetary rewards for tasks performed in the home; second, there are no job descriptions or universal standards of achievement for the production of home goods; third, the value of goods and services produced in the home is not included in the national income if the woman performs them herself, but is included if they are performed by a substitute and then only at the lowest wage level; fourth, the home market worker reduces her responsibility if she performs well, while the labor market measures success by increase in responsibility. These differences create complex problems of prestige and achievement.

Susan R. Orden and Norman M. Bradburn
"Working Wives and Marriage Happiness" [1]

LET US FOCUS now on woman's economic role and the changes taking place there. The fact that it has split down the middle into work for a labor market and work for the home in the home, as Susan Orden and Norman Bradburn point out, doesn't reduce its influence on woman's other obligations and activities, but it changes the effect. Women used to expect to work "throughout the whole of their adult lives," as Eli Ginzberg reminded us earlier, but they worked in a framework that included the rest of their lives and often included the rest of their families.

The first of the great social changes of modern times, the rise of the middle class, produced the home that was occupied by one family plus servants, with close relatives sometimes included: a widowed mother, a spinster sister, but essentially a small family group. The economic tie with "the big house" of the neighborhood was gone, but women usually worked as hard as they had before, and they continued to train their children in the useful skills they knew. Thus, there came into the one-family home some of the economic activities which the little houses had previously left to the great ones, while sending their children to these centers as apprentices, servants, or farm laborers. By the nineteenth century, single-family, middle-class homes were centers of domestic production, though of course of a narrower range than the manors of medieval times. They were no longer dependent on the big house, and though they were supplied by industry and commerce with a number of goods, a lot of the processes needed to prepare these goods for use went on at home. It was a change of great economic and social significance, but it was not as abrupt or as psychologically divisive as the split in women's lives that followed when the next shift came. That occurred when the continuing growth and specialization of industry, plus new means of transportation which made it easy to distribute cheap consumer goods, joined forces to take away from the middle-class household much of the activity which had come to be centered there and remove it once and for all to factory production. Families don't make things anymore, they buy them.

The result has been to fragment woman's tripartite traditional role even more since there are now two distinct areas in which women work. Not only are they separate in space, they differ in the demands they make and the rewards they offer. Home market and labor market operate to different standards and have a very different emotional tone to them. When, in the past, economically valuable work was done at home, this division didn't exist. Such work was undertaken with the same people, family and servants, and in the same place as purely domestic tasks. There was often a great deal of overlap.

Farm wives, for instance (and most families lived on the land), very frequently produced for the market as well as for the family. There were special kinds of farming or crops that were traditionally under their care. Our grandmothers often got whatever cash they saw in "egg money" simply by keeping more hens than were needed to produce for the family alone. In a valuable recent study of the village of Chanzeaux in the Anjou region of France, Professor Laurence Wylie of Harvard describes another method by which farm wives there still supplement the family income. The herb camomile, which is used commercially in tisanes, aperitifs and hair dyes, comes almost exclusively from a small area around Chanzeaux. It is the woman's cash crop *par excellence,* grown and harvested by them, the children, and a very few old men who are past other work. In addition to this specialty, Wylie goes on, the gardens and barnyards of Chanzeaux's farms are "like the camomile patch . . . woman's domain. Virtually all the fruits and vegetables consumed by the family are normally home-grown, from squash and scallions to peas and peppers. The barnyard is stocked with pigs, chickens, ducks, geese and rabbits, but these animals are not raised for home consumption alone. On very small farms, the sale of rabbits, angora fur, chickens and eggs may account for as much as a tenth of total income. An intelligent, efficient farm wife is absolutely essential to the successful operation of a Chanzeaux farm," [2] just as she was in America a century ago.

Or less than a century ago, for though such a way of life seems distant today, in terms of actual experience a pattern very like this vanished from America quite recently. In the early years of the New Deal, in fact, when the Great Depression was ravaging the United States, a plausible and rather popular proposal for dealing with mass unemployment was to send starving city dwellers back to the farm, on the assumption that they could at least feed themselves there. Implicit was the belief that anyone, given forty acres and a mule, would know how to set about subsistence farming. Now the idea is as dead as the dodo, though the dream of happy living in farm communes has a romantic attraction for some of those unsatisfied with our present way of life. Back-to-the-land movements of this kind, however, are oddities which—so far, at any rate—lack the economic base to make them viable. The dream of a simple life in a do-it-yourself group is far less important and influential than is the longing to get away from the pressure and ugliness of the city which has produced the pressures and ugliness of dormitory suburbia. The urbanization of the American population has become irreversible in our present society.

Urbanization and industrialization have changed everyone's way of living, not only that of women, but, as in so many other matters, the changes for men and the changes for women are different. To put it at its simplest, men work in the labor market and they therefore work outside the home—with a very few special exceptions, mostly in the arts. Their work and their homes are

separate. Women's lives are divided, too, if they work outside the
home, but the division falls in a different place. In their homes
they work for the welfare and well-being of their immediate families as their great-grandmothers used to do. But if they have to
work for money, they can't make it at home. They must turn to
the labor market and, like men, work as part of an industrial or
commercial enterprise. Whether it is large or small, they work
with people to whom they are not related, at a schedule they do
not control and usually at a job that bears no relation to what they
do in the rest of their working time at home. This experience can
be very valuable indeed, if only because it keeps women in touch
with the way the world runs. But it means that while men almost
all work in just one way, women who work work in two ways.
The change from one sort of work to the other may often be
stimulating, but it contributes to the part-timeness that is so characteristic of women's lives. They are the original moonlighters.

This relatively new need to leave the home in order to do work
that will bring a monetary return is what raises the question that
plagues so many mothers: "Am I depriving my children of the
emotional support and care they need from me if I take a job
outside the house?" The current emphasis placed on the mother-
child relationship, which we discussed in the last chapter, obviously sharpens this pressure. Central to today's argument over
woman's proper role is the dilemma presented on the one hand
by the fear of "maternal deprivation" and, on the other, by the
lessened importance of woman's economic role in the home. To
deprive a child of his mother's care, women are told with considerable authority, may derange his personality and prevent his
growth to happy normal maturity. This nightmare possibility is
the more haunting because, in spite of the force with which it is
stated by doctors and psychologists, there is no way in which its
likelihood can be measured or even defined. The possibility exists,
that is, as a threat, stated universally but felt privately and felt,
consequently, as an added weight on the narrow duality of mother
and child. The connection with a wider society, which is really
part of the context, is easily overlooked. But fundamental to this
agonizing personal dilemma is the lack of support from society to
mothers in the changed situation which forces them to work out-

side the home if they want, or need, to do economically valuable labor.

We shall consider this problem again when we talk about the actual experiences of women working in the labor market, but here it is important to insist that the difficulty can't be solved by means of a mythic absolute. Such a solution is invited by the mythically absolute injunction: "Don't deprive your child of the care he needs," as if an equally universal dictum from on high could be cited in response: "Children need their mothers' presence to exactly this extent, and if you follow these guidelines you will not fail them or need to feel guilty." Even when one is sure that there is no such rule, it is sometimes hard to think past the nagging need for it.

In fact, one can only try to handle the question of children's need for their mothers' care on an empirical basis. Put in a realistic framework, the answer will depend on circumstances: on the age of the children; on the possibility and quality of available mother substitutes, day-care centers, kindergartens and schools; on the woman's own feelings about her need or desire to work, or the pleasure or lack of it she feels in staying home—and, of course, on the family's real need for her earnings. But let us remember always in considering the problem that this is a *new* question which exists in a framework of time and circumstance. This particular difficulty has never arisen before, and its present solution, therefore, is best approached on a pragmatic, day-to-day basis. Mythic absolutes will only confuse the situation by presenting it in falsely universal terms which involve emotions that will get in the way of reasonable common sense. What we can do most usefully is look at the new differences and old similarities between present circumstances and those of the past, so that we can judge the context surrounding the problem and see how the split in woman's economic role affects her whole situation.

If we look first at the women who stay in their place at home (which is the majority of married women in America, but not an overwhelming majority), we see that they escape the split in their interests and activities felt by women who leave home to work. Most signally, they are spared any distress over leaving their children. At the same time, however, they lose their direct, personal connection with the world of productive and economically valuable work. Nothing they do inside their homes brings in any direct economic return: no egg money, no income from a cash crop, no pay for fat geese or angora fur. Of course women working at home make an indirect contribution to their husbands' ability to support the family. Certainly they raise children (or strive to raise children) who will be able to look after themselves and earn their living when the time comes. But these rewards, both material and psychological, are separate from the wife-mother's own experience. Women at home, working at their own pace in their own place, are protected from the harsh pressures and boring burdens of making a living in the world of commerce and industry. They are out of the rat race. But by the same token, they are not in the running for its prizes. They experience the success meted out by the external world only through others and not on their own account. It is part of their role, that is, to live vicariously.

Does this matter? I think it matters very much and in many ways. For one thing, it supplies another example of how women's lives differ from the norms of today's experience, and differ by a time lag. Just as most people used to live lives in which their social roles were laid down from birth as women's still are to a considerable extent, so most people used to be confined—like women in the home market—to receiving a great deal of their experience vicariously. Over the centuries the mass of human beings has been barred by class or caste or some other hierarchical arrangement of status and roles from receiving the gratification of tangible countable return for their own individual labor. Until recently, most men participated in the drama of life by watching others act it out for them, whether the scene was the court with its pageantry, the church with its ritual, or the arena with its games and circuses. Only in modern times have men come normally to expect to receive earnings, in money or status or respect, which are related to them individually and which come as a result of their own work. Today they do expect a material, and a public, return which can be valued by comparing it with the returns that go to others. Modern economic man knows where he stands. Because of this—and no doubt because there are many areas of life in which he *doesn't* know where he stands—he values himself by the return his work brings in, and he expects to enjoy it himself.

Women, in their jobs as homemakers, don't know where they stand. As Orden and Bradburn say, "There are no job descriptions or universal standards of achievement for the production of home goods." [3] In addition, the rewards they receive are private, not public, and certainly are neither countable nor comparable to rewards going to others. What women think of as their return for working at home is the affection of their husbands and children, their pride in contributing to the happiness and success of their families, and indeed these are fine rewards. But again, they are *vicarious* rewards, as well as being personal ones. They are valuable on a different scale, in a different frame of reference. The question of economic return for home labor gets lost, and with it is lost a means of judging one's own value by objective standards. There is really quite a difference between saying to oneself, "I am a good cook because people who love me tell me I am," and saying, "I am a good enough cook to make my living at it."

Women working at home, then, are in an archaic situation in this other sense that what they do there stands outside the money economy and the values related to it. This time there is a further anomaly; this particular archaism has overtaken women rather recently. It used to be quite usual for them to earn by work at home, even if their earnings were generally less than men's.

One can very well argue that ours would be a healthier society if more labor, involving wider areas of activity, were to find rewards that had nothing to do with money. Part of the original attraction of the Peace Corps was certainly that the wages paid there bear no relation to the importance of the work done. The very fact that they are so low immediately invokes another standard of accomplishment. Many people, the young especially, but not only the young, resent the emphasis placed on money values in today's society and would like to see other standards, like the personal satisfaction derived from work well done, replace the cash nexus. Unfortunately personal satisfaction has got itself thoroughly mixed up with money values in our world. With only the smallest exceptions, the value of what we do and make, and thus the value of the "being" that comes from "doing," is reckoned at its cash value. Teachers and policemen, supposedly the leaders

and guardians of society, are willing to tie up communities for
weeks while they strike for higher overtime scales or better pension rights. Public service is expected to pay salaries commensurate with those of private industry. Even judges have considered
going on strike.

Women in the home market, then, are pretty nearly alone in
being required to value their work by standards which are not
money standards. That situation may be (often is) pleasant enough
in itself. To be spared the need to make a living in a competitive
economy liberates the individual and leaves him free to turn his
energies and imagination to activities in other fields. So, in the
nineteenth century when most men worked long hours, women
formed the largest part of the audience for high culture. Before
the government was drawn into social work, they made up the
bulk of the volunteers who administered charities and dispensed
welfare. Indeed, women are still active in these fields, though less
is done by amateur volunteers and increasingly more by paid and
trained professionals. But of course, most notably, women at home
have spent their energies in the home for the benefit of husbands
and children. The dwindling of the economic side of woman's
traditional role has increased the time and imagination which she
can give to her other roles, once she is protected from the rough
world of competitive earning. Sometimes, however, protection
turns into insulation from reality.

Let us look directly now at the psychological effects which the
disappearance of woman's old home-centered economic role and,
with it, her direct tie to the outside world has produced. First,
we have noted, is the loss of an objective standard by which to
measure oneself and one's actions. Our great-grandmothers may
not have been able to support themselves easily by their earnings,
but—like the farm wives of Chanzeaux today—they could look
beyond the family for a judgment on their abilities. Some of them
turned out goods that went to market and had to pass the test of
salability. But even if they didn't, their repute in their own communities supplied a public yardstick. Mrs. Appleton's pickles, Mrs.
Matthews' baked goods, the special dyes Mrs. Mayhew used for
her yarn, Mrs. Lockhart's quilts—these might win only local fame,
but they existed apart from their makers, and they were judged
in public by the peers of the makers. Such a reward may be no

more tangible than ribbons from a county fair, but it is substantial in its own way and it offers a place in a hierarchy of social values.

There was more to it than ribbons, however. Public judgments of this kind simply reflected and represented the existence of a whole area of competence in housewifely skills. Women knew from their own experience whether or not they were successful homemakers and housekeepers because the things they did and the things they made had purposes and uses and they either worked well or they didn't. Women had their own crafts. They made clothes and mended them, washed them by hand, preserved them from moths and made them over for younger children even in this century. Earlier they would often have spun the yarn and woven the cloth and made the soap. Recipes were handed down from mother to daughter, not just for meals, but for the kind of large-scale preserving that would make a summer's bounty see a family through the winter. Any little girl who has envisaged woman's role as involving the ever-ready, never-failing competence of Mrs. Swiss Family Robinson has caught a glimpse of the ideal of woman-as-provider.

Not only were these activities meaningful in themselves and a source of pride because they helped to keep the family going. Beyond this, they had a continuity of value that remained present throughout a woman's life. They helped her to identify specific skills and find areas for realistic self-approval. Learned in girlhood, they tied her life together across the years, giving her a lasting identity and becoming a strand which opposed and defied the fragmentation and temporality of her other, emotional, roles. It was as a housekeeper or cook or needlewoman that a woman at home could see herself as something more than a part-time amateur and see her personality as secure and continuous throughout her life.

We cannot regain that world, and even when we talk of the good things it offered, we should never overlook the terrible drawbacks of narrowness, of drudgery and of frustration which it often imposed on body and spirit. But when we examine woman's role today, we must also take account of the gaps which exist there now that women at home have lost their old tie with the production of economically valuable goods, and thus lost, too, the chance of being judged by the objective standards of an outside community, no matter how small. Those standards represented "the reality principle."

Without them, women at home, "managers of emotions" in Keniston's phrase, must reckon their successes in private and personal terms. Their skills are no longer to be related to the quality of material goods, but to feelings and temporary aesthetic effects. Good wives should be able, for example, to assess the emotional content of a social situation, map out the personal connections within it and either resolve it if that is called for, or make use of the dynamics present for their own purposes. Mothers are expected to use the affection felt for them by their children to direct the children toward right ways of behaving. But all these goals are ill-defined. Because they are, a feeling of success may have more to do with feeling than with success.

The fact is that with no outside standards to reckon by and with no opportunity to win rewards through their production of things or by respect for their professional abilities, women's concentration on personal feelings tends to make all their judgments personal, private and emotional. And these indeed are characteristics which are often attributed to women. They are expected to take general remarks personally, to vote for candidates because they are handsome, to change their minds easily and to cry at the movies. Many of them do. An important reason—not the only one—is that their lives are lived on the emotional, personal side and they lack practice in the technique of abstract, rational decision-making.

Even the products which women at home may still turn out have ceased to have public economic value. Nothing debars woman today from cultivating special housewifely skills, from cooking and preserving or designing their own clothes, or covering the dining-room chairs with exquisite needlework. These activities can be very satisfying—but they are satisfying, again, *personally*. Their meaning has changed. They are no longer necessities, but luxuries, and even when a woman goes into business and sells a specialty, she sells in the luxury market. When she works for herself, her work is a hobby, and the fact she can undertake it marks her as dowered with more leisure than most of her sisters instead of as part of the workaday world.

Women at home, therefore, can judge the success and the meaningfulness of their lives only by personal, emotional values. This fact introduces what the economists call a leverage factor. Women who think well of themselves will go on doing so, judging their accomplishments optimistically. There is nothing wrong with that. Self-approval can be a reflection of the strength of mind and security that carry an individual through bad times and help him to undertake new and necessary tasks. But self-approval which never has to be related to any external evaluation tends to grow into smugness. Caught within a small and personal world, a woman may come to regard it as the universe itself and to close her ears to the demands of a larger community. The complacent, canasta-playing ladies who can't imagine other people's lives and needs and don't want to try provide too frequent an example of this danger. On the other hand, women who undervalue themselves and who have no objective standards that might offset their own harsh judgment are all too apt to feel that their work is unimportant and their lives meaningless.

Self-satisfaction at one end, self-pity at the other—these are the poles of the "only-a-housewife" syndrome. They are not mutually exclusive. One woman may experience and act out both. If fear of confronting the wide world keeps one at home, it is very likely that one will set up mental barriers against the world outside and reject opportunities to know it better. At the same time, one may feel uneasily and inescapably that everything is happening somewhere else, that one is not only isolated but excluded from the centers of life. Certainly a desire to escape from limits and blindfolds is one of the drives that push women to work outside the home, into the labor market.

For women at home, then, the loss of a direct tie to the outer world means a loss of cognitive knowledge of how things work and of real standards to test oneself against. Psychologically this lack of know-how makes for hesitancy and a shrinking back within oneself from responsibility and connection. Of course it isn't meant to do so, but to give women who are sheltered from the need to work a chance to celebrate other values—warmth, affection, the cultivation of feelings, gaity and pleasure. The trouble is that it's difficult to provide and enjoy these things in a vacuum. When the outer world is totally excluded it becomes impossible to imagine it. If this is the case, the sheltered being may develop quite inappropriate, even fantastic, reactions to any given situation. Some nitwits, in short, are born; but others are produced by lack of contact with anything real.

This is one result of vicarious living. Another is the need not only to act, but to *feel* through others. Acting through others produces manipulation. The need to feel through others can engender the sort of overinvestment of emotion in one's children which Keniston identified in the mother-son relationship common among the alienated young men he studied. The same kind of situation was noted by psychiatrist Edgar A. Levenson of the William Alanson White Institute of Psychiatry in an investigation of college dropouts. Characteristically there existed here, he reported, an "intense mutual dependency" between mothers and sons, so close that it sometimes "virtually ruled out the youngsters' rights to privacy or a life of their own. Even in their early twenties the dropouts felt they could never do anything their mothers didn't know about." [4]

We might regard this attitude on the mothers' part as the counter-threat to maternal deprivation: maternal identification, which is sometimes (and rightly) felt by the children as a devouring of their own personalities. For, to their mothers, these young men were not individuals, but functions of themselves. This is not, of course, a sex-determined attitude, but one called forth by the situation in which success has been denied to an individual. Fathers, too, whose lives had been unrewarding ached to live through their sons. The failure of the children provoked from their parents the question, "What have I done wrong?", a question denying the children even the right to fail by themselves. The proud mother of "my son, the doctor" is a milder variant of the type, but her situation is the same. Her children are the only tangible product of her life, and if she is to win any approbation for her work and justify her days, it will be by sharing the awards they win. To the extent that she has been denied the chance to win any other prize, and persuaded that her main function in life is to raise children, society has pushed her into that attitude.

Maternal pride in the accomplishments of one's children is natural enough, even if its exaggeration is not pretty. What is more disturbing is the determination to limit the opportunities of children, and particularly of daughters, which also turns up among mothers who have invested emotion in vicarious living because they have never enjoyed true autonomy. A woman isolated from the world with her children will fear the loneliness of losing them. College-trained daughters, following professions that set them strange goals and lead them into unfamiliar ways of living, will leave their mothers behind, unable to keep in touch. Such a mother may feel that even her daughter's success is not worth a lonely old age. In addition, women who have come to terms with the limits that society has set on their ambitions may resent their daughters' hopes or, more kindly, feel that they are saving them from disappointment by urging them not to set their sights too high. "Don't try, don't care too much, don't break your heart," is motherly advice that is sometimes wise and often seems so; it can never be entirely selfless.

One other effect of the lessened importance of woman's role as a worker in the home market remains to be noticed. As we have seen, mothers and children no longer work together to produce goods which will supply the world outside the household, as the women and children of the Chanzeaux harvest the camomile crop. In Orchard Town, New England, the chores that children are expected to do pertain only to the home and are done within it: they clean their rooms, pick up their toys and help wash dishes. So they too are indirectly affected by the loss of the economic tie between home and the external world where their fathers work. They can't observe that world; it has to be explained, and it is often explained by mothers who don't know a great deal about it either. Even when the fathers take a hand, there is no natural, casual way for children to learn much about the world of work into which the men vanish in the morning. In the old world, activities went on in full view of the public. A smithy, a shipyard, a rope walk were all places where work was demonstrated as well as done. A tour of Daddy's office does not produce the same effect.

This has been noted often enough, but the point I want to emphasize here is that the isolation of children with their mothers from the world of work is another factor which increases the importance of the emotional tie between them: they are not only isolated *from* a world, but *in* another. This other world has its own special characteristics. Is it possible that the sudden rise in drug use among the young is related to a view of the world as an interior place defined only by emotions, where real processes of cause and effect do not operate? For that is, in fact, a fair description of the sheltered space assigned to women.

Meanwhile, the decline of home-based productive processes not only emphasizes the emotional content of family life, it also lessens the continuity of woman's role. The emotional give-and-take of child-raising changes profoundly as the children grow. With the loss of regular chores that have to be done year after year, the discontinuity of women's lives increases. Their activities have always been diverse because of shifting day-to-day demands. But now most year-to-year demands change at least as much. Perhaps for ten years a woman's most important work will be the hugely rewarding task of mothering young children. But even while she is most deeply engaged in it, she knows that it will end, and will end inevitably, because of the sheer passage of time, not because she as a person has brought a piece of work she began to a successful conclusion. The part-timeness of women's lives applies, thus, to the course of their activities.

It is in this sense that women can validly be spoken of as a minority. They aren't a minority numerically, but their lives are a bundle of minority activities, temporally as well as socially. There is always some central situation commanding their attention in which they are part of a group set off from the whole. Women at work are a minority of workers as well as a minority of women. Women at home are a minority of the population. And very often any activity they undertake is something at which they will spend a minority of their lives. The consciousness of being part of a minority which women so often feel can be very limiting to them (as well as being thoroughly irritating to rational men who point out that more than half the population is female), but it has its roots in the fragmented way of life, the demanding role changes and shifts of interests and activities which women experience.

It may be, paradoxically, that this feeling of being in a minority is what persists longest and is felt most widely by women, a feeling that is akin to that of limitedness, and of being distant from centers of action. Even women who penetrate the world of power seldom do it directly: they are wives, hostesses, mistresses of salons or tycoons. Close to power, they must still act through others; and because they act through others, shielded by them, they often act without a full sense of responsibility for what their action will bring to pass. They will not bear the brunt of the results of their action, so they act frivolously, feel in secret, enjoy intrigue. These are the faults expected of women in power, and they are faults that the barriers raised to shelter women tend to produce.

For vicarious living, which means acting and feeling through others, should not be confused with living in affection and community *with* others. That is participation, and everyone who experiences it, whether within the family, in an orchestra making music, or in a political-action group working for shared ideals, is enriched by it. But let any of the group be debarred—by custom, or law, or even their own feelings—from moving out of the group into their own individual relationship with the world outside, and the joy of community is jeopardized. The need to use others as instruments for action or feeling will adulterate it. So many women come to see their families, or others to whom they are connected by bonds of affection, not as people but as implements to gain satisfactions that are purely selfish, satisfactions they cannot lay hands on honestly and directly if they are unable to act and feel for themselves. And if that is all they see, that is what they will teach their children.

CHAPTER 14

The house is often a refuge for women. But escape from life leaves no life at all. Women comply—because husband, children, church and state seem to expect it—but there is usually at least a wistful longing to break out and a well-founded suspicion that they are missing something important. Working class women are easily trapped; most lack the courage, the know-how to break through. They stay in their cages, quiet and desperate, working out unhappy compromises with their spouses, very often battling for position or giving in and taking a beating.

The brightest days of my mother's life were her first days of work—as a school janitress—during the Depression. The "glamor" wore bare but it still beat staying home. The job offered new hope, new routines, and a regular pay check. It was the beginning of a new life of labor, hard labor, but it offered her what it offers every worker—warm and varied associations with other workers, and the ironic sense that, despite her low-man status, she was after all her own boss with her own source of income.

Patricia Cayo Sexton
"Speaking for the Working-Class Wife" [1]

IF WOMEN AT HOME share a feeling of limitedness and distance from power, if, as Patricia Sexton expresses it, they experience "a well-founded suspicion that they are missing something important," is there another, different common denominator of attitudes among women at work? We can't deny that a sense of being limited exists here too. Most jobs are pretty dull. Centers of power, controlling levers of action, are still distant—as they are, after all, for most men. Comparing woman's role to that of a captain of industry is neither fair nor sensible. But women in the labor market, even in limited jobs, do have real advantages over women at home that can't be shrugged off. Mrs. Sexton puts her finger on them when she talks about the kind of participation in work, even

hard, dull work, and the control over their lives which women feel
when they join up with the working majority of human beings.

The Depression years, when Mrs. Sexton's mother went to
work, seem distant now, part of another world. But in 1962, when
the article from which I quote appeared in *Harper's*, Mrs. Cayo
was still working at the sort of job that offers no romance whatever
and still finding it satisfying. She was a mechanized seamstress in
the Ford Highland Park plant in Detroit. "She still rises at 4:30
A.M.," wrote her daughter, "returns home at 3:30, does her house-
work, eats, naps, reads the evening paper, takes in a little TV. If
the weather permits, [she takes] a customary drive down the main
street of town, and retires at 10 o'clock. That's it and has been for
almost twenty years." It certainly isn't a thrilling life for a middle-
aged woman, but this one quite positively didn't want to give it
up, retire, and be looked after by her successful sociologist
daughter.

One reason was that vicarious living had been replaced by
active participation in events even if they were routine, rather
humdrum events. Mrs. Sexton gives us the background: "My
mother's only point of contact with the outside world used to be
through my father and yet she complained that he did not talk to
her enough. Of course, he was a taciturn man, but few workers
talk much to their wives. They have little to say about their jobs
(the same routine), and little common meeting-ground. Unlike
most middle-class men, they have interests, tastes, experiences
often very different from their wives. So there is little rapport; the
man would rather talk with his bar-room buddies about baseball,
leaving the stay-at-home wife starved for adult talk.

"A job gives a woman something to talk about and someone to
talk to; it makes it easier to stay alive and alert, to keep up with
husband and children; it gives her organized purpose. More than
this, it helps her face advancing years, when children scatter,
[and] life changes." [2] If there appears to be a contradiction here
between Mrs. Sexton's remark that "men have little to say about
their jobs," while "a job gives a woman something to talk about,"
the solution, I think, lies in this: one talks about even "the same
routine" with fellow workers, and especially about small variations
and incidents, where one wouldn't with outsiders because it would
be too much trouble to explain the background. Women with jobs

do this at work, and also, because they are fellow workers with their husbands even if they are not employed in the same place, it is easier for husbands and wives to talk at home. They both know what work is like.

Independence and participation in the present, then, offer a woman an important return for hard work with strangers at an imposed timetable. Another reward is a sense of control over one's future. A paycheck that is your own gives you a tangible, countable sign of your individual value and, together with the pension rights that usually go with it, it means some security and continuing independence in the years ahead, after "life changes." In 1962, to continue with the example Mrs. Sexton has documented so well for us, her mother was planning to retire after a few years on social security plus a pension. No luxury here, but no charity either. She had built a solid barrier against becoming a welfare case or a burden on her children, and had done it on her own. She did not have to fear the indignity and shock of the ugly reversal of role which can terrify the suddenly old, suddenly poor widow as her children wrangle over the practical, unpleasant question, "Who will look after Mother? Where will she live?"—those same children who once, as babies, depended on her for their very lives. A working woman, even one with a routine job in an automated plant, can hold onto something of the old feeling of continuity in her life, which only participation in the external economic and social order can supply. Part of the normal, workaday world, she is also an individual who feels herself valuable because she is valued and paid in her own right and is not simply part of a family constellation.

I have talked this much about Mrs. Sexton's mother because her case alerts us to one of those perfectly obvious, fundamental facts that tend to get overlooked in the mythic overtones of the debate about woman's place. Most women who work do so because they need the money. They work at unglamorous jobs, not in careers— and they always have. If we look at the figures on the sort of jobs women do, we find that less than 20 percent of women in the United States labor force can be classified as professionals, managers, officials, or proprietors. This is a figure that has held steady for a generation. Clerical workers, sales workers, service workers outside the home and operatives in industry (like Mrs. Sexton's mother) have included more than two-thirds of working women ever since the Second World War. Even in 1940, this sector amounted to 57 percent; and the 10 percent difference between that year and the two-thirds brought about by the changes made by the war was made up of women working at least as hard on farms and in domestic service.

This suggests something interesting about the context of our mythic statement that woman's place is in the home. We have seen that, as far as history goes, it is very much a middle-class myth. It rose with the bourgeoisie as the late Middle Ages gave way to modern times, it spread with the increase of their influence, and it took hold after 1700 ever more strongly as they began to dominate the norms of culture. This is naturally not to say that other societies didn't and don't limit women's activities and rights too. Of course they do; but the myth as we know it reflects a society that can afford to hold women off the labor market and keep them at home in a more or less Veblenesque situation, where their contribution is more expressive than productive. It appears, that is, to be a middle-class myth from the standpoint of economics as well as of history. The large majority of women who work have been pretty well exempted from the argument over whether or not they should. They have worked because they had to, and for a good long time too. Those working-class wives caught at home, of whom Mrs. Sexton speaks, are a relatively new phenomenon: a product of an affluent and *embourgeois*-ed society. Even in prosperous mid-nineteenth-century England, one out of every four married women worked at some job which gave her a professional classification other than "housewife"; and this was over and above the huge but uncounted number of wives who worked, as they always had, in their husbands' businesses and shops.

The myth, of course, tells us that Victorian ladies in just these years either married or, if they didn't manage this feat, fell to the charge of their brothers or married sisters and ended life as those ubiquitous necessary maiden aunts. If money to keep them vanished, they were faced with the rigors of existence as a governess or a companion. The only other choice was prostitution—thus the myth, with its expected imperative: "Get married! Stay home! Leave man's world to men!" But most Victorian women were not, in fact, ladies. Some of them did indeed become prostitutes, but others worked in mills and factories and other people's houses, sewed in sweatshops or as visiting seamstresses, washed clothes, sold flowers, apples and nuts, watercress and whelks, danced on the tightrope and swept muddy crossings. They were the poor, and they were outside the reach of the myth.

If their descendants today, women who work because they have to, are not still outside it, it's because myth is protean. The idea that women have a special place and require special treatment has both invaded the ways of thinking of a working class now grown increasingly comfortable and middle class-minded, *and* adapted itself to the labor market. The latter result is in part due to the untiring efforts of socially conscious folk, many of them women, to protect working-class women from exploitation. The first wave of feminists never did clear up the intellectual ambiguity in which they maintained that women deserved the same rights as men and more protection. In fact, this is a good deal less irrational than it seems: women were being treated worse than men in some social and economic situations at the time. They needed legislative action to protect them from actual abuses. But of course the idea of legislative protection for women accords with and reinforces the dictum that they have a special place and special requirements. This isn't the only reason why certain jobs have been earmarked as female. Man's world is always more willing to welcome working Indians than competitive chiefs. The jobs that were first opened to women were jobs that the chiefs don't much want for themselves. Not even the most violent anti-feminist is likely to declare that women mustn't file papers in offices, clerk in shops, put through long-distance calls, or teach school in the elementary grades. This is woman's place in the labor market, and as economic need forces women out of the home, an effort is made to contain them here. It is only when they start to move out of jobs like these that they begin to make waves—like the girl jockeys who ran into a boycott by all the male jockeys when they first tried to ride *in* races, instead of simply training horses *for* races, where they had been accepted for years; or like the women in engineering—there are around eight thousand of them in the United States—who are hired for junior jobs, but find it difficult to move up to where they will be "in charge."

Thus, woman's place in the labor market tends to become traditionally defined and, wherever possible, related back to woman's role at home. When myth is under pressure from actual events, that is to say, it will change, but it will try to make its changes consonant with its old rules and definitions. Indeed, this is part of its dynamic of survival, this tying together of old and new, and it is also the reason why "traditions" can appear and spread so fast. Necessity may be the mother of invention, but invention is best packaged as being a new version of an old custom. We are all looking for rules and structure, all anxious to do things in the normal, "s'pozed-to-be" way. And it is easy to see why: the world is so terribly complicated, and so demanding at the same time, that we cannot sit down and think out every move. We depend on the social system we have evolved, and if we are to get anything done at all in one area, we have to act in other areas by the human equivalent of instinct—that is, by playing roles and taking situations for granted. So we take for granted the idea (among many others) that it's perfectly all right for women to work in the labor market if they do jobs that are "suited" to them, and that these will resemble the ones they used to do at home.[3]

It sounds so reasonable! Thus, Mrs. Sexton's mother is a seamstress. Elementary-school teachers look after children. Secretaries work as assistants and aides in support of active, dominant males. Receptionists pretend to be hostesses. Telephone operators facilitate interpersonal relationships by speeding communications. Name the feminine job, and there will be a way to work it into the old, accepted pattern of support, nurture and skill at managing emotions which is held to be traditionally typical of women.

But do these jobs really tie up with the old, or are we simply accepting a linguistic connection instead of a real one? If the job Mrs. Sexton's mother held at Ford's Highland Park plant was that of a mechanized seamstress, the emphasis has to be on the adjective, not on the noun. She was actually running a small machine, not exercising graceful, ancient feminine skills with needle and thread. Elementary-school teachers today are frequently more in need of the talents of a lion tamer or a squadron leader than those of a nurturing mother. What mother ever had to deal with a family of forty children all the same age, often from backgrounds with which she is not familiar? Any good teacher will want to nurture them—but she won't do it successfully if she tries the

methods she would use with her own intimately known and
responsive baby.

As for assisting the dominant male—is that in fact what women
used to do in their economic role at home? Sometimes yes, particularly on the farm, but then they were more another pair of
hands than they were women working at feminine skills. In the
latter case they usually worked on their own schedule in their
own place, as free-lance artisans and craftsmen. In the time of the
great houses, the chatelaine was sometimes called on to be as
dominant as any male while her maids either worked in teams,
processing food or cloth or other necessities, or they used the
special skills they commanded on their own, craftsmen again. If
there really is an analogy between woman's traditional occupations
and those that she undertakes with full acceptance in the labor
market, it seems to be a matter of words and names rather than
what she actually does. If there is continuity, it is of the role
assigned to women, the expectations projected onto them.

This is not to say that woman's place in the labor market is
established by myth, for it is, of course, established by economic
considerations. But economic considerations have a terrible apti-
tude for getting tangled up with myth, by way of psychology and
received ideas. When women step out of their role they very often
upset the people they are working with. That makes for trouble,
and trouble costs money. At this point a balance appears. Is it
cheaper to keep women working in traditional and accepted ways
only and lose the potential talent and energy they might bring to
new jobs? Or will there be a big enough payoff to make the trial
worthwhile?

In itself this is neither a mythic nor a moral, but an empirical
question, and it is usually solved empirically—though not always,
for the myth may have got into the psychology of the decision-
maker himself. In good times, when women are needed on the
labor market, it's easier for them to break into new and better
jobs. Girl jockeys are now racing. At the height of the Wall Street
boom, two women brokers had seats on the New York Stock Exchange, though one later retired. During the 1968–1969 season
the St. Louis Symphony included eighteen women musicians playing everything from the flute to the double bass. There are women

housepainters and women taxidrivers, and women members of the
Seafarers Union have been demanding equal pay for equal work.
Black and Decker, machine-tool makers, started canvassing wom-
en's colleges for job applicants when technical skills were most
in demand. The INA corporation, a Philadelphia-based holding
company, reported in 1970 that it employed over two hundred
women in "judgment-level jobs," ten times more than it did a
decade ago. And of course, during the Second World War, women
worked almost everywhere in heavy industry, including shipyards
and steel plants. Their acceptance then was tied to the need for
their labor.

But when that need declines, the myth becomes more influential
in the context within which empirical questions get their answers,
complicating decisions and raising painful emotions. Women who
are passed over for executive positions on the grounds that men
don't like to work for women naturally feel very bitter about it.
On the other hand, some men *don't* want to work for women, and
that emotion can't be ignored as unimportant or illusory. The
myth of female power and the unconscious fear that it provokes
are deep-rooted and pervasive, and their existence is a fact of
economic life.

Another fact of economic life is the normal part-timeness which
affects the way women live and pursue careers in our society. They
keep getting married and leaving their work to have children, or
quitting because their husbands have been moved to the West
Coast. Whatever problems this may raise within a marriage (and
most women go where their husbands go without question), it also
presents a difficulty for business management. Women who leave
to start families step off the escalator. Many do so planning to go
back to work when the children are in school, but when they do
they will have lost six or eight years. Their skills will be rusty, they
won't have kept up with new methods in a business that's sensitive
to change, and they have obligations at home. At the simplest
level, they may have to leave work for a week if a child is sick, and
they want to take vacations when their husbands do. A more
subtle disqualification for the superior sort of job that few women
hold is that they're not usually able to fly to San Francisco or
Tokyo on an hour's notice, or spend three weeks checking out a
new installation in McKeesport. It would be economically impos-

sible to give them jobs that demand this ability, even if the plant manager in McKeesport could be expected to welcome a female boss with delight, and many executive jobs do demand it.

This is the sort of thing we take for granted. It is so close to the heart of the myth that we don't see it as myth at all. *Of course*, we say, women can't be dedicated to their work in the way that men are. *Of course* their families come first. And they do come first for almost all women. Maybe they always will. Maybe they should. But that does not mean that we can ignore or gloss over the *effects* of this pattern which limits all women, whether they have families or not, and puts a ceiling on the energy and emotion any woman feels she can afford to invest in her job. For she really doesn't have an equal choice of job first, family first. Our society tells her to put her family first, and any woman who disagrees has got to fight the pattern and face the consequences of playing something of a negative, and therefore unpleasant, role.

It isn't only career women who feel the repercussions of mythic imperatives and evaluations. One-half of the human race is told to accept the fact that it is not to act, and to live, for its own primary purposes. That affects all the human race, one way or another, because secondary women react with powerful men and, even more influentially, with the children who are now isolated in their care. Perhaps this stratification of society by sex is a necessary, or at least useful, simplification of life. Perhaps it is even good, in the sense that enforced unselfishness and willingness to sacrifice one's own immediate desires may be better than no unselfishness or self-sacrifice at all. Most women, at any rate, accept the dictum that men act and women support them. But nothing on earth can prevent the dictum, and women's acceptance of it, from affecting the rest of life, with results that range from the trivial to the profound by way of the frightening, the absurd and the utterly infuriating.

We must all expect, in our lives, to experience absurdity and irritation and manage to dismiss trivia without magnifying them. None of us can have everything he wants, none of us is free from boredom and drudgery. Men's lives contain them in large quantities, and men's commitment to a life of work in the world of the status quo can often be stultifying, can blind them to the need for innovation, can confine their interests to narrow, specialized goals, can face them with wearing, exhausting tasks which don't bring a return that matches the effort put into them. This is and always has been the human lot, whatever dreams of an apocalyptic future may promise. Any social system is going to bear harder here than there and create gaps in understanding between this group and that, however defined.

What's more, the position of Western women in the labor market today is obviously favorable enough to bring more and more of them into it. The limits set on ambition may be annoying to those who run into the limits, and costly overall, but they haven't stopped women from emigrating from their place into man's world whenever they can find a spot and a job. They do indeed work at lower levels than men, and at lower wages when they are on the same level, but apparently it is worth it.

Worth it, of course, to them, the women who work. And here we come around again to the question of the priority of one part of woman's role over another and the problems of a working mother. Women who work because they have to are plagued just as much as those who work because they want to by the thought that they may be leaving their children neglected and their husbands bereft. They do not only like but need their paycheck, and they may tell themselves that their work helps the children by guaranteeing them a better standard of living. Sometimes it's only women's work that brings in a living at all. They are not immune, however, to the same concern about maternal deprivation that bothers their sisters who could stay at home if they wanted to. These women must work, and a society which offers little care for the children while they do so bears hard on them indeed.

We might remember, I think, that although our present situation, where all economic work is done outside the home, is new, mothers did work hard in the past and certainly did not spend all their time with their families. Millions of children, in fact, throughout century after century, have been raised in large part by women who were *not* their natural mothers. I do not mean only the children of the kibbutzim, but all those babies put out to nurse, left with grandmothers or older sisters, and sent away to school (or, earlier, to the great houses) when they reached "the age of reason," an age which is and has been thought of around the world with considerable uniformity as being about seven years old. In our own cultural past (that is, in medieval Europe), when the only formal schools which existed were devoted to training boys for the church, the rest of the folk—noble, gentle, or serf—learned by doing, in a kind of general apprenticeship to the adult world, and they learned a lot of it a lot of the time away from home. Even when formal education came to be thought of as desirable for the laity and upper-class boys were sent to school, girls and boys from the lower classes continued to learn in the old-fashioned way: it was only the daughters of the rich and great who were kept at home with a governess. The rest learned by working, sometimes with their own parents, who were not necessarily more tender than strangers, but very frequently while boarding with friends or relations or in the home of some well-placed notable, to learn manners as well as crafts. The institution of the *au pair* girl which still survives in Europe is a legacy of this manner of teaching domestic skills, household management and savoir faire.

No doubt, one may say. This happened. But were these arrangements good for the children? How can one answer—except to say that the human race survived them as it has other ways of life that seem strange today, and that the customs themselves must have been socially useful and psychologically satisfactory enough to endure? Five hundred years ago an Italian observer declared that the cruel English didn't love their children since they sent them away from their homes to be raised by others when they were no more than seven to nine years old. The English are still doing it and still being chided for it, but the system did not prevent England from producing, in the same five hundred years, a literature second to none, an empire larger than ever existed before, an economic system that revolutionized industry and political institutions that have influenced the world.

Certainly all children need loving care, need attention and instruction, and need adults to model themselves on. But must all these needs be supplied *only* by their natural parents? We might recall once more Shakespeare's remark, "Homekeeping youths have ever homely ways." The small community of the family can get too small rather rapidly and—like the Jewish families of the ghetto which the founders of the kibbutzim wanted to see forgotten—become stifling and binding rather than supportive. Or it can simply not be various enough. I was amused to receive, as I considered this question, a letter from a friend pointing out that models other than their father can be very useful to boys. My friend and his son lost their tempers at each other very thoroughly one day (he wrote), and his son declared, "See, now, you have given me both angry genes and a bad example."

In effect, how much is done for children by parents alone depends very much on the society in which the family exists, on the social and economic demands that society makes on the parents in other ways, and on the help it offers them in bringing up their children and instructing them in the mores of the community. We are most conscious today of the changed situation that arises because women are working outside their homes more than they have in the past, but the departure of fathers from the close circle around the home, where their activities were easily seen by their children and sometimes shared by them, certainly had a large effect on child-raising too. Obviously there is a minimum of close and affectionate care that every infant must be able to depend on; it was physically greater in the past when there was no substitute for mother's milk than it is now. But it is awfully easy to base a superstructure of myth on this need which can hamper both mother and child by emphasizing and prolonging an intimacy which is proper to the early years, but a burden to both later on. When "later on" begins is not simply a matter of emotion or of a family situation, but a question that depends on community size, community custom, community closeness and the kind of work done there.

Keniston's young men in the alienated group would have been better off if their mothers had put some of their energy into doing a job outside the home instead of projecting their ambitions onto their sons. Women who work in the labor market, in fact, often find that their bonds with the world outside can widen the world of their children. Sometimes they find themselves closer to their children because they have their own knowledge of the world the children are growing into. Women who have gone back to a university for a degree in order to go on with earlier careers remark that their school-age children are not only sympathetic to a studying mother, but impressed and proud of her serious purpose. "It is very important," wrote Talcott Parsons in his study, *The*

American Family, "that the socializing agents (that is, the parents) should not themselves be *too* completely immersed in their family ties. . . . Specifically this means that the adult members must have roles other than their familial roles which occupy strategically important places in their own personalities." [4]

For the family, as Parsons rightly insists, is not a system but a subsystem. It doesn't exist for itself, turned in on itself, but as a means to prepare children to grow up and take their part in the larger organization, the social system. Mothers who know something about the larger organization can help children understand and cope with it better than those who don't. Even if they believe that our social system stands in great need of correction, as many women do today, they can still be more useful to their children in dealing with it and in evaluating it realistically if they have been out there in it and have arrived at their own informed judgments about its faults and advantages.

In the end the problem remains empirical: not whether women should work, but how those who want to, or need to, *can* work without leaving their other obligations unsatisfied, in this case without neglecting their children. And here is where the myth comes in. For if the myth is taken at face value, if society assumes implicitly that women shouldn't work because their place is at home, and regards women who do work as flying in the face of custom or even nature, then there is no need for society to do anything to help them out. No need for day nurseries or nursery schools or public health nurses who can come in when a child is sick; no need to find new ways of making domestic service a pleasant, decent job so that middle-aged women, their families grown, could come in regularly mornings or afternoons to help young mothers. No need to suggest to industry that steady part-time workers can solve some of their problems and are worth training, or to universities that a young woman with a child might take her law degree part-time over five years just as well as full-time over three. No need to accommodate custom to facts, so that an increase in women workers doesn't have to mean an increase in desperate compromises, family strains and unnecessary dislocations in business. No need to think and plan about the social shifts that are actually going on and thus ease their impact instead of letting it develop toward explosive force. And no need to try to bring fathers back into a closer relationship with their children and thus enlarge the family world.

For even when there is large agreement that women have a perfect right to work if they want to, as there is today, the effort to change customs and institutions may lag very considerably because of the mythic residue at the bottom of our minds. We don't try hard enough. "All right, let them work if they want to," has a bit of an echo of "Let them eat cake" to it. It encourages, by complacency, that effective method of heading off any push for change by assuring the world that the change has already taken place, that women have all the rights they need, or at least as much as is good for them and for their families. This is the real danger in myth: it encourages rigid thinking, a black-and-white, right-or-wrong view of the world where only give-and-take can adjust institutions and social change. Closed minds accept myth most easily, but a frightened society seeks it actively.

As for marriage—do working women withdraw needed support from their husbands, put their own wants first and grow competitive and hard because they have joined the rat race and started to tussle with demands from the world outside woman's place? This is the threat that the myth hints at in this relationship. Implicit in it is an assumption that is almost never spoken but that lies at the heart of the wrangle over woman's proper place: namely, that a woman can never be exactly the equal of a man. She must be kept as his dependent lest she become his boss. And so we come around again to the myth of female power.

CHAPTER 15

... they have friends they can talk to weve none either he wants
what he wont get or its some woman ready to stick her knife in
you I hate that in women no wonder they treat us the way they
do we are a dreadful lot of bitches I suppose its all the troubles
we have makes us snappy Im not like that ...

James Joyce
Molly Bloom, in *Ulysses* [1]

WOMAN'S THIRD ROLE is that of wife. I have left it to be considered
last, not because it is the least important part of woman's doing-
and-being, but because it is the hardest to write about coherently
in general terms. Because it is the most diverse, the most changing
and the most private, it is best tackled after our look at other
aspects of woman's triple role has given us some guidelines.
Women as mothers all have jobs to do that are oriented toward
the same end. They hope to raise children who will be successful
and happy, a credit to their families, able to fit into or to manage
the world around them. Women at work are themselves engaged
in the social environment. If they work in the labor market, what
they do has an obvious public aspect and can be judged objectively. Even as housewives, each in her own fastness, they face
situations that have enough common factors to be discussed
generally.

But women as wives are individuals each involved with one
other individual, often deeply and intimately and always, in part,
wordlessly. The nuances of these relationships are infinite and
there is no objective way of measuring them or even observing
them. We are dependent on what husbands and wives tell us about
themselves, on our estimates of their behavior (which is naturally
related to our own experience), and on our judgment (which may
be good or bad) of whether they are speaking and acting what they

really feel. When they say they are "happy" or "sad" or "bored" or "desperate" we have no way of knowing how they assess these words in their own minds, or how to compare the intensity and tone of their emotions with those of other happy, sad, bored, or desperate couples. If individuals are alone with their own experience of life, couples are perhaps even more alone in their own little binary systems, for the doubling of experience increases enormously the possible differences in the way they live together.

We must, in fact, once more approach the area of myth if we are to talk of the relationships between one man and one woman in any unified way. What we have learned of its dynamics and its content will help us here, for though marriages differ in the amount of myth they incorporate, they are alike in that they all incorporate at least a little. True, the range is wide. Some couples —Scott and Zelda Fitzgerald were a striking example—appear to be sitting for their portraits as case histories of *folie à deux*. Love affairs often begin with each partner playing an ideal role that exists only in his own head. A missed cue by one or the other member of this joint venture *can* open the door to reality, but sometimes what comes in is simply another version of myth.

Of all myths, the ones growing out of the ancient and ambiguous confrontation and partnership between mother and child fit most easily into the pattern of another two-person relationship. Marriages are peculiarly sensitive to the conjoint myths of female weakness and female power. The very establishment of a marriage, even when it is an unemotional marriage of convenience, requires a commitment from both husband and wife: a mutual giving, even if it is grudging; a mutual expectation of some return, no matter how small, no matter how indirect; an agreement to trust each other to keep up appearances publicly, at the very least; and, at the same time, a mutual uncertainty as to how these expectations will be met. Even when it is not intimate or when the value to each partner is very unequal, the duality of marriage recalls the first relationship of all. In the universal symbiosis of all-dependent child who imagines himself all-powerful and the truly powerful mother we find the source of attitudes toward all later connections and the crust of love and of unappeased desire on which we gnaw for nourishment for the rest of our lives.

Marriage is a reversal as well as a renewal of the old mother-child pairing, for neither the allotment of power nor the direction of the relationship is settled in advance. In the first duality the mother was, so to speak, the representative of the reality principle. At the start, it was she who could withhold pleasure and satisfaction, could limit, control and frustrate the other member. The child, who began by thinking himself omnipotent, discovered reality by discovering his own limits and pushing against them. So he discovered his own abilities and powers, growing from dependence toward equality. But as he did so, he had reason to fear his mother's strength: he learned and grew by testing himself against it. It is very possible, I think, that a psychological source of the ban against incest lies in this fear. In order to reach a life of his own, every child has to fight free of his parents. Of these the mother is the most powerful because she is the closest, the first, the one who handled the child before language gave him any clue to the world around him. The incest ban helps the son to separate himself from his mother and take on a full social identity. Freud thought of it as a way for old men to keep the women of a tribe to themselves; but it is also a justification for young men to leave the women who loved them first—and a weapon to use against them, if need be.

Having left his mother, a man takes a wife and a new duality begins. It would be odd if the fears and hopes of the old relationship did not have some part in the new, and specifically if the ancient dread of female power did not sometimes awaken. We should not suppose, either, that women as wives have forgotten all about these lines of force. Were they not also subject to all-powerful mothers? Did they not have to fight free of the first bond, just as their brothers did? Except that, fighting, they knew they fought their own sex and would, in time or in principle, become the very thing with which they were struggling: daughters and heirs of the all-powerful mother, givers and withholders, healers and deniers. For them the struggle was also a promise for the future and a lesson in the exercise of power which they assumed would one day be theirs. This is the side of the pattern offered to women.

It is here that the idea of pleasure as a gift from woman to man begins for, to the child, the mother is the giver. By analogy, the woman as object of sexual desire takes on the aspect of giver. What she controls and can give or deny is not, of course, the same material comfort that a mother gives a child, but rather the emotions that are associated with that comfort. Sexual needs and the appeasement of these needs call up the echo of an earlier pleasure pattern. "The lineaments of gratified desire" are those of the infant that has nursed and drunk its fill. Beyond both immediate and reflected pleasure, however, the sexual act does not take place without arousing some other emotion, whether it is fulfillment or frustration, and whether it is directed toward the self or toward the partner; and any kind of enduring two-person relationship will be embedded in a highly complicated system of feeling. The more a society values sex (and ours today values it very highly), the more weight the emotions surrounding the act will assume. The idea that women are the givers in sex ties in with Keniston's description of them as managers of emotion, experts in feeling. Their responses, their pleasure and their ability to qualify the pleasure and the responses of men are, therefore, a very important source of power, important enough to be frightening to men.

The meaning and value of sex in our society is a subject I will consider later at some length. Here I want simply to comment on its constant and trivial use today on the surface of life, where it appears as a *lingua franca* exploited for a host of superficial purposes. If we look only at the surface, we are tempted to discount it as having become a way of selling cigarettes or automobiles, a step toward getting acquainted with strangers, a trendy pastime for a wet afternoon, with "straight" sex such a cliché that even the ads are getting kinky and aping the baroque and gothic exaggerations of art. One can be irritated or amused at this exploitation, but there is obviously a reason for it, and the reason is exactly that sex in itself is not (or not yet) a trivial amusement. For most of us, its subterranean reaches are the unique source of profound and transcendent emotion. The appeals that are made to it in fiction, good and bad, films, good and bad, and commercial advertising represent an attempt to reach the depths of emotional truth which still exist within us, what Dostoevski called the springs of life. For most people, the way down to them through religion is blocked, and though the way down through drugs is becoming more frequently traveled, it is still far from being institutionalized or even accepted. Sex is the surest path to the source for whose streams we yearn in order to irrigate our desert existence.

Women in private, women as wives and lovers, are thought of as presiding over these springs of emotion to whose presence we were guided, in the first instance, by the mother figure from whom we learned to feel. Women give value to life because they are the guardians of emotion and the guides to its expression. When men act in man's world, they hope to find fame and esteem there and so receive the public rewards of society, but it is women whom the pattern designates to be givers of private joys, healers of wounds suffered in public, replenishers of pride and courage and honor. The ability to feel for others, with which they are credited, allows men to share (and thus to unload a part of) the disappointments and denigrations that are an inevitable result of ambitious action in the external world where no one triumphs all the time. In the world at large men are required to act with restraint and dignity, whether in defeat or in success. They must accept rewards modestly and hide discomfort and hurt under a cloak of apparent indifference. Men turn away from the public arena in real need of a chance to feel their own emotions to the full, to cry and curse and exult, and to find someone who will respond and share their experience, who will validate it by sharing it and so declare that it is not simply fantasy. From time immemorial it has been a part of woman's role to offer men the place in which to act out their feelings, to authenticate them, and in the end to determine and pronounce on their significance.

There is an interesting by-product of this situation which offers women such enormous, secret power. The association of women with the acting out of emotion is an important reason why men feel so uneasy when women move out of their place into man's world. That world is governed by public rules of restraint and dignity. Emotion is not appropriate. How, men ask themselves, can we trust women to behave properly here when we know from our experience in woman's place how emotional these creatures are? The custom by which men put aside their public etiquette in woman's private place habituates them to think that women can't assume rational restraint when they are abroad. In private, men are allowed to be unfair and personal when they ask for sympathy and comfort. The very fact that women give them comfort under such circumstances makes men suspect that they don't put much stock in being fair. Men are so conscious of the barrier between man's world and woman's place that they find it hard to believe that women can move from the one to the other as freely as they do themselves. Who knows? Perhaps they can't. As long as women are expected to be more emotional than men and find a real source of power in acting out and encouraging emotion it will be difficult to find out, for social expectations program behavior very efficiently.

It is agreed, then, that men, in return for being the actors in the external world, allow women to preside over the springs of feelings in the interior world of woman's place. We have considered the effect on women of the need to act through others and to feel vicariously as a part of the experience of others. Let us now consider the actual transaction in which men turn to women for gratification of emotional need. Do they see it in the same terms? I very much doubt it. We can take as an example the exchange we noted in Chapter 3 at that meeting in a black ghetto where a social worker addressed a group of well-intentioned young whites on causes and cures of drug addiction. "The only way a man can be a man," he said, "is if a woman is a woman"; and a girl listener asked, "How do the girls help the boys? Do they talk to them, draw them out, give them sex?" "They have to listen," was the answer. "A woman shouldn't compete with a man, she should make him aware of what his capabilities are." [2]

Both question and reply clearly accept the premise, which the girl states in so many words, that sex is a gift from women to men, a supreme gift which helps to form one's ability to deal with the world by shaping emotions. She wants to be active about it. He tells her that her anxiety to give can be felt as aggression by men in a precarious situation, unsure of their place and power in society. Don't try to "draw them out," he says, just listen. Let them make the running. And when it comes to sex, sit still and wait to be asked. Don't compete. By listening—that is, by patient concern and attention—make him "aware of what his capabilities are." For if sex is a gift, then, like other gifts, it is most valued when it is asked for, least valued when it is pressed on the recipient by an overeager giver.

What we see here is the pattern of negotiation common to all confrontations between two people who want to strike a bargain as buyer and seller. The seller may present himself, but the buyer must act first, for it is his desire that triggers the bargaining. The negotiation, that is, begins at a slightly different time for each member. For the man, the request he makes is the first step in the bargaining. For the women, the bargaining doesn't begin until the question has been asked, though she must be ready to respond. The man is the inaugurator of the situation, which is of course a position of power; but he begins by asking for something and so must consider the possibility that he won't get it. The woman's position of power in the orthodox ritual is secondary to the man's, and later. No overt situation exists (for her) until he asks his question. But then the logic and phrasing of the process imply that she doesn't have to worry about whether she is going to get something or not. Her only decision is whether or not to give. Of course the question of her own pleasure exists, but it is internal and private as far as the traditional pattern goes. In that pattern, she is asked and thinks about giving, the man asks and worries about getting. Standard operating procedure (as our social worker reminded the girl in the audience) precludes her from giving without being asked.

For the man, if the gift is hers to make, it is also hers to deny, and he therefore faces anxiety about a possible refusal. The greater his need, the greater his anxiety, for at the very heart of desire lies the possibility of its denial. The woman can refuse him absolutely or, perhaps worse, can mingle her acceptance with refusal by lack of response. She may give only grudgingly and stint him in half a hundred ways that leave him with an angry residue of humiliation or that, at the very least, exact gratitude: an emotion that can only be pure if it is spontaneous. When he most needs completion and fulfillment, she has the power to deny it to him; and this is a terrible power because it is wielded when he is most vulnerable and can only be wielded because he *is* vulnerable. There is a fairy-tale quality to the situation, for the only weapon that can wound him is the one he himself turns over to the woman when he comes to her with his burden of emotion and desire. He needs her and she can say No; or, not quite saying No, say Yes, but . . . or Yes, if . . . and so make counter demands or (it may seem) blackmail him.

Here is a negative role we have not yet touched on: the bitch. If the witch is the dark shadow side of the mother role and the shrew the negative of the public, pleasing woman whose business it is to charm men, the bitch shadows the private, loving woman. When she should give, she is greedy. When she should be serious and listen (thus assuring the man of the weight and dignity of his problems), she is frivolous and chatters. She knows secrets and tells them—or teasingly hints that she will. She can wound with a word, will betray any trust if the fancy strikes her, turn children against their father, take a pretty fool for a lover and lie herself blue in the face for the pleasure of lying. Then, in a moment, she can become a tearful, self-righteous martyr.

We know her in the world, we know her in literature. Tolstoi, in *War and Peace*, gave her to Pierre as a wife; Hemingway gave her to Francis Macomber; Byron was sure he had met and married her himself. Flaubert knew her so well that he transcended the stereotype. "Madame Bovary, it is I," he said, and made her a human being caught in a trap of ignorance and circumstance, not simply a shadow. Emma Bovary is a tragic bitch, the larger and more terrifying because we pity her. Because we understand her troubles, her small, impossible fantasies, her boredom with her life and her awkward husband, we cannot simply sum her up as bad in herself and by nature. Emma is the bitch in her background, her provenance clear, a product of life as we know it. We can't withdraw from her. She is not only Flaubert's "I," she is connected with all of us who are part of the world that made her and that recurrently makes her again.

For if the witch peeps sometimes from behind the face of the loving mother, if every child has caught a glimpse of her because no child can ever be given all he wants, the bitch is a part of many, many marriages. The witch comes first and sets a pattern, but the bitch lives longer. Children, after all, grow up. The witch-mother fades, the good mother too is outgrown, and the tension of the relationship relaxes. But marriage is a continuing relationship, even though the duration may not be for life. In fact the frequency of divorce today increases the number of pairings. It makes new pairings possible, and in those, too, a man who has fled from a bitch may find another waiting, and a new chance for disillusion. It is very likely that a greater proportion of adults are married today than at almost any other time in history. Certainly they are linked more exclusively in pairs and pairs only—two-person families are now 35 percent of total families. Old maids and bachelors are less often met with. Some of those who are encountered will be part of fairly settled homosexual pairings, and such pairings, I suspect, approximate more closely to patterns of marriage than they did when other two-person relationships were more common: fraternal pairings, or those of master and servant, knight and esquire, teacher and disciple. Many of the divorced and separated are so temporarily, between partners, while even individuals who form no continuing ties may find themselves in occasional pairings, for they will not be as celibate as they were when morality or lack of money kept them pure, and when the clan or the extended family or the big house or a religious order provided them with an adult group to which they could belong and where they could feel at home, when loneliness was more often alleviated by religion or kinship or community ties than it is today. The advent of the nuclear family is part of a social process that tends to produce pairing, in the dominant patterns of marriage pairing. We usually think of it as signifying a household of two generations only, but it is also, typically, a household containing *two adults* only.

Two adults can live together in an infinite number of ways, I repeat, but nonetheless there is one factor present in every two-person relationship, and that is the possibility of greater intimacy and interdependence than other patterns of family formation offer. For some people such closeness can be the apotheosis of delight. Two can grow so near and so much a part of each other that giving, withholding, questions and negotiation are submerged by the miraculous intervention of what it is simplest to call love. Love breaks all laws and overthrows all rules. But it cannot be programmed into any relationship at all: *"Il n'a jamais, jamais connu la loi."* For many, therefore, the mere thought of utter transcendent intimacy can be very frightening indeed. To deliver oneself into the hands of just one other person means that one reveals oneself a great deal more fully than by giving a bit of oneself here and

another bit there: one gives oneself away, one becomes helplessly
dependent. The other person, the other member of the couple,
knows so much about the first! Can one really dare to make over
this power to someone else, someone with whom one is alone in a
duality that includes no makeweight, no one else to turn to?

In the big families of yesterday, marriage pairing was not so
claustrophobic. There were allegiances and alliances that could
offset the all-one's-eggs-in-one-basket aspect of the duality. Sisters-
in-law might band together, a man find support in a bond "against
the women" with his father-in-law or a young uncle, even develop
an understanding with a mother-in-law who might agree that her
daughter was behaving in exaggerated fashion. From my own
childhood, I remember how my father and the young woman who
married my mother's brother would raise their eyebrows together,
signaling a mutual amusement at the antics of the rest of the
family, "the Perfect Filleys." It was a very gentle comment, but
it allowed each of them a moment of objective judgment on the
Perfect Filley each had married and to whom each remained
devoted. In truly difficult circumstances, this kind of support can
operate as a needed channel to external reality from a pairing
that seems too demanding.

If it is the man who is frightened of such threatening intimacy
(and it isn't always, even with marriage still the approved goal for
women), it is the dark side of the mythic female figure who stands
at the center of his fear. Bitch and witch, she is the woman who
does not respond. Sometimes she refuses entirely. Sometimes, on
the other hand, she makes demands herself, unexpected and un-
explained. Sometimes she does both. She recalls and reconfirms the
mother who says no, the mother who does not listen, who pulls a
child here or there and ignores his wants while imposing her own.
She is the wife whose cries or whose rejoicing take men by surprise, who is "moody" or "hysterical," not a "manager of emotions,"
but one who gives in and is overwhelmed by them. In short, she
is a woman who seems to be unaware of the obligation she owes
to the role she has agreed to play in a one-to-one relationship. In
that inner space which is (so the myth declares) sacred to women,
the priestess still chants on the tripod, the sudden winds blow
from the abyss, and the poor petitioner never knows what answer
he will get.

Some petitioners opt out of the deal altogether and turn to pairings with their own sex on the assumption that here emotions will be more familiar, less frightening, more controllable and easier to share. Some shy away from any sort of intimacy that may involve them in these disturbing experiences. Some follow the pattern of Don Juan, whose talent it was to walk into the antechamber of a relationship and there perform the acts usually carried out in the bedroom, so that he could depart again before the outer door had swung entirely shut. There, in the semi-public situation of courtship, woman's role directs her to be pleasing rather than loving: love belongs to a later stage. Obviously, it will please Don Juan if she goes to bed with him, and when two partners meet who ask no more than to please themselves by such an encounter, all goes well. The trouble comes when one of them must do more: when, for example, Don Juan is asked to unmask and present himself as a man with a face, and not as a phallic stud; for that means intimacy, and intimacy may mean permanence, may mean responsibility and response to a woman as a whole human being, which is not only a time-consuming affair but one that calls on a man to be a whole human being himself. The player of Don Juan's role finds that difficult and sees such an encounter as meaning that he has been caught instead of being the active agent, the catcher. The old double-standard pattern of sex allows the Don to couple in man's world with impunity, for if a woman strays out there it's her own fault. She should have stayed in her own place, with her male kin to protect her. She broke the rules when she let him lure her out, and she must pay for it. Don Juan has no standing in the sacred enclosure, woman's place, because—like the bitch—he cannot support the mutuality in which two human beings meet each other wholly and must therefore expect not only to have their needs met, but to meet the needs of the other.

These are the negative roles of loving, as seen by men looking at women and women looking at men. Negative roles are not only reversals. They can also be thought of as extremes, the limits of the usual, warnings of what not to do. In the traditional scene, a man steps out of his world into woman's place and makes a ritual gesture by asking her for something. In the ordinary course of events, he is supposed to be the powerful one, in control. Now, he indi-

cates by asking, he is abdicating his control. Here we come around
again to the different meaning of his gesture to himself and to the
woman he approaches. He sees this abdication of power as a concession in itself, a favor already granted. To him, it is not a small
favor, for not only does he cede control to her, he takes on a new
role, that of the petitioner.

In our society today, the agreement to play a new role carries a
greater significance than it used to. In a mannered and structured
system, where classes and groups and hierarchies were clearly
defined, men expected to have to change their behavior according
to the company in which they found themselves. The knight paid
homage to the baron, the baron knelt to the king. The king, in
turn, was expected to bow (at least privately) to the will of the
Church. And the Pope, to indicate his obedience to the law of
God, would ceremonially wash the feet of the poor. Over the
centuries etiquette had grown up to define and legitimize these
changes in role behavior, and consequently they were less disturbing than today because they were more frequent and better
understood, part of an overall structure of conduct and belief.

Now, however, we live much less in a world ruled by etiquette
where we think of ourselves as making formal appearances and
behaving differently but naturally in different prescribed situations. In our world, individual values are held to prevail and to
determine the proper way of behaving. One should try to be the
same person everywhere. So when men, going into woman's
place, are expected to behave in an unusual way and to accommodate themselves to women's rules, they feel such a change the more
because this doesn't happen to them very often. An element of
unfamiliarity appears, both internally and externally, and this is
disturbing. They are not only giving up some control over the
exterior world, but are acting differently within themselves. A
man who jeopardizes his identity in this way, by choice, seems to
himself to be making quite a concession.

So asking a woman for something comes to feel, to him, not
just a first step in a bargaining process, but a favor *already* granted.
He has not simply advanced the proposition that they go to bed
together, he has paid part of the price for getting the answer
"Yes"; and he expects that this down payment will carry some
weight. Ask enough times, he feels, and the answer "Yes" is really

due him. A woman can say no a few times, but not for very long. If she won't say yes, she should remove herself from the situation. And once she has said yes, she is not expected to say no again. She mustn't say it, at any rate, without some plausible, acceptable (to the man) reason for her refusal. "I don't feel like it right now," is not an acceptable answer.

So much for the traditional male attitude. The point of view of the woman has its own, different, emotional logic which also goes back to the putting of the question. Why is she asked in the first place if she can't say no? The fact that a question is put to her ought to mean that she has a choice and can say no without being reproached for it. If it doesn't mean that, the question is partly a fraud; and women, like all groups that are not fully autonomous, are only too familiar with the apparent request for permission which is really the cloak of a demand. Why, moreover, isn't "I don't feel like it" an acceptable reason for saying no? After all, if the man doesn't feel like it, he doesn't ask, so the situation doesn't arise. If his feelings are valid, why aren't hers? (Don't women ask men? Of course they do. In an intimate relationship of love and trust it hardly matters who asks whom; often there's no "asking" at all. But we are talking here about the patterns of behavior by which pairings are established. There, women who ask men are often very frightening for they can appear as an epiphany of the unpredictable woman who wants too much and can never be satisfied, who embodies the myth of female power. A recent novel by Kingsley Amis, *I Want It Now*, began with a girl demanding immediate sexual relations with a stranger. She turned out to be entirely frigid, her demand an aggressive reaction to her dominance by her mother. The plot of the book related her lover's reeducation of her to a more "normal" relationship.[3] The moral, thus, turns out to be, Don't believe a girl who wants it now —she's in trouble.)

Why, however, should women want to say no? The man's side of the negotiation finds this difficult to understand, and part of the mythic content of the situation is a male suspicion that women say no capriciously and don't mean it. Plenty of men have found, after a certain amount of persuasion, that women who first say no often turn out to enjoy themselves once they are bedded. They say no, men suspect, just in order to exercise their power, to amuse themselves by making a man work to get what he wants, and wait for an answer. They *like* using this power of theirs to create hang-ups and problems.

Men are absolutely right in their suspicions. Women do indeed enjoy playing games and putting them through the hoops. The only odd thing is that, having got this far, more men don't ask themselves *why* women do this. (Though not so odd as all that, perhaps, since by the time the question is apt to occur to him, the man is either in bed or in a rage, and not inclined to think analytically in either case.) *Of course* women enjoy exercising power when they can, both over their husbands or lovers and over their children too. In woman's place, as part of her traditional role, it is only in intimate situations that she can use power and feel its rewards. The more she is precluded from acting for herself in man's world and limited to managing emotions in woman's place, the likelier it becomes that her need for autonomy, her search for identity (she hears about such things too) and the unused energies she possesses will come to expression in private because they can't be put to work in public. The negative role of bitch is almost built into woman's role and it surfaces at the heart of the duality of marriage if this is the only place where she has a chance to exercise power.

It is sometimes easier to follow such situations in a society that is foreign. Let us look again at the Marri Baluch, whose culture is basically different from ours but carries some traits reminiscent of Western attitudes in the not-too-distant past; attitudes, indeed, whose effects have not yet been forgotten. The Marri elder and the woman of his tribe, whom I quoted at the head of Chapter 7, speak from the two sides of a very large sexual gap. Among these Moslem nomads of Baluchistan, a mountainous near-desert region of West Pakistan, custom allows women very few rights indeed. They are property, first of the father or of his clan if he is dead, then of the husband. Women are kept in strict purdah, so far as a nomad people can enforce this traditional segregation and separa-tion of the sexes. They have no public standing whatsoever and can be represented in any social relationship only by a male relative. Marriages are made by purchase, usually when the bridegroom's father buys a girl for his son. She then moves to the family camp of her husband's clan, and anything she owns becomes his except for such small belongings as she can lock away in a box and carry about with her. Anthropologist Robert Pehrson, who, with his wife, lived with the Marri for some time in the mid-fifties, describes woman's work thus: "In the tent camps, the woman expects to grind flour, cook and bake; fetch wood, water and dwarf palm (from which is woven mats, ropes, tents, sandals and so on); plait, sew and embroider; strike, pack and pitch the tents; milk; and to the extent the husband directs, do a share of the herding and the harvesting." [4] The men are away a good deal, traveling and trading, but the plowing and sowing of crops is their business, and so is much of the reaping, threshing and herding—the last of which also takes them away from camp.

Isolated from her own family, subordinate to an often absent husband and to his male relatives, what does a woman do to defend her interests? She uses three classic techniques: first, she plays men off against each other—that is, she distracts their attention from herself by "making trouble." Then she forms alliances with other women, mutual non-aggression pacts to keep each other's secrets. Third, and most pertinent to our present discussion, she minimizes her contacts with her husband by withdrawing from intimacy. As a result (Pehrson writes), "Marri men see themselves as opposed by women, as fighting a continuous battle against female recalcitrance and laziness." The women know it and enjoy it. "You know," said one, "it's all women's business, the giving or the stinginess, the helpfulness or the lack of helpfulness." [5]

Against this background, so eerily reminiscent of nineteenth-century petit bourgeois attitudes, it is hardly surprising to find that Marri sexual attitudes are also recognizable. The sexual act itself is thought of ambiguously. It is at once polluting and highly valued. The woman is the polluting agent, but mutual desire between the sexes is taken for granted. There is much love poetry, and the Marri's favorite Moslem saint is famous for his passionate love for a beautiful mistress. And here we come to the point of these passions: *they never occur between husband and wife*. There, the traditional emotion can reach such a peak of hatred that the Pehrsons recorded being "approached by women who wanted poison to kill their husbands, and the most extreme case, which awed even the Marri themselves, was the woman who put a curse on her own children in hatred of her husband." Romantic love, passionate love, is always adulterous love; is expected to be adulterous. In fact, if a woman finds herself by some chance in love with her own husband and he with her, this deviant relationship is felt as shameful and will be hidden.

It is private, secret love, outside and opposed to all legal bonds, which gives beauty and value to life among the Marri Baluch. Reading the Pehrsons' reports, one feels oneself adrift in the further reaches of romantic opera or the dreams of twelfth-century troubadours. Love tokens pass from hand to hand carrying the whiff of danger: a cap embroidered by a woman whose husband must not see what she is doing; a pebble wrapped in a scrap of silk bringing the message, "My heart has become dry as a stone since I have not seen you." Poetry recalls the fleeting bliss of passion. "Now my lover has come," sings a woman. "He sits far off with other men. My husband forbids me to see him—a curse on my husband, all of his days." Her lover begs, "Come once more to the hidden valley, gathering wood for your evening bread. Come to me waiting in that valley ere your camp moves to far grazing lands." The thought of parting is always present: "Find a new lover when I migrate," a woman says, hoping for and receiving the answer, "I shall grieve, my heart will break for you and for you alone. All other women are as dirt; by my beard, I will love only you." [6]

All this is perilous, for a man has the right to kill an adulterous wife and the deed still takes place—unless, learning of his intention, she shames him by killing herself first. In spite of danger, the love relationship is almost universal. Preferably it occurs between partners who belong to different camps. But most important, it is completely voluntary. "The man should plead with the woman," say the Marri. "She must be won by charm, because he is a good lover, not by force." [7] He must come out of man's world, that is, into woman's place and ask for her kindness.

Among the Marri, then, love and marriage have become polar opposites. This can only have happened because their form of marriage is incapable of supplying the emotional satisfaction that men and women need from each other. The husband's power has grown so great that it is self-defeating. How can one love a crea-

ture whom one owns? She has lost the power to say no, and so
her yes has no value and can bestow no virtue. It is exacted from
her instead of being chosen by her. She has nothing to give
because everything has been taken from her. The myth of female
weakness has come true, and the result is desolation. So the
trapped husband turns away from the wife whom their culture has
made destitute to another woman. Of course she is someone else's
wife, for Moslem feeling is strong enough to ensure that unmarried
girls do not take lovers; but in the outlawed love relationship, the
woman regains the power she has lost in marriage, the power to
act voluntarily. "It is the only relationship in Marri culture in
which men and women are jurally equal," notes Pehrson.

One more point which turns us back toward the source of myth.
Lovers share food and drink in mutual trust, while husbands are
forbidden, by an absolute taboo, from touching food or water
from which their wives have eaten or drunk. Aside from lovers,
the only other situation in which Marri of both sexes eat together
is that of mothers with their children (and, by extension, brothers
and sisters together). Here is an extreme case of the familiar
Moslem idea of closeness and fidelity expressed by sharing bread
and salt, and we see clearly how it goes back to the mother-child
relationship. Trust begins there, and when adults need to celebrate
mutual trust and love, they share a meal. So men who have taken
too much from their wives dare not eat the food they have
tasted; while the same men sanctify the love relationship by
sharing a meal with another woman, as they once did with their
mothers.

Carried to extremes, the myth of female weakness has called
forth a new manifestation of the myth of female power. An unbalanced relationship has created its own strange external balanc-
ing weight as men have found that power can be bought at the
expense of pleasure and intimate, trusted support. A woman,
silenced and compelled at home, turns into a bitch and a hater,
willing to curse her own children. Meanwhile, outside the dry,
fenced garden, love grows like a weed where it has freedom, and
where men and women meet as equals.

CHAPTER 16

The singular is not Love's enemy;
Love's possibilities or realisation
Require an Otherness that can say I.
W. H. Auden
For the Time Being [1]

THE LOOKING-GLASS world of the Marri Baluch furnishes an exaggerated example of what happens when too much power collects around one role in a relationship. There, male dominance has grown so great that it has destroyed the balance of marriage. So much is demanded of women and so little given them that they possess no store of happiness, no bounty from which to offer comfort and joy to their husbands. Because they have lost control over their lives, their responses within marriage have been reduced to minimal gestures, mere semblances of affection and support.

What has happened is that the role of wife among the Marri has been squeezed dry of any spontaneity, any possibility of real emotional expression. As we saw earlier, roles impose a mutuality, or reciprocity, of action within the relationship they serve. The example of Marri marriage tells us that the action a role prescribes should not ask too much from the player, or the role will tend to turn into its negative shadow. Within marriage, Marri women are not granted even the illusion of controlling their actions. There is no area open for creative choice or imaginative impulse, no pleasure and no "play" in either sense of the word. The only possibility for autonomous action in these circumstances is to do what is expected, but to *feel* in opposition to the behavior exacted; to offer hostility instead of affection, and nurse hidden impulses to attachment for another until they can be freely given outside marriage—since this is the only place where they can be given freely.

This is not a complete picture of Marri marriage, of course. Very obviously there are external social and economic reasons for the institution to continue, or it wouldn't do so. The kinship structure that regulates daily life, the lines of political power, the passage of property in an orderly fashion, all these elements are interwoven with Marri marriage and help to keep it alive. Moreover, since Marri men, like all Moslems, are allowed four wives, they can, in theory, avoid the intensity of a hostile one-to-one relationship, though in fact few men are rich enough to take more than one wife. Still, the polygamous rich are naturally the most powerful element in society, and if they are most satisfied with the status quo, they are also most capable of maintaining it. Marri marriage, consequently, continues; and Marri adultery continues with it as a method of alleviating the emotional distress that this kind of marriage engenders. Adultery supports marriage.

Something of this sort must certainly have occurred at other times and in other places when male dominance within marriage grew too great and too restrictive. I suspect that the twelfth-century Courts of Love and the romantic servitude of knight to lady celebrated by the troubadours grew out of the need of men and women to meet in a relationship which offered another, different balance to male-dominated marriage. Of course the cultural flowering of the high Middle Ages didn't appear solely on psychological grounds; it was a product of the relative political stability which followed the end of the Viking raids, and of the economic benefits produced by a developing technology. Yet as part of that flowering, women were assigned an unheard-of power in emotional life, a power which ran counter to the old structure of marriage ties. All of which suggests that men were finding the emotional rewards offered by man's world unsatisfying. They needed, in Auden's words, some "Otherness that can say I," some element of society which they did not control and which would respond only if, and as, it chose to. Again, a counterpoise to the main pattern of society had been found, and though it was an apparent contradiction, it worked to support the social structure.

The brutally sentimental nineteenth century made a different social adjustment, but the division of women into "good" and "bad" and the setting off of "lust" from "pure love" also provided an apparent contradiction which was in reality a counterweight.

Here, the extramarital sex that supported marriage was provided by prostitution much more than by adultery. Love was divided into "sacred" and "profane," a situation which is usually thought of from the male point of view as offering a chance for eating one's cake and having it too. We might note, however, that whatever this pattern exacted from "good" women, it did provide a thoroughly acceptable reason for them to say no to demanding males. Marriageable girls had something to bargain with, their virginity, which it was within their own power to promise or withhold, and this did provide a social balance for women who had lost most of their economic base for bargaining. We are all familiar with the difficulties this situation provided for men and women alike, if only because the psychological dislocations to which it gave rise formed the material for Freud's work and shaped his theories. In social rather than psychological terms, however, it was another solution to the problem of providing a counterweight to an unbalanced marriage relationship. It didn't, incidentally, help girls of the poorer classes from whom the "bad" women were drawn— another example of the middle-class bias of the myths that assign women a special place.

Unbalance of this sort can crop up in many relationships other than that of marriage. All healthy and productive human situations must offer their participants the feeling that they have some choice of emotion and action, some control over circumstances or some gain from these circumstances in other areas of life. Unless people feel that they get enough out of a connection to make it worth their while, in marriage or at work or any other place, they will either break it off or, if they can't, they will begin to withdraw from it psychologically. This is true not only personally but socially: the limits to participation in relationships that are insufficiently rewarding are either alienation or rebellion.

Our recent social experience offers an example. During the fifties, young people seemed to their elders rather silent and withdrawn, uninterested in participating in social and political action. In the sixties, this withdrawal became overtly hostile to the establishment, positively negative. The young did not simply refuse to participate, they began to affirm their opposition by their behavior. Feeling that they had too little control over their lives, too little foreseeable future, they began to act quite the way Marri women do. Their attitude toward their parents and the society which they felt to belong only to their parents became that of sullen anger. Not only were they being denied control over their lives (they felt), they were being refused any chance to work out another way of life, for society did not want to believe that a different pattern might be valid and valuable. Their clothes, their behavior, their speech, their music—all these cultural manifestations became outspokenly provocative and defiant. Successfully so, in a purely emotional sense, for, as we have seen, this kind of mythic defiance frightens those who feel that it is an attempt to overthrow their own system of beliefs, their own understanding of the order of the universe.

Then, in America, the draft for the Vietnam war began. Instead of responding to their demands and needs (the young men felt), the generation of their parents was taking revenge on them for making these demands. Far from trying to make the situation better, to listen and understand and allow them some larger degree of autonomy, the people in power were making things worse. No longer did they simply refuse to imagine a different sort of future, a different sort of social balance; they had begun to act out the role of the mythical ogre. The fathers were sending young men to death. The young exploded in rage, and the rage and the explosion were felt far beyond America.

All this much to the surprise of the establishment. For the elders had been persuaded that they were simply going about their business, administering power with little thanks for their efforts. In fact, they believed they had been doing quite a good job, not merely running things efficiently, but actually spreading social justice and increasing prosperity. Remembering the blight of depression which had struck their generation when they were young, it seemed to the men in power that they had in fact created a better, different future and rendered it effective in the affluent present.

It wasn't a present that pleased the young or an affluence that extended to those who were the victims of social, not economic, deprivation. And so a government and a society which had taken its own good intentions for granted began to reap a reward of hate and hostility without quite understanding how this had happened. Indulgent fathers in their own eyes, they were indignant to find themselves being treated as tyrants. The reaction of the young—and, again, it is akin to the instinctive behavior of Marri women in their situation—was to force the powerful to act like tyrants. The universities became the locus of this demonstration because it is there that the final stage of education for living takes place. Consequently they are the most sensitive place to register contempt for the sort of life this education has been created to support, and to demand another sort which will give rise to other values and patterns of relationship.

The dynamics of the situation have now begun to push the opponents of the establishment past demonstration and protest to political action. How successful this may be no one can say, but it is at any rate an attempt to grapple with actual problems in the actual world of events: alienation has become rebellion. This is a great gain, for it is an effort to get hold of some sort of control, not simply to react against not having it with sulky, stubborn anger. But whatever happens here and now, it is clear enough that the strains of any social system produce psychological, and moral, reactions and that these take a toll. They may, nonetheless, be long-lived. Open tyrannies have flourished throughout history. Bad social arrangements can drag along for centuries even though the balance of power within them approaches that of slavery; slavery did. But these arrangements can't exist without affecting their victims, those who enforce them and the whole of society which allows this enforcement.

Hatred between husbands and wives, the fury and despair of slaves, the rage of young men and women against a world that seems both false and unresponsive—these emotions cripple those who feel them and lose human resources of energy and imagination for society. The dominant class, reacting in turn, uses its energy to hold the rebels down instead of thinking ahead for the good of the whole membership of society, which is the only valid reason for an elite to exist. Sometimes it clings to inflexible and irrelevant rules. Sometimes it dithers about, trying to adjust to change and not succeeding because it misses the point of what is felt to be lacking, concedes without appeasing and wins a bonus of contempt from those who hated it to begin with. Sometimes it does both. Hostility blows like dust on the wind. Distrust becomes good policy for everyone because no overall premises for action can be agreed on; and any action therefore grows more and more difficult to take. It becomes a cliché to say that we can go to the moon but can't reclaim Bedford-Stuyvesant—but that doesn't make it any less true. By regarding our impotence as a truism, we emphasize our acceptance of impotence.

Control of some kind over the surround of life is the deepest psychological need of every human being; and since appeals to ethology have become so popular, it may be worth pointing out that that's true of animals too. A dog will sit where he's told as part of the social contract he's made with his master, but it *is* part of a contract of trust, that is, of a real relationship; while any cat will demonstrate his independence of judgment by arising and inspecting the site on which he's placed and thinking it over before he sits down again. Only in the depths of psychotic disturbance and despair do creatures accept being treated as things; and even here I think, with Ronald Laing, that they sometimes do it like Marri women, as a form of revenge and satiric comment on the stupidity of the powerful. When the strong treat the weak as objects to be manipulated, when the elite absentmindedly speaks thus of the masses, the weak and the masses take their revenge even if the strong don't know it, even if the revenge amounts to no more than "goofing off" and playing dumb, even if it reaches the exquisite art of doing exactly what the master says and never anything more, turning *oneself* into a thing. At this last extreme the slave can deny the master the pleasure of commanding or owning another human being by ceasing, in that relationship, to *be* a human being. Then any connection between them expires and leaves the master alone in an empty world. He can find human companionship only when he accepts the human needs of his companions, beginning with their need to control some sufficient part of their lives.

I have dwelt on this obvious point here because, though the need to recognize the human reality of another member exists in every relationship, it is greatest where one and one makes a duality. One does not achieve full humanity by oneself or retain it alone. It is an outgrowth of reciprocity, bestowed only by that "Otherness that can say I." The value of such a bestowal depends on one's own acceptance of the reality and independence of the other. We have seen some of the difficulties that arise within the mother-child duality if each fails to see the other as more than an extension of personal needs. Then mothers manipulate children for their own ends, and children imagine an impossible world which exists only to gratify their whims. Only when and as each gains some objectivity about the other's real talents and desires, strengths and weaknesses, can either deal with the real situation in which they live. The worst maternal deprivation may be that which fails to grant a child proper respect for his individual identity.

This need to realize the other obtains as well in the adult duality of marriage if the marriage is to be more than a social device for producing children and passing on property. I have emphasized the possible variations of feeling and behavior within marriage, and one could in fact write an encyclopedia on its versions, potentialities and pathology and still stumble on a new kind the next day. Nonetheless, marriages which are satisfying (and in our society marriages which aren't are more easily dissolved than in many other social systems) do all offer husband and wife some kind of positive reward: social status, emotional support, economic benefit, sexual pleasure, a haven against the pressures and demands of the world—one could go on, but it is here that the great differences in marriage enter. For our purposes, it is enough to say that some kind of a reward must exist, and so must an opportunity to give as well as to receive. In order to give, both partners must feel themselves rich and secure enough to want to give to the other; that is, in sufficient control of life to think beyond themselves. This is true both in sexual relations and in the rest of marriage. Let us begin with the latter because we will understand our present attitudes toward sex best when we place them against the social background.

Marriage begins with choosing. In our time the choice appears to be made almost entirely by the marrying couple and its range is very wide indeed. At the outset, then, bride and groom control their lives by choosing each other. Now, the right to choose is not the only factor which permits an individual to exercise control over his situation, but it is a very important one and also a *conscious* one. When we make a decision, we know it, and this knowledge in itself makes conscious decisions seem to be special

turning points, even though many other factors may be present
too. Among these factors, which also contribute to the control of
personal situations, may be named continuing commitment to a
choice already made, willingness to see things through to the end
of a period or a process, repeated small actions that work together
to maintain an equipoise or achieve a desired end. The companionship of marriage, indeed any companionship, grows up on the
basis of mutual undertakings of this kind. They ensure trust and
permanence.

In the past they probably figured more largely in the general
conception of marriage than they do today because the element of
choice was smaller. The first choice, that of selecting a husband
or wife, was a good deal more restricted. The extended family and
even the community itself felt involved in every mating. Marriages
were arranged directly or were controlled by being limited to a
group of possible partners. The religious establishment had a
word to say. A very large part of the choice that did exist was
exercised not by the couple, but by the head of the clan, or the
mother's brother, or neighbor-parents who felt that marriage between their children would tie landholdings together in a sensible
way. It is also very likely that later choices about life were fewer.
Children came or did not come. Most people were committed to
a craft or a way of life which they could not change. No doubt
life as a whole was no more stable—disasters, famines, war and
disease were rife—but the chance that one could *choose* to act
against such catastrophes with any prospect of acting effectively
was very small. Often one simply chose which saint to pray to,
which god to consult; but in so doing one did not act oneself, one
invoked a higher power.

Obviously marriage is different now in Western society. We feel
ourselves to be individuals, responsible only to ourselves. No one
is really involved in a marriage except the couple who make it.
They are thought of as choosing each other on the basis of mutual
affection and shared emotions, motives which have largely superseded social and economic reasons for forming alliances. And
because they are thought of as selecting each other, the mutual
choice is generally felt to mean that husband and wife embark on
marriage on equal terms; not, that is, that they expect the same
things from it, but that by taking each other as partners they are

equally committed to the marriage, and committed in the same way.

I would like to explore this idea, though the question of what "equality" can mean in the relations between husband and wife is more tricky than it seems. We tend to use the word unthinkingly, both because egalitarianism is a commonly accepted ideal and also, I think, because when we imagine a duality, we tend to see the proper relationship as a balance, and a balance of two implies equal weight. I have used the word *balance* several times myself, but let me here qualify it by pointing out that a balance within a relationship cannot be static; "being" is affected by "doing," and a relationship is a continuing process of action and behavior which adjusts itself to changes in action and behavior.

So "equality" seems to me unsatisfactory as a description of a desirable relationship because, for one thing, it is too static. Equal status, we may say, is the same status; but if we are talking about actions and processes, "equality" becomes too small a word and too confining a description. I think it should be enlarged by introducing the idea of *reciprocity*, a word I have also been using. One need not get back exactly what one gives if the return is emotionally valuable enough to feel rewarding. Husband and wife needn't do the same things if their actions are mutually supportive. Sometimes they may do things that are very much the same, sometimes things that are very different. As long as each comprehends and respects what the other does well enough to share the experience of the doing, different occupations and responsibilities will extend the range of a marriage and enrich its content. In this context, equality is a mythic demand. Equality of action is impossible and would be impoverishing if it were possible. Equality of emotion is impossible *to judge* because feeling can't be measured. A mutual reciprocity of giving and receiving which is satisfying to both partners seems to me the sustaining value of any relationship, and particularly of the duality of marriage.

In practical terms, we may well ask whether husbands and wives do make an equal commitment in marrying and, if not, how their commitments differ if each chooses the other. The answer comes down to another question: Does each stake as much on the choice? And here, I think, we find that there is a difference, perhaps a lessening difference, but a difference still. Men face at least two major choices in life. For them, choosing a wife may well be less important than choosing a career. In addition, many men continue to be faced with the need to make a fair number of conscious decisions, more or less vital to other people, in the course of their ordinary occupations. This is not true of the large majority of women. Taking a husband is still by far the most important decision they will ever make in their lives—not necessarily the most important *action*, but the most important *choice;* and in their traditional daily occupations, conscious decisions affecting other people do not loom very large. Their control over life continues to be more the old-fashioned kind, where small continuing, or repetitive, actions direct the course of events.

A generation ago Talcott Parsons, in a study, "Age and Sex in the Social Structure," considered this difference in the way men and women experience marriage. "In the case of the feminine role," he wrote, "marriage is the single event toward which a selective process [that is, a process of choice] in which [a woman's own] personal qualities and efforts can play a decisive role, has pointed. . . . It determines a woman's fundamental status"—which is, then, bestowed by the husband. Once her marriage choice is made, the patterns into which a woman's role may lead her don't have much effect on the status that society assigns her, but are more "a matter of living up to expectations, finding satisfying interests and activities." [2] Such activities are personal. They don't connect with the outside world importantly enough to change the way the woman is thought of there. No doubt this is somewhat less true than it was in 1942 when Parsons wrote it, but it is still true enough. Most women, when they marry, commit themselves to being thought of publicly as an adjunct of their husbands, and most women will not do anything later on their own to change the situation very much. So they commit more of the future to marriage than do men.

Let us not dismiss this obvious point as merely obvious, for the different weight of commitment made by partners at the outset of a marriage has some less obvious effects as the relationship wears on. The fact that women tend to regard the most important decision of their lives as already made, once they have married, makes them readier than their husbands to settle down and sit still in the situation at which they have arrived. It contributes, that is, to the passivity which is so commonly taken as characteristic of women, and also to the conservatism expected of them. For why should one be vitally interested in a future about which one can do little? Responsible thinking, creative imagination are everywhere tied to the possibility of action. In the orthodox view, women who have married and made their choice have little maneuverability left. Society, their husbands and they themselves imagine that they will provide the continuity of life, the backdrop for the actions of the man and the readying of children to grow and arrive at the stage of decision-making. The French phrase expresses the situation rather well: such a woman is a *femme faite*, a woman formed and "done."

But increasingly women are finding this "doneness" unsatisfactory. Our investigation of woman's role has shown us again and again that there is less to be done in woman's inner place than there used to be, and fewer direct connections between it and the outer world of men. In spite of the repeated emphasis on the vital importance of mothering and the threat of maternal deprivation to children, the *time* spent by women as mothers of young children is growing shorter both in proportion to a lengthened life-span and in actual duration. For one thing, most children live to grow up today. Two hundred years ago a family of four might be the survivors of eight or ten children born over twenty years. Now they will almost always be the only four children, born over a period of ten or twelve years. Once they are off to school there is less actual work to be done at home, and what is done there is more isolated from the rest of life outside.

Consequently women are feeling greater pressure to take action that will change their lives again. A settled pattern of living, from marriage on, is turning out to be unsatisfactory to many. Fewer women see themselves as settling down at twenty or twenty-five, and what one does after thirty or thirty-five is becoming more and more of a challenge. Women are getting to feel that the male tempo of continued action is one in which they want, and have a right, to share. In 1942 Parsons, writing about America as "a society where such strong emphasis is placed upon individual achievement," was well aware that many women were already plagued by the feeling that the timing of their lives was out of joint. The American woman's "absorption in the household is greatly lessened, often just at the time when the husband is approaching the apex of his career and is most heavily involved in its obligations," he wrote.[3] *He* is busiest away from home just when *she* is at loose ends within it, and the contrast increases her feeling that she is out of things.

Even today there is still no direct and easy way for her to get into them. Her earlier activities may have been pretty well prescribed by the traditional pattern of keeping house and bringing up small children, but there is no pattern, in our world at any rate, for being a wife, and certainly no pattern for being a middle-aged wife. Helping one's husband "get ahead" by some dazzling display of executive wifemanship is a talent not commanded by many women, nor are there really many situations that call for it, while it has some built-in perils of the sort we have examined in talking about vicarious living. Projecting one's ambitions onto the career of a husband can be as dangerous and touchy as projecting them onto one's children. As for broader activities outside the household, what Parsons calls the "humanistic aspect of the feminine role," they have been only dimly defined or, in his word, "institutionalized." "It is not surprising," he adds, "that [the] patterns [of the feminine role] often bear the marks of strain and insecurity." [4]

What Parsons is saying is that women who don't want to sink into peaceful hebetude in their middle years find themselves confronted less with a choice than with a dilemma. Today, again, this is less true than it was in 1942, but although possible alternatives are evolving, they have not yet got to the stage of presenting clear, connected courses to follow. Women who want to "do something" find that before they can decide on something to do, they have to create the possibility of doing anything. That often means rethinking and revaluing the whole pattern which one's life has followed and which one imagined it as following, and the pattern involves not only one's own personality, but the relationships built into the pattern—most important, of course, family relationships. So even now a woman who is not content with the position she finds herself in and the future it offers can't turn to a ready-made alternative, but has to devise one.

We need hardly recall the Marri Baluch again to note that one alternative to an unsatisfactory marriage is a search for a love relationship outside marriage. This would seem to land us in the middle of today, for the decade of the sixties is supposed to have seen a great increase in extramarital sex. Very likely it did see a substantial increase; though since the sixties also saw a remarkable growth in overt talk about sex, one can't be sure how much was action and how much was publicity. In any society as emotionally involved with sex as we are now, what is *done* will always differ, sometimes widely and wildly, from what is *said* to be done. As sociologists John H. Gagnon and William Simon remark in a recent book, *The Sexual Scene,* "One senses that there is more talk about wife-swapping than there is wife-swapping and that the rates of participation are extremely marginal. The structure of talk about sex has an extremely complicated relationship to behavior, and even when the structure of talk changes there is little evidence of behavior following in any direct manner."

This is certainly not to say that behavior won't change or that it won't be affected by talk; but it will change in a complicated way, influenced by social considerations and by the ability of individuals to imagine themselves as participating in change. As Gagnon and Simon go on to say, "The moment of change may simply be the point at which new forms of behavior appear plausible," [5] a statement which is true of social adjustments generally, as we noted in Chapter 11. Since we are still talking about the social aspect of marriage rather than its internal value, it is important to note here that, for all the publicity, the sixties did not see a significant shift in the way our system of marriage works at the public, external level. Promiscuous or not, marriages go on getting made. The reason is that our society long ago worked out a pattern for adjusting marriage to the existence of a fair amount of extramarital sex as a social constant. As yet, this pattern has been flexible enough to absorb whatever changes have actually occurred.

The pattern—it's no great discovery—is one that preserves the social stability of marriage as an institution by letting married people change partners. Though prostitution was certainly the greatest support of nineteenth-century marriage, a percentage of our ancestors, like the Marri, maintained their households by staying with husbands or wives but setting up relatively permanent adulterous relationships on the outside, so that marriage and adultery went on together in a symbiotic relationship. Even during the nineteenth century, however, the American pattern began to diverge from this earlier European arrangement and to become what it is today. Here it's usual for marriages that turn bad to be followed not simply by extramarital affairs, but by divorce and remarriage between lovers. For us, it is not adultery that supports marriage, or prostitution, but divorce; and this situation began to develop a good long time ago. In 1886, to take a representative "high Victorian" year, when there were just over seven hundred divorces in Great Britain (the European country most similar in culture to ours, where the divorce scandal involving Sir Charles Dilke was shaking society), there were more than twenty-five thousand in the United States.

Divorce rates have been rising lately (though even the 1969 rate did not quite reach that of 1946, when hasty war marriages were breaking up all over), but the rise has not been spectacular enough to change the long-term trend. Promiscuity may have spread in Suburbia, but not as a revolutionary change. Other classes, and places, in America have been familiar with affluence, leisure and permissiveness long enough to make their accommodations, and Suburbia has simply taken over these adjustments. If the bourgeoisie has been busy shocking itself lately, that is, after all, one of its continuing pleasures. Thus in America, and in western Europe where American patterns of living have been spreading, the most recent increase in extramarital sex has not made a significant difference in the external order of life. The *plausibility* of divorce has been taken for granted at least since the twenties.

The right to end a marriage for personal, emotional reasons, then, is very much a part of our approach to the relationship; and since we see marriage as specializing in emotional rewards, this is not surprising. The common impulse is not to sustain a marriage by finding satisfaction elsewhere, but to end the marriage and set up a new one which will provide the comfort lacking in the first. Now, if the pattern is followed in the regular sequence of marriage, adultery, divorce and remarriage, what happens at the role-playing level is not significant. One changes one's life by living out the same role with a different partner, not by shifting circumstances into a really different pattern which would involve changing one's activities and taking on a different role. Men sometimes change their lives more by changing work roles—jobs, companies, locations—than they or their wives would do by divorce and remarriage. Of course people who get divorced and stay divorced find themselves in new situations; but in fact most divorced people end by remarrying, and a good proportion remarries fairly fast. Married to a lawyer after divorcing an accountant, a woman finds that she is still acting out her triple role of wife, housewife and mother (the latter often under more difficult circumstances than before). In all probability she doesn't change her social status very much, particularly if she marries someone with whom she was having an affair when still married. The men she met then would normally have been of equivalent standing to her own, which was basically dependent on her husband—as of course it still is. She takes her status in the new pairing from her second husband just as she did from her first. A man's new wife may move up, especially if she is younger or if he met her through his work, but his old wife is more apt to stay about where she was.

At the external social level, then, the sequence of divorce and remarriage is not very important. Of course it is, or can be, at the personal level. Most important of all is the idea that it *may* be, that one's life can be transformed by such a change. This is certainly a standard component of daydream for any woman who is suffering from the kind of nostalgia, emptiness and confusion about who she is and what she wants to do that Parsons was writing about. Daydreams like this, the exercise of imagining another life, define and determine the kind of change one can see oneself living through. The more one dreams a changed life, the more plausible it becomes and the more ready one is, therefore, to embark on it. And yet I think one may very well wonder whether an adulterous wife, in our present society, will ever find her romantic dreams satisfied as rewardingly as are those of a Marri woman or a bourgeois wife a century ago. What she gets if she acts out her dream in real life is not, essentially, a new kind of relationship (as the others did or do), but simply the same relationship with a new man.

The alternative is to look for a new role instead of a new man. As we have seen, one exists, though it's not often thought about in the same romantic mood: getting a job. In fact there's a sort of farcical embarrassment, a resonant awkwardness, in considering the two things together. Stylistically they don't match, and the statement that a woman can get as much out of taking a job as out of taking a lover may well appear not just absurd, but callously, tastelessly dunderheaded. No man likes to be put on a par with a typewriter. Am I really suggesting that a woman who feels unfulfilled might as well be offered the second as the first? Or a course in library science? Or an M.A. in guidance? That a paycheck will be as satisfying as an orgasm? That instead of embarking for Cythera, she should take the subway to Wall Street and a job as a financial analyst?

There are various answers to these questions, beginning with the statement that I am not suggesting anything, but simply observing and reporting, and to a reporter it is evident that "getting a job" is becoming a plausible solution to the vague discontent of married women who aren't sure that they are getting all they expect out of life. I agree that there is an element of farce in talking about going to work as a substitute for falling in love, but this is partly due to the context, romantic and charged with emotion, with which we surrealistic Westerners surround the idea of sex at present and which we deny to most other areas of life. "Taking a lover" is phrased in romantic style, but how often does it really denote a grand passion? Even in the heyday of nineteenth-century romance, the passion of Anna Karenina and Vronsky was paralleled by the distinctly unromantic affairs in which Emma Bovary trapped herself. Love as a bolt from the blue is one thing. Love as a means of assuaging boredom and greed is another. To fail to discriminate between the two is a failure of the imagination.

At the level of life, of what people really think and feel and do, we know perfectly well that there are women who are happy, or happy enough, with their husbands, but who are dissatisfied with the surrounding context of their day-to-day existence, who feel that they are not sufficiently connected with the rest of the world, who want to use more of their talents. It's perfectly possible that, under certain circumstances, some of them will find that an affair with a sympathetic man will widen their world and show them experience through new eyes. On the other hand, the vague uneasiness that bothers them may be satisfied simply by getting out into the world, trying new kinds of work and making new connections with other people at this level. We have seen that paid work, autonomous activity and contact outside the home provide a sort of "psychic income" that can change a woman's valuation of herself. Outside the sweep of grand passion, the emotional effect of a love affair often works out as just that—a rise in one's self-esteem because someone else has listened, been pleased and admiring. As an addendum, it might be noted that getting a job and having an affair are not mutually exclusive activities. And a good few women who have decided on divorce find that they have to get a job as a result. Some testify that the job has changed their lives more than the affair, or the dream of an affair, that set off their decision to divorce.

The point I want to make exists outside any comparison between the relative experiential value of an affair versus a job: both are now plausible possibilities in the minds of women who are not finding their marriages sufficient to occupy their energies. And of the two, getting a job is the newer possibility and the one which probably offers the largest area of self-exploration. Just thinking seriously about going to work can be valuable, because it invites one to imagine oneself connecting with an active world of events. Even a woman who decides against a job may find that she experiences a reawakened sense of control over her life because she has involved herself in a serious choice about her future.

Of course the idea of going to work is not "new" any more than is the idea of divorce as a way out of an impossible marriage situation. Careers for women have been possible at least as long as divorce has been plausible. But there has been a rather startling increase in the number of women who think about work as a distinct possibility for them, even though they are married; not, that is, as an alternative to marriage. Some really astonishing figures turn up in a survey done during the sixties by a young English sociologist, Hannah Gavron, for a doctoral thesis at London University. Mrs. Gavron interviewed young mothers in their middle twenties, equally divided between middle- and working-class backgrounds. Some of them were working already. Mrs. Gavron asked the rest, in the course of lengthy interviews, whether they, too, planned to work later on. When she added up the figures of those who were already working and those who intended to get jobs "as soon as the children are in school," she found that nine out of ten of these women were either working or planning to.[6] (The percentage was almost identical for both middle- and working-class mothers.) Now, we must assume that there is a fair amount of wishful thinking in these unexpected figures. No one imagines that 90 percent of married women will ever really hold jobs. But the point is that 90 percent of a very typical selection of women in their twenties were thinking about it as a real possibility, and thinking about it, moreover, *before* the new feminist movement came to life in the late sixties.

This increase in plausibility is a new phenomenon, and it bears witness to an important social shift. In a very short period of time, just about a generation if we take Parsons' description of the married woman's plight as a *terminus a quo*, women have begun to present to themselves as a serious idea the possibility that they will spend a good part of their lives married but also working outside their homes as individuals. And that this will take place as an enterprise they inaugurate for themselves in middle life. They expect, that is, to make a crucial decision for themselves after the traditional marriage choice. This gives the prospect of existence an openness that is a really new phenomenon.

Will it change the overall pattern? Will it, as a few early feminists thought and many of their angry opponents alleged, overturn the social structure and put an end to the family? We have lived for three generations or more in a world where careers for women were conceivable, but they have almost always been conceived as an either/or proposition: either a family or a career; and this dichotomy is by no means out of our thinking today. Will the twin facts of more women working and many more women considering it as a possibility finally herald the downfall of marriage as an institution?

Or will marriage-as-an-institution draw upon this new phenomenon as a support-by-way-of-escape-valve, as it has drawn at other times and in other places upon adultery, prostitution and divorce? If these apparently contrary circumstances can help to keep marriage alive, why shouldn't woman's right to hold down a job?

CHAPTER 17

Human beings, being mammals, spend an inordinate—but scarcely disproportionate—amount of time involved in institutions whose task is to make into an orderly and predictable entity the expression and control of sexuality, replacement of the population, succession to rights and offices, and education of the young. [It has been] claimed that the nuclear family is universal in pursuit of these ends, and often other ends as well. Whether or not this universality is more than an epiphenomenon of the mammalian mode of reproduction is open to argument. . . . But what is not open to argument is that there is a wide variety of ways in which human beings can mate, reproduce, and train the young.

Paul Bohannon and John Middleton
Marriage, Family and Residence [1]

WITH MARRIAGE as protean an institution as the two distinguished anthropologists quoted above declare it to be, it's difficult to see why we should find it odd that women's rights can operate as one of its social supports. We have seen that many other contradictions work out as counterweights, preserving the situations they appear to discredit. Being less hampered by dogma or doctrine than are religious institutions, marriage has from time to time incorporated within itself any number of disparate principles and practices and survived by adjustments and accommodations. This is not at all an indication of weakness. On the contrary, the almost universal incidence of some kind of marriage makes clear how valuable a system it is: otherwise why bother with it at all? Pliant enough to change, tough enough to endure, marriage absorbs the tensions that modify it. Once modified, it then in some fashion passes the effects of these tensions back to society in constant interaction.

If at present we hesitate to see women's rights as a prop to marriage and think of them more as a challenge, this is due partly to memories of the old feminist movement and more to the appearance of a new one. The militant rhetoric of Women's Liberation and its obvious mimetic connection with other "revolutionary" movements stamp it (in our eyes) as an agent of change. We have had a good deal of practice in getting used to agencies of change lately, and one result has been to accept them, whether we like them or not, into intellectual coexistence. But having accepted them as being *there,* we don't particularly try to arrive at a theoretical compromise position which will adjust the new to the old. Let everyone, we say, do his own thing—expressions which are passé to those who coin them being still potent with those who take them up later. This is particularly so because we see marriage now as an entirely private, personal and emotional arrangement. The result is that arguments which support it as a prop for social stability feel false, stale and old-fashioned. And indeed why support marriage, or attempt to bring together the old and the new, if its function is purely emotive?

In fact, its function is greater than that, for the definition given by Bohannon and Middleton continues to be valid. But the way we represent marriage to ourselves is increasingly as a fluid deal between husband and wife. Divorce as a possible end to one pairing and the gateway to another is built into our thinking, and now the experiments in diverse ways of living associated with young people, "new" people, the trendy rich and hippie communities are having their effect too. All of this suggests that marriage must once again exercise its capacity to be flexible and accept adjustments. It will do so most easily when we are least conscious of them.

The adjustment which has proceeded furthest with the least publicity is the return of middle-aged middle-class women to work outside the home. As we have seen, it has been increasing both in the actual number of working wives and in the plausibility of this way of life. Now a left-wing women's movement has sprung up and is calling attention to the effects and defects of this hitherto rather subterranean social drift. The right of a woman to a paycheck has been more or less taken for granted lately. Today demands for an *equal* paycheck have turned public attention to the whole situation—including a great deal beyond the mere economics of women at work, which means a great deal that is not taken for granted.

There is much to be said for doing this—Bring things out in the open! Show how women are being cheated and imposed upon!— and a certain amount to be said against it. Change which isn't cried up in this way may take place rather easily and produce fast results if its goals are definite and its immediate effects not too abrasive; while change that is proclaimed in heated speeches and presented in theatrical demonstrations will have great impact as far as emotional reactions are concerned, but is likely to be implemented only with difficulty. And not only does such a campaign kick up a backlash; so long as part of its aim is publicity, getting publicity will drain off its energies and satisfy (or seem to) its purpose.

These are generalities. If we take a moment to look at the first stages of the Women's Liberation Movement, we observe that it is as yet without defined goals that are widely agreed on and exists largely as an exploration of the problem and a channel for expressing emotions. In addition, its relations to other radical groups are ambiguous. It needs, therefore, to find an identity; and the rhetoric, gestures and demonstrations it has been specializing in are a very necessary step for further development. Unity of feeling must come ahead of reasoned programs in any organization. In fact, at the beginning, programs *are* gestures: they confirm loyalties by asserting that a real future exists in which real action will be taken. Conceptually, Women's Lib is not a revival of the earlier feminist movement, being much more an application to women of the Negro drive which has progressed from Civil Rights to Black Power. But, of course, it is seen objectively as being a revival, which means that there are ready-made attitudes to be revived and applied to today's women militants.

These hand-me-down attitudes have (so far) assured that Women's Lib isn't taken very seriously. We have noted that laughter is always the first reaction to a change in role behavior, a defensive reaction which is useful because it permits a degree of play in the social situation, so that innovations can enter bit by bit. To a certain extent, then, the corollary holds true: as long as a change is derided, it can happen. But revolutionary movements insist, quite rightly, on their dignity. They reject minor changes as tokenism. If the women's movement is humorless (an attitude for which it has been attacked), this is partly because women are refusing to stay within limits where change is not upsetting and can be taken as amusing by the powerful.

Which brings us back to the other party in the present confrontation between women and the establishment: the powerful. As we noted at the end of Chapter 8, the powerful are not at the moment in love with the power they hold. The complexity and the stubborn resistance of the world today to any individual efforts extend to the efforts of the powerful. "All, all of a piece throughout; Thy chase had a beast in view; Thy wars brought nothing about; Thy lovers were all untrue"; Dryden's words describe well the impotence to act effectively which has robbed our rulers of any pleasure in decision-making. They are guiltily afraid of the repercussions of responsibility, pessimists unhappy with the world but hardly able to do more about it than anyone else and as ready as revolutionaries to find relief in rhetoric instead of action. In this situation, change *per se* is not necessarily something to be refused; perhaps it might even work! But demands for change that will actually and openly force our decision-makers to decide something are irritating, if not frightening.

In short, change is more possible today than it was when the grandmothers and great-grandmothers of today's feminists were first making the issue of women's rights; but the old mocking and hostile labels still linger in memory, and they will be brought out and attached to the new movement as it begins to appear serious. This will lay emphasis on the divergence from traditional views of woman's place rather than on the continuity in our ways of living. Useful adjustments will then be taken as attacks on a mythically valuable status quo.

For demands that women be liberated have a special emotional effect, not simply because of the sexual challenge implicit in them, though that certainly counts, but also because of a tendency common among us two-sexed animals to divide the world into neat dichotomies. We see things as opposing entities, this *or* that, not as gradients of more-or-less. Not only is the desire of one sex to change its traditional place taken to be a threat by the other, which will be disturbing at the very least. Our yes-or-no, either-or approach to the world and the way it works makes it overwhelmingly easy to believe that any change means destruction. Like so many binary computers, we tend to think as if our switches were

set to on or off. Negative roles, for example, which reverse the
expectations and attributions of traditional roles, are much easier
to assume and impute than are new groupings of traits and actions. Thus, a demand for change will often be seen as the threat
to put down anything and everything old with a ruthless hand.

So it is in our time, and so it was with the general reaction to
the campaign of the first feminists for a new definition of woman's
place. We can learn something about public attitudes to demands
for women's rights from a brief review of past history, beginning
with the fact that one of the standard attacks on the suffragists
was the assertion that these brazen creatures wanted to do away
with marriage. In fact, however, barring a few eccentrics, the old
feminist leaders were not at all anxious to meddle with the institution. True, one sometimes gets the feeling, reading their writ-
ings, that their restraint was based either on timidity or on considered policy: Don't wake up the monkeys! But it was a policy
that was adhered to, for most of the feminist leaders, most of the
times, were reformers, not revolutionaries.

It is hard to see how they could have been anything else and
remained a group cohesive enough to get anything done. They
have been criticized for not fighting for more than the vote, on
the grounds that the movement fell apart once the vote had been
won when there was still much ground to be covered before social
equality of the sexes had been achieved. The trouble with this
hindsight view is that there was *so* much ground to be covered.
No one could agree on an objective other than the vote and, at
the start, the old movement was as diffuse in its aims as is today's.
No more then than now was there general agreement on what
"equality" meant; and to the extent that the demand for women's
rights involves private, personal and psychological aspects it was,
and is, difficult to see how public action can ever provide what is
wanted.

What this means is that if one uses political means, one should
aim at political goals. When the feminists did finally sort themselves out, their central goal was the political aim of achieving
the vote. If it doesn't seem a charismatic goal today, that is largely
because its effect has been absorbed and is now taken for granted.
In any case, we should not downgrade the difficult campaign

which finally gained it or refuse to learn from its strengths and weaknesses.

One obvious effect of focusing on a political campaign with a defined goal was to suppress other amorphous, and unconventional, demands. The vote would not be won by women carrying banners inscribed Free Love. The feminists needed the support of respectable women (it was a long time coming) and, even more, they needed the votes of men who were the exclusive possessors of such things. Whatever their private thoughts and reactions to marriage (and many never married, or married unhappily), they were not about to launch a frontal attack on holy matrimony and the sacred institution of the family. Not that their restraint convinced the most bitter of their opponents: the attacks on them were unpleasant and rebarbative, and there is little doubt that their militant descendants may expect to hear them again.

Nonetheless, they succeeded; but as the critics of the first feminist movement point out, reducing a crusade to a campaign has its dangers. Because the approach of the suffragists avoided questioning received ideas about woman's role, it invited an over-investment of emotion in the goal it offered, and in so doing imported a familiar kind of mythic ambiguity into the heart of the struggle: the ends pursued could not, even when achieved, produce the results that were promised. On the one hand, the reformers declared what many women truly felt: that they could no longer accept the sort of lives which were prescribed by the narrow limits of their traditional place and activities. But on the other hand, the solution they offered—the vote—was not commensurate with the problem. By declaring, sincerely, that it was, the suffragists guaranteed that any victory would include a defeat. Indeed, they spoke ambivalently, though again, I am sure, sincerely. At the same time that they demanded change, they assured their listeners that the change would not really be very big: this, of course, was intended for the ears of the establishment. Not much would happen, and yet everything would happen. Or, to put it simply, liberated women would save the world, but would not upset it. One is reminded of Lyndon Baines Johnson addressing the Southern Establishment on the question of civil rights.

The world didn't much want to be saved. It seldom does; and

in those years the powerful still enjoyed the exercise of power. The world was convinced, moreover, that if women accomplished anything at all beyond making fools of themselves, there would be a great deal of upsetting. No matter what they might say, women who moved out of their place into man's world would, men believed, grow coarse, hard, unfeeling and unfeminine. They would accomplish nothing—that is, not much would happen—but at the same time they would cease to be fit for their tasks as wives and mothers: everything would happen. The sexes agreed on all but the locus of change. You won't change anything in the world, said men, but you'll change, that is, you'll ruin, yourselves. Not at all, replied women. We won't change ourselves and our standards, but we'll apply them to man's world, we'll raise its moral values, we'll bring them up to our own. We'll change man's world by making it match woman's place. You'll masculinize yourselves, said men. We'll feminize the world, said women.

In the end, both sides appear to have been mostly wrong, which is hardly unusual for general predictions on the course of events. Both women and the world have changed, but the causality is far from clear, and any connection between votes for women and the loosening of restrictive marriage customs is particularly obscure. "Free love" is a good deal more respectable than it used to be in middle-class, propertied circles, but one suspects that the lessened economic importance of the family is a factor here along with the general secularization of our society. The effect is that marriage has moved toward its opposite pole and incorporated a bit of free love within it, so that the community which Ambrose Bierce once described as consisting of "a master, a mistress and two slaves, making in all two" has lost some of its suffocating narrow rigidity. In short, marriage has adjusted itself to the sexual latitudinarianism which the first feminists denied as an aim, while any positive and direct effect of women's right to vote is hard to trace in the inner or in the outer world. Any feminization of the latter has been due to large social forces which have made physical strength and endurance less important than ever before.

If marriage is now going to incorporate working wives as normal, usual members of its duality, we may suspect that it is not going to do so in the most obvious, direct fashion. On the face of it, we would suppose that women who work because they have to would be those who rock the boat least. In fact, women often think so themselves: at least, some of them assure their children that Mummy is working only to get money, not because she wants to—even when Mummy knows she wants to. She is afraid that the children would be upset if she seemed to want to do more than be their mother. This is evidence in itself that work for married women is not yet accepted as normal and plausible, in spite of the number of them in the labor force.

Yet such studies as have been made indicate that women who work because they have to upset the equilibrium of the family more than those who work because they enjoy it. We must tread carefully here, of course, and allow that economic pressure in itself can be generally disruptive and upsetting to the husband and father who feels ashamed of failing to do his job as breadwinner for the family if his wife works too. Then, it's obvious that people who are compelled to undertake a task, any task, and certainly an unexpected and demanding one, come to it with less pleasure than those who do it out of choice. One would hardly expect all women who have to get jobs because their husbands aren't able to support the family to do so in a spirit of Christian charity and spiritual joy. Many will resent the compulsion, and some will feel scorn for a man who fails to make a good living and shame for having chosen to marry someone who falls short of their expectations.

External factors are also present. Families where women have to work just to keep going will tend to be marginal families with lower than average educational backgrounds. The jobs open to women who have not, for example, finished high school remain drudge jobs, monotonous routines which cannot be valued highly in themselves though they do offer change, companionship and the income which means so much both practically and emotionally. In addition, it is often harder for women who live in small towns or suburban areas to find any sort of work, let alone that which is interesting, for there simply isn't the range of openings available in cities. Lack of seniority means lower wages for women and earlier layoffs even if they work at the same level as men. All these elements come into the equation which, like all social equations, has to be made up from random factors lying around at the time and can't be elegantly arranged and tested in a laboratory.

Still, there it is: the families of women who work because they want to are distinctly better off emotionally than the families of those who work because they have to, according to a study, "Working Wives and Marriage Happiness," made by sociologists Susan Orden and Norman Bradburn.[2] (I quote them at the head of Chapter 13.) They determined that "a reluctant recruit to the labor market" experienced "a significant reduction in her happiness." This was true both when she balanced "recent positive and negative experiences" and when she considered her marriage long-term. It was also true for husbands of wives in this situation. On the other hand, women who were not working simply because they had to, women who answered "Yes" when they were asked, "Would you work if you didn't need the money?" found themselves in a pleasanter situation. Both husbands and wives said they experienced more tensions than when the wives stayed home, but felt that overall these were balanced out by greater satisfactions. In addition they noted that they enjoyed more companionship and sociability. Certain commonsensical facts turned up: women with pre-school children found themselves less well-adjusted if they worked, but this negative result was not true for women with children of elementary-school age. On the whole, too, there was an evident tendency for part-time work to be more favorable for the best marital adjustment than full-time work.[3] With nurses and nearby grandmothers largely a thing of the past, this is what one would expect.

Orden and Bradburn don't suggest that women who work outside their homes in the labor market are bound to be happier than those who stay home. What they do say is if women *choose* to work outside, there is nothing to show that their families will suffer and a definite indication that tensions which do develop will be offset by emotional rewards within the family, plus a bonus of wider companionship outside the family. The real crux of the matter is choice. A generation ago Talcott Parsons was noting that the outlook and attitudes of married women reflected their feeling that their greatest decision, marriage, had been made once and for all and had left them with little more control-by-selection over their lives. Today these young colleagues of his see the possibility of choice reintroduced into the lives of married women.

"A woman's freedom to choose among alternative life styles is an important predictor of happiness in marriage," their summing-up begins; and they mean happiness for both partners. In fact, their conclusion considers some future possibilities for increased choice and continuing positive reactions: "Efforts to extend this freedom [of choice] should have positive effects on the marriage happiness of both husbands and wives." Indeed, if women could receive the economic support of the community, if restraints to their free entry into the labor market were removed, Orden and Bradburn believe that "there is evidence to support the contention that there might well be a strengthening of the marriage relationship for both husband and wife." [4] In short, woman's right to choose to work may turn out to be another support-by-escape-valve for marriage.

Sociologists are often accused of laboring the obvious and of fixing unnecessary, distracting, or meaningless numbers to widely accepted generalities. No doubt some of them do. But this judgment is partly due to a misguided reaction by the lay public to the nature of sociology. Sociology must look at the obvious, at "what we all know." That is its field of inquiry. Having looked at the obvious, counting it—which means approaching it as if it were new—may open the mind to new aspects of the familiar and certainly forms a better basis for judgment than do hazy assumptions. Besides, what sociologists come up with is often far from obvious in its implications. To say that the freedom to choose how to live contributes to the happiness of the chooser is obvious. Equally obvious, one happy member of a relationship will promote general happiness therein more than a sulky one does. But if we go on being obvious for another moment, we see that freedom to choose entails freedom to change, and within a relationship the change is not confined to the psyche of one participant. It implies freedom to break up a situation that has hardened into discomfort. It is often a nuisance to change, and in some cases hardly worth it. But in some cases it is very much worth it, and in a few fortunate situations it can bring the saving force of imagination to bear on old difficulties and begin the development of new solutions and resolutions whose influence will extend beyond the immediate situation.

This kind of adjustment to a new situation at once involves the roles people play within it. The roles themselves are resistant to change because they demand repetitive action: they must, if they are to be clearly understood. They bind separate acts together into *behavior,* which is a pattern of action that has become familiar enough for easy interpretation by other participants and by the outside world. When one does something out of the ordinary, and goes on doing it so that it has to be seen as something more than a blunder, one calls for a reassessment of the whole situation by the others involved in it. This is never easy, and it is more difficult when the roles have not simply grown out of the activity, like professional roles, but have been ascribed on the basis of some personal attributes, like sex, particularly when these attributes are related to gradients of power or prestige. Our investigation of feminine roles has made very clear that they assume an inequality of power and prestige between the sexes: men are top dogs. Now, one must really be determined or driven if one acts very unexpectedly very often in the face of adverse public judgment and the disapproval of the powerful. To turn that statement around, one must be indicating clearly that a role is outworn, a social situation changed drastically, and the old behavior no longer appropriate.

So when a team of sociologists tells us that our assessment of a situation is faulty because people are not behaving the way we expect them to, they are often signaling to us that circumstances are changing. Let us, then, note this information: it seems that, one way or another, women who work because they choose to are at present less menacing to their marriages and disturbing to their families than women who work only because they have to, and probably less disturbing by far than our traditional hand-me-down moralistic views have led us to expect.

What sociologists often leave out, on the grounds that it isn't their business, is what it feels like inside—inside the situation, and inside the role-player or role-changer. Now, part of the proper function of literary fictions (the creation of which is my primary trade) is to imagine such feelings and set them down believably. Not only are they important in the present, these emotions influence the future because they fuel the mythmaking machinery. Unfortunately, it's characteristic of the present age to hold "fiction" synonymous with "untrue." This isn't so. Good fiction is always concentrated truth, or the apotheosis of fact by the discovery therein of a living, active drive to become—a process trying to enunciate a principle which will survive until it, in turn, is falsified because it no longer expresses true feelings. I shall not, however, dispute the present Spirit of the Age by introducing a piece of imaginative fiction to illustrate the feelings of ordinary women who are involved in a change of traditional role, but only point out that much knowledge of this kind is contained in fiction. In fact there is no need to call on fiction when there are many women in this situation who are perfectly capable of speaking for themselves. They speak more diffusely than would a fictional character, but what they say converges on one meaning.

A few years ago I sat in on a workshop course, given at Barnard College, whose purpose was to help orient women who wanted to go into, or back into, the business world. Between fifty and sixty attended each semester, and the overall number ran into the hundreds before the project ended. All the women had families, though a small minority (under 10 percent) were widowed or divorced and an even smaller minority had no young children living at home. Their ages ranged from the late twenties to the mid-fifties and, a requirement for the course, all held college degrees: the intention was to achieve reasonable homogeneity in the group. All of them had got far enough along with acting on their decision: "Consider getting a job," to arrange to be away from home all day one day a week for ten weeks.

The atmosphere at the first session was euphoric. I think this was not simply a holiday feeling of being out of the house, away from one's chores, on a workday. Most of the women present had had to make too many complicated arrangements in order to get away at all to feel very holidayish about it. I believe that it was just the satisfaction our sociologists have been talking about, the happiness that comes with the freedom to choose. These women had not yet chosen to go back to work and, in the end, many did not so choose, or at any rate not at once; but they had chosen to get themselves into a place where they could think about it seriously and talk about it as a real possibility and devote their minds to practical ways and means. And here they were.

What they were offered was nothing that seemed to me of

enormous value in itself. They listened to lectures, some good, some useful, some vague, some depressing and rather condescending, on what it's like to work in this profession or vocation or that one, how to go about getting a job, how to present oneself to an employer, what has to be tackled in setting up on one's own. They seemed to me, at the time, to listen too docilely. I would have welcomed more questions and discussion from the floor. There was very little. But I think now I was wrong, perhaps because the college setting misled me. These women were not students whose business it is to bounce ideas around and challenge premises in order to learn how to think. They were people who were preparing for action. If they listened unquestioningly, ready to take everything in (and I thought they did), it was because they needed to take in all they could get hold of that might turn out to be practical as an approach to man's world. They were perfectly capable, it turned out, of filtering out what was unusable and using what was pertinent.

I suspect now that some of the most useful products of that course were not evident on the surface and had nothing to do with what anyone said. The first of these by-products was habituation to an outside routine: get to class by ten o'clock Tuesday, every Tuesday, and get your homework done first. The second was the reintroduction to the world of paper work. They wrote reports and book reviews and curricula vitae and criticized those of others. They practiced explaining themselves and some of their ideas to others. They were back in the communication-with-strangers-and-adults world. Of course it wasn't totally strange. Many of these women were active in various kinds of volunteer work both in their communities and in larger fields. But now, and perhaps this was most important, they were doing it all on their own, by themselves and for themselves. They were neither Andrew's wife nor Timmy's mother, nor helpful Mrs. So-and-so whom one knew from the PTA and the League of Women Voters. Not only were they unknown to the rest there, *no one was asking them to do this*. It was a favor to no one but themselves and they had to find their satisfaction within themselves, for they could expect no gratitude and no pleasant moral glow, no vicarious living.

Three years later I wrote to all the women who had been present at the spring semester I'd attended, to ask what they were doing. Had they followed through on the "get a job" idea? Had it worked out, if they had? And how? If they hadn't, had the experience changed their lives, either at home or abroad? A considerable number were generous enough to reply, and it is partly from their answers that I have gathered the reactions which I summarize here. In addition, the leader of the workshop had kindly permitted me to go through anonymous replies to an earlier questionnaire sent to previous participants. Though its purpose was different (to discover how effective the training had been), the answers proved to be complementary.

Let us begin at the beginning, with the motivation that brought several hundred women over the years back to the schoolroom. For some, it was boredom, pure and simple. In others, boredom combined with self-dissatisfaction and a feeling of being left out. Several used the term "identity crisis" to describe a sense of bewilderment and uncertainty of aim "once the children were grown." Some were sharply aware of the psychological dangers of vicarious living. "I think it's best for me to have my own interests rather than hover over [my children] all the time," wrote one. Another declared forthrightly that unless she had some other vital interest she "might well become an interfering unpopular mother-in-law constantly involved in her children's lives." [5]

Such fear of possible peril to others in the family from one's own lack of a grip on the world is about as close to a generalized, other-directed motive for getting out of the house as any member of the group reported. True, a number of them, particularly those with whom I was directly in correspondence, spoke of an uneasiness about the world and about American policies both at home and abroad. Far from being bound up in themselves, they looked at the world, criticized it and saw themselves as part of it. Typically, however, they are not crusaders—which is what one would expect. Women who want to go back to work in the world accept the world, by and large, though often with reservations. Crusaders are more apt to head straight into volunteer organizations whose declared aim is social change or political readjustment, whether by reform or revolution.

I don't mean to suggest that women who plan to change their personal lives by getting jobs for themselves are thinking only about themselves. It could be that they need the assurance of being able to hold a job, and so resolving that identity crisis, before they can move toward larger considerations. Some of them may turn into crusaders; and in a vague way, many felt disturbed about the way things in the world were running even as they considered how best to get out there and help run them. The connection between such concern and one's own active work in the world showed up in the desire, expressed over and over again, for "significant work," a job "doing something that will help people." In part, I believe, this apparently condescending phrase masks a great modesty and a great sense of ignorance. If they knew what would help people, and felt capable of doing it, they would be more specific; and as they find out, some of them become so.

Humanly speaking, the process works something like this. Selfishness comes first; and that, I think, is absolutely valid, because it supplies a driving motivation. In some sense, selfishness *always* comes first, even when one talks about women who have ended with jobs that are obviously and fundamentally valuable and helpful to society. Whether it is boredom, the sense of being left out and passed by, shame over wasted time and talents, the prospect of an empty future—these menaces weigh on the self, eat away at one's personal value. Women who feel them—not all women do, needless to say—are acting quite selfishly when they decide to do something about it. It follows as the night the day that, once the decision is made, one hopes that some good may come of it; that it will be *not only* selfish, personal, trivial; that one will find "significant rewarding work" to do, work that will "help people." We might note that selfishness enters at this level too: how much easier to justify "significant work" to one's friends, one's children, one's husband, oneself than more mundane pursuits!

None of this matters, because the work needs doing. The reasons for doing things, we should remind ourselves from time to time, are not directly related to the effects of what is done. We tend to be overly moral about motivation today. Perhaps this is because we live in an era of automation, where it is easy to overlook the necessary action that intervenes between intention and result. One of my correspondents, for instance, is working with a psychiatric clinic charged with investigating families in which "the beaten child syndrome" has produced a beaten child. Another started work as a volunteer in the elementary grades of the public schools helping children with reading problems. She got so charged up about the need that she is working for a master's degree in Remedial Reading while continuing to do two days of volunteer work a week. Another who has been spending three days a week as a volunteer in the psychiatric clinic of a New York hospital has just received a master's in Social Work. Three years ago one might have dismissed their desire "to help" as naïve, but no one could so dismiss the results of their activities.

Not everybody is this socially minded. One woman reports that she works as a substitute teacher and hates it. Now divorced, she does it for the money. The money allows her to do other work that she loves and may one day make a living at, reviewing films and plays, writing and reporting. She is, she says, thoroughly happy out in the world, rushed and driven and coping. Matching her is the woman who went back to graduate school for a refresher course in her scientific field and discovered that she was pregnant. Her daughter is now two, and she is thoroughly happy at home.

Other women stayed home, too, having thought their circumstances over in the light of what they learned from the workshop and having decided that they did not want jobs. For one it was a question of age. She couldn't get the sort of job that would interest her, she decided, without going back to school. In her fifties, she weighed the volunteer work she was already doing against the years of study and opted to go on as a volunteer. But she had faced the issue and made a conscious decision, and this in itself was valuable. "After examining the alternatives," she writes, "I had a greater appreciation of the things I had been doing and the freedom of choice and mobility afforded me." Another typical reaction was that of a mother of teen-age daughters who decided to stay at home for a while, continue with volunteer work, but direct it and coordinate it so that it could serve as a foundation for a future job. This is not wishful, for volunteer work is often a stepping-stone to paid employment. Occupied in this way, women begin to gain confidence and some want to go on to work that seems more serious and demanding. Another woman with teen-age children who did go back to work at a college where she is now Director of Student Activities wrote, "I think it was my semi-professional unpaid work that made me itch for meaningful involvement."

That sounds as if, for this woman at least, "meaningful involvement" implies a paid job. That isn't entirely true even in this case,
however, for along with her job and with work for a master's
degree in American Studies, she has continued to do some of the
unpaid work she had been doing before. Another correspondent
sums up the meaning of "meaningful" when it is equated with
paid work as follows: "To me the central question has never been
one of whether or not to work, since work is another way of saying that one is making oneself socially and economically relevant.
Work implies continuity and the effort necessary to become good
at doing something of value. Work one must, to maintain self-
respect and to enjoy a sense of achievement—and to occupy time.
Thus the question is rather what one defines as work, at various
stages of one's life, and under what circumstances juggling one's
family life to fulfill a professional obligation is desirable. . . . There
are halfway solutions, for some total solutions, via volunteer work,
but to me they lack the essential reward of getting paid, the proof
of one's value on the marketplace."

Clearly, then, for many women the ability to make a living as
an individual is becoming psychologically important in the same
way as it is for men. A paid job is "meaningful" because it measures one's ability in terms that can be judged publicly and
equally with others—it's worth money, but money here isn't
merely a medium of exchange, it's a standard of ability which has
nothing to do with femininity but only with human capability.
This not only bolsters the ego, but allows a woman to know that
she can meet the world and satisfy its demands without dragging
in feminine wiles or appealing to it as a special case. A sense
of one's proper value is a fine antidote for the defensive feminine traits frustration can engender and which even the most
rabid anti-feminist deplores—self-pity, timidity, silliness and self-
consciousness.

The one motive for going back to work of which I found no
trace, overt or disguised, is the one traditionally suspected and
feared: the desire of a wife to compete with and outdo her husband. In my own experience, it is nonworking rather than working
wives who seem to fall into open expressions of marital hostility,
like the wife of a senator, now dead, but distinguished in his time,
who cried, "Shut up, Joe!" across the dinner table of a Supreme

Court justice when she decided her husband was being long-winded, and shocked the young career woman sitting next to him —me—into near catalepsy.

Her attitude is matched all too often among angry and frustrated wives and mothers who feel somehow cheated by life because they are not part of what seems to them "the real world." It is from their lips that one hears attacks on the value of the work done by their husbands; it is they who imagine (without any real effort to do so) that they can successfully compete with professional men at difficult occupations. Nancy Milford's biography of Zelda Fitzgerald documents the obsessive competitive drive which set this talented, underoccupied woman to trying to write and, at the same time, blocked any successful effort at it. For Zelda, writing was something to do because Scott did it, not something to do for its own sake as an independent enterprise; in token of this, the material she used was always the material *he* used.[6] It is very difficult for anyone who doesn't have experience of working in the world of affairs to realize the demands there and to judge what is done objectively. Today, as we have observed, women at home are more cut off from economic activity than ever before. What happens "out there" comes to them via their husbands, and their emotions about the husbands and the external world can get hopelessly mixed up together. Frustration at being left out, anger at not doing work of value, is projected onto men in an ugly way.

The women at the workshop seminars who decided to go to work, either at once or after graduate study, felt quite different. If anything, they were overconscious of the strain that holding a job or getting a graduate degree might put on a marriage. Many of them speak with warm gratitude to their husbands for emotional support as well as for practical help. They knew they were often asking a great deal in the way of cooperation, and they were sometimes conscious of anxieties over whether it was worthwhile. Even for a role-changer, change isn't easy. Those who hung on and went through with it report overwhelmingly, though not unanimously, that it was all right in the end. "My husband wouldn't want me to leave my job now." "The pluses outweigh the minuses." "He's really very proud of me. He talks about it to his friends." "My husband and children have benefited from my being in a better frame of mind." "The attitude of the family progressed from mild alarm to real enthusiasm."[7]

Many husbands, of course, were not this adaptable. They actively disapproved of working wives. Some wives were perfectly happy about that. They write that they enjoy entertaining their husband's business friends; they enjoy the freedom of not being tied down to someone else's schedule, so that companionship with friends, visits to museums and concerts are always possible. They feel life to be too rich for them as it is to want to change it. They find the volunteer work that almost all of them speak of doing both personally satisfying and objectively worthwhile. They want to be present and ready to answer their children's questions when the questions are asked. They did not look for paid jobs because they chose to stay home, and they don't feel frustrated and angry about it, though occasionally they complain that women who *have* managed to combine home and career are sometimes rather smugly superior about it.

But there is another category, and this is inhabited by women who did want to work and whose husbands opposed it. They are definitely not happy, and particularly in the anonymous replies to the Workshop questionnaire, they speak their minds about what it means to have to write: "I am still doing the same type of volunteer work because my husband refused to let me get a paid job." "At present," wrote one, "I am taking care of my baby and the other children—and the biggest baby of them all, my husband." A remark as bitter as that is rare. Most of the women who want to work and have run into a husbandly veto have gone in for persuasion—or perhaps nagging? "I am still Mrs. Chief Pinch-hitter for my husband this winter, that means almost full-time work; but he is growing more tolerant of my ambitions." Or again, "I think I am gradually winning my husband over to the fact that some kind of part-time work is essential for me." Another reported on the tensions of her situation: "You'll see that I've answered both yes and no to the question about family approval. This paradoxical answer is what I feel my husband's reaction to be. He mouths approval and even praise. If, however, I'm unable to listen further about his topic of conversation because I must do my homework, he's not understanding of the situation. (By the way, when I mentioned this to him, he denied it completely.)" [8]

The pattern that emerges, when we leave the emotion aside, is consonant with what our sociologists report. Women who are

doing what they choose to do, whether it is working or whether
it is staying home, are happier than those who do not have the
choice. But I believe that we can see from this glance at what it's
like inside—and that means including the emotion and taking it
seriously—that there's a further conclusion to be drawn. This is
it: married women who work, work with their husbands' consent
and often with their approval. Married women who want to work
and don't receive their husbands' consent *don't work*. It may gall
them, they may be nasty about it, but the masculine veto appears
to be effective.

The traditional social contract by which all women are expected
to begin their duties by tending to those located in woman's place
is still widely observed. It's true that recently many young husbands have come to feel that they properly have a part in baby-
tending, child-raising and even household chores. But almost
always this help is seen as just that—help to a wife in her role
but not really as an extension of the male role. And husbandly
opposition to outside work for women still exists, even if it's
sometimes almost unconscious, just the communication of unease
and disturbance over the idea of a wife with a job, so that the
woman says, "He'll be lost without me," which is flattering if frus-
trating. Or it may be the kind of flat opposition that pushes a marriage toward divorce—though I doubt that this kind of disagree-
ment produces many divorces by itself. More likely a marriage
that splits on the issue of a job for the wife was shaky before. For
most married women there is no doubt that marriage is still the
stronger force when they think in terms of either a job or the
marriage. The exceptions are almost always clearly situations
which involve women with special, directed capabilities or talents,
women who were aware when they married that a career had to
be part of their lives.

This being so, and I think it is pretty much the median, or
average, situation, why suggest that recognition of the right of
married women to take jobs can work out as a support of marriage? Because, for one thing, the value attached to marriage is
obviously still very high even in the eyes of women who want
jobs as well. It is worth a compromise. And because, for another,
most husbands won't and don't apply a veto. To say, descriptively,
that feminine roles still follow the old tradition and assume that

men are top dogs isn't to say that all men act like dogs in the manger. Marriage is worth a compromise to them too. Today the typical male response to a wife who wants a career or a job is that which a young English woman reported succinctly in the London *Sunday Times* of December 7, 1969. When she told her husband that she wanted to attend a teacher training course, "his first reaction was one of total amazement that I should want to take on extra work but he said he would never stand in my way." [9]

To sum up the trend behind the headlines and slogans, what is happening appears to be this. Many married couples include a working wife. Her job is an understood thing between them, either because she was working when she married and kept on or—as in the more easily analyzed cases we've been considering— because she decided to go back to work after staying home for some years as a housewife and mother. Implicitly in the former situation and explicitly in the latter, her husband agrees to her doing so. Her job thus becomes a part of the marriage and its context, for both husband and wife actively (if sometimes unconsciously) adjust their marriage to take account of the wife's outside activities. Her decision to work is ratified and the old pattern of wedlock changes and expands to contain it. A new equilibrium has appeared, and what we think of as being a normal and usual sort of marriage has become more varied and less restricted.

CHAPTER 18

We are faced with an unintended, unguided, but irresistible revolution in all human relations, from the marriage bonds and family controls whereby personal life has traditionally been ordered, to the religious and patriotic loyalties that were wont to rule people's wider activities. Such a change in the human scene requires and effects a change in the concepts with which we operate practically and intellectually, but few people realize that their basic social conceptions have changed. . . . Our profoundest metaphors have lost their moral import.

Susanne K. Langer
"The Growing Center of Knowledge" [1]

THUS FAR THE FLEXIBILITY of marriage as an institution, even monogamous marriage, has assured its continued existence. It can adapt itself with ease to varying social circumstances and moral imperatives. It can keep a woman in purdah or let her work outside her home at a job which has no connection at all with her family duties, a job where she works, like a man, as an individual pair of hands or compendium of skills which happens to fit into an empty slot in an impersonal industrial or commercial operation. Marriage can insist that it is eternal or permit divorce; and divorce may be total and final or (as in part of West Africa, for example [2]) it can work out as a series of progressive, secondary marriages with a wife moving from one husband to another as she is claimed, staying for a while, going on or back to an earlier mate and settling finally where she chooses. Marriage can shrink to a narrow one-plus-one pairing or form the framework for a clan-sized household of relatives descended from or clustered about the central couple. Any study of marriage customs turns up an enormous variety of ways that people can live together, and in addition it underlines the fact that through all these mutations, something that we are willing to call marriage goes on.

But what does it feel like inside? I have put off considering the sexual element, both in and out of marriage, until we had taken account of the external social and economic factors which affect the position of woman's place in man's world. I chose to do this because it is all too easy to think of sex as a thing in itself, a unique value absolutely self-justifying and impossible to compare with other human interests and activities. When we do think of it in connection with the rest of life, we tend to see it as a prime mover, the hidden power source behind any number of other aspects of existence. No doubt—as Freud's work indicated—strong lines of force do run this way. But, as I suggested earlier, the emphasis we put on sexual experience today may very well be due in part to the decline of other powerful and compelling emotions and events, such as communal celebrations, religious faith and others which I shall discuss shortly. In order to talk about the value of sex, we shall have to allow that its value can be compared to other parts of our emotional lives. And indeed, as Gagnon and Simon point out in their book, *The Sexual Scene,* "sexual behavior is learned as all behavior is learned—through the complex interaction of cultural and psychological factors. This means that sexual behavior can be expressive of a wide range of nonsexual motives and interests." [3] Which is to take the Freudian pattern and reverse it: the lines of force run both ways.

As always, it is easier to talk about the past or about the customs of Baluchistan or West Africa than it is about our own world. Both our private feelings and the externalized emotions that have crystallized into mythic beliefs get in our way as we come closer to home. Our opinions of the way things are going seep into our judgments about today's conditions and adulterate them. This is especially true of a subject so emotive as sex; and when we start positing a sexual revolution, we have added another topic, the effect of revolutionary change, about which it is difficult to be objective. In my own view, what we are experiencing is less a sexual revolution than the huge, overall change Susanne Langer describes, in which sexual attitudes and behavior are naturally involved; but this does not make objectivity any easier. On the contrary, it means that no shifts in values can be taken to apply only to the field in which they appear to take place, but must be related to others which, in turn, affect the first. It hardly bears repeating that one man's promiscuity is another's natural search for happiness, and that the emotions we attach to words like "freedom" and "license" and "honesty" and "ruthlessness" and "escapism" and "responsibility" and "selfishness" are so mixed up with each other in our personal estimates of what's going on that every statement about today's moral climate or sexual behavior has to be examined for its own built-in compass deviation.

We do, however, have a few indisputable facts, and one of them is certainly revolutionary. Sexual activity can now be totally disconnected from the possibility of pregnancy which was, in the past, always present; not present as an inevitable result, of course, but as a possibility that inevitably demanded consideration. Of course other efficient methods of birth control beside the pill have existed for years, but using a condom or a diaphragm as a precautionary measure which had to be taken at the time of intercourse still made its own clear reference to the chance of pregnancy. And, in fact, these methods had psychological drawbacks if only because they demanded a certain amount of thinking ahead. The pill, working chemically instead of mechanically, and taken as a routine like taking vitamins, has turned pregnancy into a matter of choice not just for the few but for the many. Beyond this—"It's done what psychoanalysis could never accomplish," a doctor said to me recently. "It's freed women to enjoy sex without fear of getting pregnant." Scares over side effects from this or that type of pill may occur, but they are not going to interrupt the long-term change.

This dramatic new chance of controlling their lives which the pill offers women is bound to affect personal relationships as well as social structures, including most prominently the institution of marriage. How will it do so? Many of those who fear that a sexual revolution is in process, and also many of those who hope for one, believe that an increase in sexual freedom, such as the pill makes possible, will put an end to marriage once and for all. It will make woman's place co-terminous with man's world and turn every individual into a free agent, bound by no obligations: in short, a version of Pornotopia inhabited by a "now" generation which rejects the past and refuses to imagine a future.

This is not a possible world. It is a projection of the sort of mythic fear which equates change with destruction and the sort of Utopian dream which has been bound by frustration into an always desired, never fulfilled, demand for transcendent (in this case, orgasmic) pleasure. Looked at logically, such a world assumes that the only reason to marry is for the enjoyment of sexual relations, and that all sexual relations are equally valuable and equally ephemeral. They are cut off entirely from the rest of life; or else the rest of life is assumed not to exist. They set up no reverberant relationships, have no consequences and therefore no meaning. But whatever the social changes that the mighty shifts of our time are bringing about, we delude ourselves (and frighten ourselves, with unfortunate results) if we imagine that the future belongs to plastic people instead of ordinary human beings endowed with memories and hopes.

The idea that marriage exists to legalize the enjoyment of sex is an old idea, but it is part of romantic popular mythology rather than actual experience of life. True, two people who marry and form a couple expect to couple, but that is not the only thing they expect. Usually they intend to found a family as a center of companionship and social life. Even if they don't plan to have children, they see themselves as a family bound together in an alliance which is both within society and separate from it. Kenneth Keniston's remarks, which I quoted in Chapter 1, about the high value placed today on family life and personal private happiness indicate that marriage is still expected to offer an atmosphere of sustaining emotion and warmth which goes far beyond immediate sexual gratification.

Of course sexual pleasure is an important part of the emotional content of marriage, and how important it is relates, in some fashion, to how easy it is to come by sex outside marriage. But the value we attach to it depends on a great deal more than that. Our present valuation goes back to that earlier sexual revolution, set off by Freud's work, which began in the early years of this century and which has had a profound effect not just on our mores but on our thinking. Looking back, one can say that as far as our behavior goes, the Freudian revolution seems to have made sexual experience more widely available than it was, though for the dominant male, prostitution had always offered easy opportunities. On the face of it, the relatively greater availability of sex for anyone who wants it, since Freudian doctrines on the subject invaded our thinking, would seem to make it less highly valued than when he first wrote. But this is not so at all. The law of supply and demand doesn't work here; and one reason is that Freud's teaching did not stop with the idea that sex is normal, universal and of interest to all ages. It also declared that sex and its expression are *of enormous significance* to every man and woman, not merely outwardly, but in the basic formation of character.

This philosophic view of sex has profoundly influenced the value that our society assigns to it, but it is not by any means part of the attitude of every other society, either past or present. It is anachronistic and misleading to imagine that the sexual experiences of our ancestors were the same as ours today, any more than are the experiences of, say, the West Africans, the Polynesians, or the Chinese Red Guards. Granted, orgastic relief of tension is physiologically the same everywhere; but the meaning assigned to it is not the same. One has only to think of poor Alexander Portnoy, whose penis was his sole private possession, to see that a culture in which genital play is accepted and common among children will assign a different value to the lonely pleasure of masturbation. Of course, in discussing possible changes in sex roles and marriage customs, we must start by trying to understand what sex means to us today. But by the same token, the very fact that we know its meaning can change and has changed rapidly within our own culture should warn us not to assume that we know how its value and its expression will be projected forward. Human beings are full of surprises and their behavior can't be predicted mechanistically.

As a help to judgment on possible changes now we might look quickly back at the most recent shifts in our attitudes toward sex. Interestingly enough, if we glance at the common view of sexual relations a hundred years ago or so, about the time that Freud was born, we find that for one group of individuals, at least, the enjoyment of sexuality was a very good reason to marry. This group was made up of the respectable women of Europe and America, who could not experience normal sexual relations at all except within wedlock. It is hard to get an idea of how they felt about this from direct evidence for, like Disraeli and his religion, no respectable woman ever told. But something can be inferred from some well-known incidents of the high Victorian years.

There is, for instance, the really startling bitterness with which John Ruskin was attacked by highly respectable ladies and gentlemen when, in 1853, his wife made known the circumstances of their marriage: a marriage which had gone unconsummated for six years, during which husband and wife habitually slept in the same bed.[4] Effie Ruskin, however, was still a virgin, a fact which she had to prove in order to end her marriage by obtaining a decree of nullity. Her virginity may seem as astonishing and sad to us as Ruskin's neglect of his wife (he maintained, by the way, that this was due to "an aversion to her person," not to impotence, but Effie was considered extremely attractive by her friends and acquaintances, so her husband's declaration emphasized the fact that he was—in this context—a very queer bird indeed). The Victorians, as we would expect, took Effie's virtue for granted. What we might not expect is the rage and horror with which Ruskin's behavior was condemned, reactions in which it is quite clear that part of his sin was cheating his wife of the sexual exercise she had every right to expect. In the marriage bargain he had failed to live up to his contract.

Very good. But that was not all there was to Victorian marriage, for it had a public social aspect which had nothing to do with private sexual relations, and everything to do with position in the world. Indeed, there is some reason to believe that Effie Ruskin might have gone on putting up with the private side of her marriage if she had continued to enjoy the social benefits which it had afforded in the past. At any rate, the Ruskins had lived for some years in apparent amity while Ruskin was studying "The Stones of Venice," for his book of that title, and Effie enjoyed Venetian society, where she was entertained and admired. It was only after their return to England, where Effie found herself cooped up in a London suburb close to her disagreeable and demanding in-laws and restricted to one trip to town a week, that she took enough interest in another young man to fall in love with him and institute her suit.

For if it was marriage in Victorian times which offered women sexual experience, it was equally marriage which conferred social status on women in a society where, except for a few eccentrics and a handful of women of great wealth or high position, one was either married or a hanger-on. This second condition complicates the first considerably. Effie Ruskin, for instance, *lost* status even

ELIZABETH JANEWAY

though she won her suit, waited a respectable time and then
married the highly successful painter, Millais. Queen Victoria
refused to receive her until, on his deathbed, Millais asked the
favor via a messenger from the Queen, who greatly admired his
work. By that time Effie was old and embittered.

In such circumstances, how can we possibly judge to what
extent women married in order to enjoy the pleasures of sex,
when they had to marry simply in order to possess any social
position or any connection with the mainstream of life? Life had
so arranged itself that a woman's personal history was based on
the passage from her father's protection and domination to that
of her husband. (When Effie left Ruskin, she went north to her
family in Perth, traveling with her father. If she had eloped with
Millais, she would have been received by no one, let alone the
Queen.) The idea of romantic love served, as we know, as a disguise for, or ornamentation of, sexuality; but it also helped to
justify the pragmatic economic and social necessity of marrying.
How many girls married in a mood of excited, palpitant romance,
how many with resignation, how many in relief at being at last
"settled," how many in a state of aggressive ambition? No one
will ever know. But there must have been many in each category,
and more who felt some mixture of these emotions.

After marriage, a wife's ability to gain any kind of freedom of
action must very often, then, have become a matter of domestic
politics which in some cases, no doubt, quickly escalated into civil
war. Sex surely got into this intimate power play, and just as
surely the power play got into sexual relations. This confusion is
not unknown today. But one may expect that the lines of force
ran rather differently at a time when women were less able to act
autonomously and more constrained to wheedle and manipulate
men in order to attain their ends. How likely were they to think
first of their own sexual pleasure? Obviously, some of them must
have; but equally obviously, many must have used sex for purposes other than sexual, must have given or withheld, enjoyed or
repressed their feelings in order to please, because pleasing was
so vital—in order to get their own way about something they
couldn't achieve by themselves, in order to keep the marriage
going because there was literally no other way to live that they
could think of. Some may have got on best as complaisant partners,

some as reproachful martyrs. Some not only put up with their husbands' adulteries, but encouraged them.

All we can say is that even when women were unable to look for sexual pleasure anywhere except in marriage, they did not marry for that reason alone. The low status of single women and the narrow range of opportunities open to them persuaded women in general (with a few exceptions, for there are always exceptions) that marriage was desirable even when it offered little or no sexual pleasure. Unmarried women were unlucky oddities, awful warnings—a view which persuaded many women to put up with personal difficulties for the sake of the position they held. And lack of sexual pleasure was seen as simply a personal difficulty, for women were promised sex in marriage, but not pleasure; were told, in fact, that experiencing it was unladylike and even abnormal. The purpose of sex was to "replace the population" (in the words of Bohannon and Middleton),[5] and marriage provided the channel through which this took place in an orderly way, while also assuring the "succession to rights and offices, and education of the young." If it permitted "the expression and control of sexuality" as well, sexuality was consciously considered as exclusively male. No doubt human affection and mutual respect raised many marriages far above this unpleasant pattern, but the darker side was there, and it shadowed all marriages, for the pattern was assumed to be possible in all.

This is the background out of which current marriage patterns grew. Even today its influence can be felt, if only by the continuing reaction against it: it is not forgotten—that is, it has not entirely ceased to be plausible as a way of life. And echoes remain in certain quarters. The status of single women is still not very high when one thinks of women only in such terms: bestsellers continue to exploit the lack of self-esteem felt by many "single girls," and to assure them that with a little know-how they can become properly, pleasingly "sensuous." Even successful women are still haunted socially and psychologically by these remnants of female inferiority.

Within marriage, too, the weight of husbandly prerogative continues to have some influence. It is much less but, as we have noted, it is still felt. A married woman who wants to work can very often do so, but she is universally expected to see that her household runs properly and her children are looked after before she goes out and shuts the door behind her. This is still her side of the marriage contract, not her husband's, and unless she can manage it somehow, she almost certainly won't work. As the Women's Liberation Movement sees very clearly, this obligation is probably the largest barrier to sex equality today, for by accepting it, women accept a special place and a special role. Women may look for help from men in getting household tasks done, and not just in America either, for some of the housewives Hannah Gavron interviewed were receiving a great deal of aid from their British husbands. But they are grateful for it, and they are expected to be grateful for it. The old pattern, in other words, has by no means been replaced by one that lets women leave their traditional triple role easily. It would be extremely difficult, in fact, to find a woman—no matter what her job—who didn't accept her primary responsibility for house and children as a duty.

This means that talented, exceptional women who want to devote themselves single-mindedly to a career still find it out-of-the-ordinary hard to sustain a marriage; or to say it another way, they have to improvise in order to do so. It was they who were breaking patterns a hundred years ago and they still have to do some pattern-breaking today. Sometimes they marry several times, hoping to find the right man to fit the conditions they need to do their work. Depending on their careers, their discretion and the milieu in which they live, they are increasingly free to enjoy sexual relations outside marriage; some of them did that a century ago. But for very able women, the choice of marriage or a career remains a dilemma as it does not for men, and even lasting marriages may suffer from passing strains. The question of "equality" in marriages like this comes down to the chance a woman has to put her work first. It goes far beyond an equal opportunity to enjoy sexual relations without reproach, though of course a woman's satisfaction with her life, which includes satisfaction with her work, affects all her emotional balance, including her pleasure in sex. We come around again, I think, to seeing that "equality" is not really the most useful goal here, for reciprocity is still to be preferred: what each member of the duality gets from marriage need not be the same, but it should be sufficient of a reward for each to continue choosing the relationship even when it kicks up some difficulties.

The shadows of old social structures remain, then, and the real changes that are taking place today are not simply sexual. "We are faced with an unintended, unguided, but irresistible revolution in all human relations," as Susanne Langer writes, "but few people realize that their basic social conceptions have changed." [6] What is happening is that the interior landscape of our lives is shifting faster than the exterior expression of our emotions. In all of this interior world, our views on sex began to alter perhaps the earliest of any. If we are having a public revolution in sexual behavior now, it is the result of a process that began many years ago. Its theoretical premises have been accepted for at least a couple of generations, for the idea that everyone has a right to pursue sexual happiness, that it is sound, healthy practice for all to achieve this enjoyment, was revolutionary from the turn of the century to the twenties, but is surely not now. It was in those years that the high value placed on a girl's virginity began to be questioned, when it was startling to declare that this condition was not really a symbol of innocence and purity, but a useful bargaining counter in the marriage market. In the Fitzgerald and Hemingway years, the old values began to seem bourgeois, selfish and isolating, and young girls aspired to become sophisticated women of the world just as quickly as they could, before marriage if possible. No doubt it was only an elite which began to act upon the idea that women could and should be independent, could choose to have sex without babies, but it was an influential elite, and one that was much talked about. As far as the plausibility of this idea goes, it was at least half a century ago that the old customary thinking about sexual behavior began to give way.

What is happening today is less the appearance (or even the spread) of new opinions about personal sexual freedom than it is the presentation of them as publicly acceptable. Sexual freedom in private has been around for quite a while, but now it is suddenly represented publicly, on stage, in films, books and magazines. And, of course, it is taking place with less disguise than formerly in real life too. This, however, has a smaller impact on society than do the recent breakthroughs in the world of art and entertainment. The shock effect of the new morality arises from the fact that anything happening "in real life" can be dismissed by those who don't want to look at it as nothing more than odd and aberrant behavior. People who act that way can be thought of as "Bohemians," as "offbeat," and in effect as not typical of the right rules of the real world. They can be ignored because they can be exiled to the category of those we regard as crazy, and so outside society. But when sexual freedom is presented publicly by the arts and the media in which they express themselves, it is validated as existing in a new way, a way that is general and must be taken as part of the surrounding culture. It challenges our ideas of normality.

"I don't care what people do," said Mrs. Patrick Campbell some sixty years ago, "as long as they don't do it in the streets and frighten the horses." We don't have to worry about the horses anymore, but what some people are doing "in the streets"—that is, where their actions are intended to be seen—is alarming and upsetting to others, because these latter don't know what they think or feel about such behavior, but can't help being aware of it. Often it's hard to consider the central situation, the meaning of the presentation, because the very fact that such things are made public is startling, literally shocking. One reacts to the shock, not to the content. Is this serious or a joke? people ask in bewilderment. Are we being provoked or preached at by those who wish to corrupt us and undermine our traditional society? In the confusion, defensive reactions come quickly to the surface. We don't discriminate among what is being presented, but try to dismiss it by denouncing it as pornography; while its supporters, equally indiscriminate, will tend to support any challenge to the old ways of thought without regard to its value. Which is all exactly what one must expect when our roles and our manners and our received ideas betray us, when we don't know how to behave because we don't understand what is happening. We retreat to old positions, find them irrelevant, and dither about distractedly before we decide that it is worthwhile (even necessary) to think about our changed circumstances, try to sort them out and analyze the experiences being offered to us.

When it is sexual experience or comments on such experience that are offered, the reactions are particularly strong because sex has for so long carried an aura of the sacred and the taboo. Consider for a moment the problem of merely talking about it pub-

licly: what vocabulary shall we use? On the one hand are the
accepted public words, euphemistic, with an air of being medical
jargon, which distance what is talked about and detach it from
any emotional connection. On the other, the old private words,
when they are written or spoken in formal public context, carry
another sort of emotional charge. They have been clandestine and
shocking for so long that their atmosphere of obscenity can't be
easily shed. What's more, their connotations are not only pejora-
tive, but ambiguous.

Let us look at a current and powerful expletive, "mother-
fucker." Why is it so highly charged? Obviously it is an accusation
of incest, insulting to both mother and son. It also calls up all the
complicated unresolved prelingual emotions surviving from the
very early mother-child relationship. By so doing it suggests that
evil lives at the heart of love. It may also awake the terror of
engulfment by the overwhelming and frightening demands of the
powerful witch-mother; and, in addition, it evokes the rage en-
capsulated within desire which, from time immemorial, has declared the sexual act to be one of aggression: the Middle English
verb *fucken* means both to penetrate and to strike. Calvert Wilkins
suggests, in the Appendix on Indo-European roots in the American
Heritage Dictionary, that this may relate back to Old English
peig-, from which stem "foe" and "feud."

Hostility is thus implicitly stated to be a vital part of sexual
connection between human beings. This is surely one of the most
psychologically familiar and least talked about products of the
division between man's world and woman's place, between the
doers and the acted upon. Is this confusion of lover and enemy,
one wonders, aroused by the fact that sexual need is so great that
one is ashamed and angered to need anything so much? In any
case, what it comes down to is that it is not now possible to use
"fuck" as an ordinary word with the assigned meaning "have
sexual intercourse," because so many other connotations cluster
around it. The same holds true for the rest of the old words, and
when we try to use them—the vernacular, so to speak—to talk
about sex, we are constantly tripped up by the emotional implications they still carry, for all of them project the idea that the
sexual act is one between active, attacking male and passive female who can participate only by seeing herself as "the one who
gives." With the old words colored so distinctly by this view we

are hardly better off using them than the prissy and priggish euphemisms which form the alternative vocabulary.

Perhaps the passage of time will defuse some of these terms, but a deeper problem remains. Sex, in fact, *is* private. Like pain, it is felt inwardly and individually on the nerves, and is truly describable only in metaphor; which means that to speak veridically about sex calls for the techniques of fiction or, better, poetry, but not for abstract generalities. Case histories—that is, non-poetic, non-fictional detail—can be useful and informative, but inevitably they *feel* grotesque. This is not due merely to our human capacity for getting hung up in confusion and shame when we don't understand our relation to events, but also because something really is missing in them. That "something" which poetry includes and case histories don't is the value of the experience. By value I don't mean moral value, or religious value, or even aesthetic value, though that comes closer, but simply *felt* value, weight of emotion, and the connection of this emotion into the rest of one's life. It is the privacy of such valuing that, justifiably, makes us hesitant in talking about sexual experiences.

The solution is to begin not with private feelings but with public behavior; to talk not about the value of sex itself, but contrariwise of *how it is valued,* of current views on its importance, of the myths we have created around it. Then we are talking about social phenomena, and here discussion of general attitudes is not only valid but valuable. What limitations surround sexual activity? What things are exchanged for it, given up for it, linked into it? What do we expect from it? What kind of relationships accrete around it? Where does it stand in a hierarchy of pleasures, or does it rank as something more important and impressive than pleasure, a higher good? Is it considered a dirty little secret or a path to the sacred? Or both? This sort of question can be pursued profitably and, indeed, the conclusions we arrive at may throw some light on private feelings. Besides, such questions are highly germane to woman's role and place, both in her own view of it and to the extent that she is seen not as a person, but as an object of desire by men.

Our present society, I suggested in passing, values sex highly and learned to do so from Freud and the discipline he founded.

This is oversimplifying the situation drastically, of course, and one cannot make or accept such a statement without asking at once: Why is it that Freud's work has become so influential, laying the groundwork for a great many of our attitudes that don't seem related to it at all? To say that it is scientifically correct is not the answer, for no proof exists; the most one can do is to say that pragmatically it has proved very useful. Out of Freud's insights has grown a body of coherent thought which has opened our minds to new and productive ways of looking at our interior lives, just as the work of Darwin, and before him of Copernicus and Galileo, opened our minds to new ways of looking at the exterior world.

None of this work has gone undisputed scientifically, and certainly Freud's is the least accessible of all to scientific testing. It might very well be more appropriate to compare his legacy to, let us say, the masterful structure of thought raised by Thomas Aquinas than to the hypotheses of those we accept as scientists. Freud's pattern of metapsychology may not in fact coincide with the phenomena "out there" in what we call the real world, and his work may be discredited and superseded. But at present it has found its way into the "web of ideas," that "fabric of our own making," by which we interpret the course of events and the significance of our lives. We cannot ignore it and, in addition, it offers a handy schema for considering emotional data in relation to each other.

If we look at this history of ideas, we see that by the end of the nineteenth century thought had run far ahead of social behavior. The "irresistible revolution in . . . human relations" Susanne Langer speaks of was waiting to take off. In art, in literature, in physics, in chemistry, even in social theory, advances had been made which were ready to turn old patterns of life upside down. Freud was part of the revolution of his time just as were Einstein, Renoir, Chekhov, Ibsen, Kelvin, Durkheim, Max Weber and many others. A new pattern was being perceived and conceived, and when the First World War broke the old molds, the change spread across the Western world more swiftly than any since Napoleon's time, more permanently than any since Luther's. All of these innovations in thought, perception and behavior were part of a long continuing process and were underwritten by the most far-reaching change of all, that in the means of production. Not that they all fitted together, of course, or that they were equally opposed to past ideas or challenged them in the same way. No revolution ever overthrows everything. Among Freud's ideas were some that were astonishing and productive of a real *bouleversement* in thinking; others fitted prevailing opinion and thus made more convincing the revolution implicit in the first. The modifications in thought and in feeling that arose during the early years of this century were great, significant—and overdue.

One way that Freud's thought fitted earlier patterns was in its emphasis on the masculine side of things, for he drew his material —naturally—from the world he knew, still very much man's world. More has been made, however, of his alleged hostility to women and his support of male dominance than is at all justified by the full scope of his work. Freud was a humanist who never denied women their human potential, and it is clear from his case histories that he saw the difficulties they faced in the social conditions of his time. Some of his more general hypotheses have indeed been used as slogans by those who oppose women's efforts to change their role; but to Freud (we should remember) his hypotheses were just that. It is his followers who have sometimes taken them as iron laws of behavior.

Another effect of his work has been less widely noted but is, I think, much more important. Freud's insistence on the naturalness and the universality of sexual drives stands in opposition to the inhibiting and inhuman laws of a world that, masculine or not, was becoming increasingly *mechanized*. While connections with the physical world were being lost elsewhere, Freud helped to break down the barriers which had been raised between men and women and their own bodily nature. His aim was to help his patients see the wounds that troubled them as caused by objective, historical events which had been wrongly invested with irrelevant emotion, and, at the same time, to restore to them the ability to feel honest physical pleasure. Sex is an activity in which we use, command and triumph through our bodies. Freud was as anxious to prevent tormenting mental activity from crippling bodies as he was to help bodily organs discharge their tensions and relieve minds from fretful strain. He understood well the strains that civilization and its discontents laid upon human beings.

In the world as we know it today there are not many activities other than sex which make intense physical demands and confer great physical rewards of relief and ease. In losing the world of the past, from which all our metaphors have been taken, we have lost the processes that underlay them. Deepest of all in the child-hood of mankind lay the Great Hunt, in which men were both pursuers and prey. I have talked a little, earlier, of how it awoke and fed man's imagination. The marvelous magical cave paintings and engravings are the outward legacy our earliest ancestors left us of their world, full of wonders and terrors, darker and brighter than ours can ever be. Did they leave an inner legacy, too, of a range of possible feeling from terror to ecstasy, a stretching of the nerves that has not yet atrophied? Certainly the Great Hunt became much more than a search for food. Its imperatives entered every other phase of life, including the sexual, for everywhere in the paintings we find sex symbols, especially the female vulva, painted or carved to invoke fertility among the herds who were worshiped as well as hunted. Science and technology began here, too, as tools and weapons were chipped and flaked ever more expertly. Meanwhile the mythic surround of the hunt, as recorded in its art where we recognize shaman-priests, and even earlier in the ritual burials of animals and men, gave birth to religion and to ceremony. In one of the deepest and least accessible caves of the Pyrenees can be seen the heel marks of dancers more than ten thousand years old, witness of the celebration of some mysterious rite in that sanctuary. And for the individual, the craft of hunting and the sheer physical skill that had to be learned and used again and again must have brought the hunter unimaginable delight in his own bodily prowess and his intellectual knowledge of his prey—as well as the immediate reward of hunger sated.

Well, this is gone. The pleasures of hunting, faded and artificial as they are by comparison, still enchant men today, but they have lost their seriousness. The very end of this ancient joy was set down in Faulkner's wonderful story, *The Bear,* and formed a background for Turgenev's *Huntsman's Notebooks.* Now that sun has set. No more, either, do we break horses. We don't put out to sea in cockleshell craft whose handling requires enormous re-sources of skill and strength; or to be exact, we do so only for fun and stay home in bad weather. We don't handle plows, or the oxteams or horses which used to pull them, or sow by hand, or harvest in a moving line of scythemen, singing together to keep the rhythm constant. We don't fly falcons we have trained, or hunt the whale with hand-flung harpoons, or the buffalo with bow and arrow. Machines work for us. Our brains are active, our bodies acted upon. And yet it is through our bodies that we feel. Part of the value that we place in the act of sex is because it is an *act*.

And an act which is felt intensely, sparking terror, granting ecstasy. Even when it is performed in a context of comic pleasure, its intensity makes it serious *per se,* in the private, interior world. Though its value may change outwardly, sex is protected from too great a loss of seriousness by the physiological intensity of orgastic relief. This unique implosion of joy sets sex off from all other bodily pleasures. As these have faded in intensity, they have fallen toward the condition of sport because they have lost their original purpose of survival: the hunt is no longer a matter of life and death; sowing and the harvest may mean famine or plenty, but not to industrial man. Success here is either trivial, distant, or taken for granted. Any sport which still retains an actual element of danger, on the other hand, develops a mystique; the more dangerous the sport, the more compelling its myth. The popularity of skiing and the compulsive devotion to surfing surely owe much to the fact that one's own expertise and daring are called on fairly frequently to save one's skin and possibly one's life. Drag racing and flying replace animals with machines, but still offer some of the challenge of danger and the reward of surviving by one's own skill. To say nothing of the bullring.

Just the same, none of them can match the intensity of reward that our ancestors derived from their triumphs over nature, because even the most dangerous sport lacks the life-and-death seriousness of a struggle in which one's existence hangs in the balance. Sport involves *chosen* encounters with risk, not necessary ones. Today the edge and savor of real peril is rare and the desperate need to triumph or die is absent. The real dangers we face today are quite different. They are so huge, so out of control by any one person, that instead of being challenging they become paralytic. Conversely, the risks that shadowed life in the past could (at times) be engaged in hand-to-hand combat, and when the outcome was favorable, the joy it conferred on the winner was of a very high order. He had won more than a game.

When in our time a man knows himself to be doing more than playing a game (whether he "knows" it rightly or not), when he confronts a real, definable risk calling for physical skill to surmount it, the pleasure he receives from winning his bout with danger climbs toward the old highs. Many pilots of World War II were more than half in love with their jobs. There was a saying at the time that, in the Air Force, flying replaced sex as topic A. "I'd rather fly than eat," was another frequent observation. Now some of this pleasure was certainly neurotic and abnormally aggressive. Men were given a license to kill. Old unconscious rages were freed, old revenges sought against enemy surrogates in long gone feuds. Planes were seen as phallic symbols and flying, for some, was an openly erotic delight. Today, a generation later, when we are not so sure that the whole wasn't, after all, a bitter game, a whole cat's cradle of Catch-22s, a great deal of disapproval gets into our judgments of those heroes of yesterday. But when we judge them in a context which takes in memories of Hiroshima and Nagasaki and Dresden, and the horror of unopposed bombing raids in Vietnam, we are introducing a component of morality which was not present at that time. We may certainly think that the pleasure the flyboys found in their job was not just excessive but unhealthy; but we have no right to say that it wasn't pleasure, or to decide how much came from working out aggressions, how much from distorted sexual drives and how much from proper pride in one's own abilities. One thing we do know is that it was both serious and intense. In this way it matched the experience of our ancestors as very few other activities do today—except for sex.[7]

The value of sex, then, is enhanced because it remains capable of giving intense physical pleasure in a world where other bodily activities have lost a great deal of meaning. Just as women's skills, once so vitally important to feeding and clothing mankind, have deteriorated into hobbies, with needlepoint replacing the spinning wheel, so men's skills and prowess have degenerated into sport. They have become adult play: leisure-time activities which imitate the realities of work. For children, such play is a necessary part of learning to live. In maturity it is a substitute for living.

Now, this is not the whole story, for play can rise toward a very different condition, toward a new and life-giving seriousness if it approaches and blends into art. This is happening in a number of professional sports: they are the real pop art. Craft, connoisseurship and dedication mark them out as being true art, in which the audience participates in a communicated, jointly felt experience. What's more, their practitioners are rewarded for their abilities by being paid—that is, they make a living, or survive, by means of their physical expertise. For them, sport is what its ancient forebears were, a matter of life and death. They live by it.

But we must stop to differentiate here between professional sport and amateur sport. Writers like George Plimpton and John McPhee are well aware of how significant this difference is—and so are the members of their audience. The whole tension of Plimpton's amusing books comes from the question they pose as a premise: What happens when an amateur wanders into the artist's world? His books explore these worlds by exploiting the daunting experiences of the amateur, clownish, incompetent and foolish, among the serious professional players. Professional sport, tending toward art, is watched and experienced vicariously by the rest of us, just as drama and the dance are. The reward it offers is the reward art offers: catharsis produced by an imagined sharing in some action, some ritual, some emotional crisis that is beyond our own capabilities. Art is an extension of life. Amateur sport is quite different in its emotional effect. It is a do-it-yourself triumph, achieved if you can, as you can, within your own limits and without transcending them. It is not art but instead the historical descendant of the work and the work skills of yesterday, its rewards gained by dogged personal persistence, while professional sport is rising toward the condition of ritual and the expression of public emotion. For most of us who are not artists, there is only one kind of physical transcendence within our reach, and that is sexual pleasure.

Our high valuation of sex today is greatly influenced by this physical background: in a world where other bodily satisfactions have lost their sharpness, it remains. But there is a social reason too. The narrowing of the world of physical satisfaction as modern man withdraws from his contact with nature has been paralleled by another phenomenon which we have noted before: the dwindling in the variety and extent of personal relationships and social bonds. We need not dwell again on the rise of the nuclear family and the distance from relatives which social mobility produces, on the fact that couples have replaced clans, big houses and tight-knit village communities. But we might recall that the most drastic effects of these changes are very recent, with the result that social isolation both is, and is felt to be, at unprecedented heights. A world in which one was born connected and placed solidly is just around the corner of the past for many people. It was often stifling, but it was comprehensible, narrow but supportive. Its American form was idealized in Thornton Wilder's *Our Town*. Ronald Blythe has recently documented life in an East Anglia English village in *Akenfield*.[8] Laurence Wylie has described two French villages in absorbing detail, both Chanzeaux in Anjou and Peyrane in the Vaucluse.[9] Two Hungarian ethnographers, Edit Fel and Tamas Hofer, have produced an equally detailed and loving study of life in the village of Atany as it was lived till just yesterday [10]—and these, of course, are only a handful of the works available. They tell us how, in the ongoing old cultures, patterns of community living adapt themselves to changing external circumstances, how old connections grip and hold. Age grades of adolescents, in France and in Hungary, become the groups of young bachelors who are bound together by the army service they do at the same time, and by the year of jovial licensed freedom they spend before it, at parties, in taverns, playing tricks on the girls they will come back to marry. Families expect to fulfill work obligations for cousins and neighbors, and to receive help in return for tasks they cannot do alone. Church ceremonies establish ties between in-laws, godparents and godchildren, which are formal and binding. A widowed old woman may choose to live alone in a peasant village, but the pattern provides that a grandson will come in every morning to make up her fire, that a daughter-in-law will visit during the day, that she will meet friends of sixty years' standing at church on Sunday and have a good gossip with them afterward. The pattern doesn't always work, and those who turn against it may find themselves isolated, but the pressure it puts on people is toward connection.

In urban industrial society these wider bonds to the community have all but vanished; and we might note that they are non-sexual bonds. The sexual connection, that is, is emphasized by the loss of other social ties just as sexual experience is emphasized by the dwindling of other bodily pleasures. Even the ties of family within the small nuclear household are slacker than they were, for families endure as units for shorter times and the frequency of meeting between adult children and their parents, or between brothers and sisters, has also been affected by social mobility. "You Can't Go Home Again," wrote Thomas Wolfe a generation ago; today, most of us have no homes to go to. The past of childhood is swallowed up in twenty or even ten years. Of course, we still form day-to-day friendships, work relationships and other social bonds, but they tend to be unstructured and easily changed if we compare them to the community and kinship ties of the past. Our current connections with our communities, indeed, are just as apt to be hostile and felt as unpleasant compulsions (taxes, the draft) as they are ties of local patriotic participation.

For us today, then, the relationship between one man and one woman is becoming the one that sets norms of feeling and behavior. In it is found the greatest, the almost unique, source of physical pleasure—sex, while around it the context of life has been impoverished by the loss of many other affectionate but non-sexual ties, in which warmth was exchanged in other ways from one person to another. Even when devotion was replaced by irritation, a sense of belonging and of obligation remained. One might rebel against a family, but the family was there. One might leave a village for a new life in the capital city or across the sea in America, but in the back of one's head one carried the possibility of going back some day, out of strangeness into familiarity. In a world full of strangers, how can one count on friends? Only the other member of the couple remains within the reach of responsive emotion. Even the consolations of religion are less sought in communal worship and ritual and more and more become goals to be searched for and valued by each man as an individual. No wonder that the certainty of sex, of instant warmth, instant connection, instant pleasurable feedback, comes to be an emotional touchstone for all the rest of life.

This is easy to understand. An unforeseen danger in the situation is that sex, in gathering such significance to itself, may become *too* important, overwhelming, frightening. I suspect that this is already happening and that what is called the sexual revolution is in part a turning away from traditional sexual relationships because they are becoming too demanding.

CHAPTER 19

Let us roll all our strength and all
Our sweetness up into one ball,
And tear our pleasures with rough strife
Through the iron gates of life. . . .

Andrew Marvell
To His Coy Mistress

DESPERATION IS NOT NEW. Our present concentration on sexual pleasure is the end product of a long romantic tradition which declares passion to be the climax of emotional experience. This romantic view has gained in plausibility as other pleasures have ceased to be central to our experience: physical skills are less necessary, communal support for the individual less frequent. The romantic attitude fills the gap by emphasizing the value of individual feeling. But how can feeling be evoked? We know that pain and threats are certain methods of awakening fear and distress. Is there a certain method of providing pleasure?

The orgastic pleasure which is the culmination of sex offers itself as the obvious answer. Today we tend to see sexual pleasure as the way to transcendent, self-validating experience, mystic knowledge via the body; and we have mortgaged our emotions to achieving deliverance by this door from the doubts and dilemmas of everyday life. The difficulty here is not with sex, which can indeed dissolve our unhappiness and dissatisfaction with other realms of life, but with our approach to it. The romantic tradition, asserting the incomparable value of passion, cuts sex off from the rest of life and invests it with a mythical status, universal and eternal beyond the modifications peculiar to any culture. Passion, it declares, is the highest good. The other view of the world, the classical tradition, is ready to comment on this attitude: it warns us that great expectations invite disappointment, that there exists a marred human world where it is perilous to neglect reason and proportion. Overinvestment of emotion, in this view, is not only the enemy of satisfaction, but the road to madness.

I have suggested before that (as is natural) many of our present attitudes represent reactions to the immediate past. Emotional reactions are never simple. Our view of sex is not just a swing to the other end of the pendulum from the ideas of Victorian morality. It also continues and incorporates some of those ideas. The differences are easy to see, the similarities less so. Thus, Victorian morality suppressed the discussion of sex and easy access to it for all but those dominant males who found prostitution a satisfactory form of pleasure. We have ended that. But it's also perfectly obvious that suppression heightened the value of sex, and this we certainly have not ended. Now, a good deal of nineteenth-century literature and customary thinking was based on the assumption that sex was evil—that the whole ordinary process was a kind of grand perversion. This is an easy-to-see difference from our current view, and it, too, is over. But a corollary went with it and had effects which linger on. For the equation "Sex is evil" invited the believer to reverse the judgment and say, "Evil is somehow connected with sex." Freud's work was devoted to disproving the equation, but liberating as it was to thought and expression, it has not entirely wiped out the underlying set of emotion.

Today no rational man would declare that sex is evil, but in a curious way we still find in sex the emotional tug that such a scheme of thought sets up. For "evil" is powerfully tempting, and when sex is put on a level which makes it as tempting (whether by forbidding it or by emphasizing its emotional rewards), the two feelings tend to blend. Evil is what we want to do but don't dare, have been told (and agree) is wrong. Evil subverts the universe of law. Evil is revolution; from Lucifer's to Lenin's, it throws down the mighty from their seats, exalts the willful child and sets him where his wishes rule others without their consent. Evil is what society can not allow: the complete swamping of the real world and the necessary social connections between real people by inner desires. I want to suggest that our valuation of sex, our overvaluation of what it can do for us, expresses more overtly the deeply buried connection between the pleasure of sex and the megalomaniac enforcement of omnipotent power as dreamed by

every infant which the nineteenth century acknowledged by suppression, though it is a connection much older than the nineteenth
century. At the level of our Christian symbols, the child's dream
of power represents original sin. The fall of man is symbolized
by Adam's yielding to the temptation of seeking such power. As a
result, he was driven from the Garden of the Golden Age.

What I am saying is that it is a good deal harder to decouple
the two drives of desire—for sexual pleasure and for power—than
appears on the surface; and the greater the investment of emotion
in sex, the harder it becomes. "Make love, not war," reads the
slogan of the flower-children, and the play on words is charming.
But present in the offer of alternatives is an expression of the sort
of dichotomy that narrows the world and reduces experiences to
these two components, matched in struggle. There really is more
to the world than that, and if sex is presented as the only way out
of our troubles, we are putting an unrealistic load of hope on it,
for we are asking a private happiness to cure the ills of society.
Moreover, as the connotations of aggression which cling to the old
sexual vernacular make clear, anger still mingles with affection in
the sexual act itself. Can sex cure aggression if it is contaminated
with it? (Am I taking a joke too seriously? But jokes as good as
this one are not falsehoods. They are alternate approaches to
customary views which are advanced "in play" so that they can
be considered without putting too much pressure on the situation.)
In short, whether we confuse sex and evil or see sex as a means
for healing evil, we are overinvesting emotion in it and asking it
to do more than is possible in the general course of events.

Let us glance back at the other psychosocial relationship which
invites this sort of overinvestment of emotion, that between
mother and child. One result of the unusual American situation
which isolates mother and child for more than 90 percent of the
time was (you will recall) a good deal of anxiety on the part of
the mother. Much more than women from other parts of the
world, the New England mothers who were interviewed on their
child-raising practices confessed to worrying about their ability
to bring up their children properly. The more they were told that
this was the central act of woman's role and the most vital of their
duties, the less did they feel sure of being able to carry it off.[1]

The analogy leaps to the eye. Overemphasize the significance of sexual experience—which means to emphasize it beyond the intensity most people are completely certain they can rise to—and you invite anxiety, anxiety which feeds on doubts and lack of self-confidence and contributes to them in a vicious circle.

A second result of overinvesting emotion, we learned from Kenneth Keniston's study of alienated young men, is that the devouring mothers who had projected their hopes and desires onto their sons were driven to ask for more than could be returned to them.[2] A satisfying companionship was impossible because they wanted more, identity instead of mutuality. This can also happen in sexual relationships. A partner who tries to lose himself in such a pairing seems to the other member not so much to be giving up his own identity as asking for the lover's. That is hard to grant; and when the response is felt to be inadequate, unsatisfied greed is added to anxiety: highly unpleasant emotions to encounter where one had been told to look for pleasure! But both can arise, as we have seen, in situations where human relationships gather about themselves disproportionate feelings of hope and obligation.

This fear of others because they not only give emotion but ask a return, this feeling of connection as obligation, haunts our era. It seems to be part of the background of schizophrenia. But if, in order to avoid it, we reject the overinvestment of emotions in others and find danger in vicarious living through others, we should be careful not to equate these perilous commitments with a sense of shared, imaginative participation in the joys and difficulties of others. And we should not go on, out of mistrust but in the name of equality, to declare that everyone has the obligation to do and to feel everything himself. No doubt each of us has a right to test, taste and try life. At a time of shifting values and changing experiences like today this sort of experimentation can be very valuable. But until men become immortal, we shan't have time to try everything out fully enough to achieve real knowledge. We are still going to have to choose among experiences and trust others to do some living and feeling for us as well as for themselves, while we live in part for them.

In the past, class distinctions and the division of humanity by its skills and their attendant roles, plus the sheer meagerness of the provision which man's environment could offer him, enforced participatory living and the sharing of experience: ritual joined with art to interpret common values, ceremonies communicated symbolic meanings. Today our command of the means of production leads us to believe that, one way or another, we ought to be able to have everything material that we want. Industrial society encourages us to want more and more. Wanting and getting become habits, and leisure to enjoy what we have grows rarer. Owning more things, we own them less because we buy them ready-made and do not possess them through the process of shaping them to our needs and taste. At the very time that our loss of contact with the natural world has diminished the pleasure we can find in bodily activities, our supposed control over it invites us to demand a share in all that's going.

It is not unlikely, I think, that this combination of circumstances is related to the increased use of drugs. They are not simply a way to escape from an unpleasant world, though they are that. But they also offer in exchange a world of vivid experience which does not tax the dreamer by asking a real emotional response from him. Of course it is actually an isolated world inside one's own head, but it doesn't feel like that, for fantasy effectively takes the place of the imaginative understanding of reality which gives life its emotional value: the phantoms one encounters seem realer than the people one meets in the dim world of actuality. Thus, drugs offer an answer to the sort of amorphous desire for experience which is an analogue to what the psychoanalysts call "free-floating anxiety." Take a trip (they say) and have some free-floating experience, a do-it-yourself life, and, at the same time, avoid the menace of intimacy with those actual folk who exist outside one's dreams and can make demands.

Meanwhile the world of material riches which seems to promise so much is also very precarious. Dreamlike, fairy-tale-like (and thus not so different from the drug world), it offers to grant our wishes and shows us, simultaneously, the ruin which lies in wait if we cannot curb our desires. A future of unimaginable change hangs over us, a kaleidoscope of possibilities that runs from the death of the planet to a planned, controlled universe which has become "man's world" in quite a new sense. This heightening of the potential for change with its accompanying threat of strangeness and loss underlines our urge to seize the day. We shrug off the uncontrollable, unimaginable future and demand to have our wishes now. Add this temporal urgency, then, to anxiety and greed and a sort of sullen determination to have what is one's *right*, which, in the case of sex, is felt to be not just an opportunity for experience, but for ravishing delight. Like Marvell three centuries ago, we long to make the sun stand still but, despairing of this, we swing to the opposite end of the spectrum of feeling and find ourselves beset with the need to make it run.

This kind of thing can get to be too much. We are reaching the stage where any kind of enjoyment, but particularly the orgastic pleasure of sex, is being presented both as a duty to one's normality and as an achievement, but not as a natural, casual happening. People worry about their ability to please their partners and, worse, they worry about their own capacity to enjoy sex. Are their feelings commensurate with those that are represented on the screen or described in fiction? Do they respond with the proper frisson to nudity on the stage—which would surely not be set before them unless it was supposed to give them quite a thrill? If not, whose fault is it? This is such a simpleminded reaction that, on the face of it, it's funny. But the grander the poetry, the more baroque the novelist's treatment of sex, the more wildly Rabelaisian the comedy, the more often do ordinary human beings find themselves wondering uneasily whether they are not missing something that everyone else enjoys.

What are the effects of such reactions likely to be? No doubt a little living helps most of us to shrug them off or at least to keep them in proportion. But in those they continue to plague, they produce anxiety, guilt, and hostility to any other person involved —all of which make pleasure even harder to come by. Anxiety is asphyxiating. One knows that something is wrong but doesn't know how to fix it. Guilt suggests that what's wrong is wrong internally, right here, that there's something abnormal about one's own reactions. Abnormality in our world is something to hide, particularly from people one doesn't trust. And how can one trust the partner one has failed, the one who has been witness to the failure? The threat of this in a less-than-solid sexual relationship is an invitation to fake the proper feelings if one can't really experience them; and the more one fakes, the more one grows ashamed and guilty and sinks into isolation, the less one dares risk the attempt to lose a devalued self in true enjoyment. Here is the dark side of sex as bodily pleasure, for the old rules of physical skills assert themselves: one can't play tennis well if one is conscious of how one should move, or dance well till the body is forgotten; and, in Japan, archers studying Zen are traditionally instructed to forget the target. "Failure" at sex not only alienates one from one's immediate partner, from the surrounding culture and its current values, but from one's own body; and *that* can open or deepen a split in the inner world which is hard to heal.

The reported background of couples whose sex life is badly disturbed, which William Masters and Virginia Johnson describe in *Human Sexual Inadequacy*, documents these general remarks of mine. The theory behind the therapy they offer those referred to the Reproductive Biology Research Foundation in St. Louis is that men and women need to break the habit of desperate striving for orgastic pleasure which (say Masters and Johnson) is preventing them from reaching it. "Fear of performance" holds these anxious couples in its grip. Husbands who have suffered from impotence "break out in cold sweat as they approach sexual opportunities," while wives of these men "are terrified that something they do will create anxiety, or embarrass or anger their husbands."

Women too find "grave self-doubts . . . translated into fears of performance." The replacement of the nineteenth-century view that women should not expect to reach orgasm is sadly often taken to mean that they must experience sexual climax in every encounter, and that the speed and intensity with which they do so is an important counter in evaluating their success as human beings. Masters and Johnson believe that "the popular magazines, with their constant consideration of the subject" have aroused "real fears of performance by depicting, often with questionable realism, the sexual goals of effectively responsive women. [A woman's] anxieties when she does not respond to the level of orgasm (at least a certain percentage of the time) are 'What is wrong with me?' 'Am I less than a woman?' 'I certainly must be physically unappealing to my husband,' and so on." [3] How tragically the need to please, built into the traditional feminine role, undermines pleasure!

The result is that both husband and wife begin to back away from the situation. Having overinvested their feelings in the promise of sexual pleasure and failed, they now withdraw their emotions out of fear of continued failure until "their emotional and mental involvement in the sexual activity they share with their partner is essentially nonexistent." And all the time our culture is busy assuring them that the door which is barred to them is the one that leads to the peaks of emotional reward.

With sexual partners more isolated than ever today, two against the world, the loss of trust in each other (or its failure to grow) is very corrosive indeed. On the one hand there lurks the fear of exposing one's weakness to one's lover, of enlisting his help in a process that one can't but expect to end badly; on the other lies the longing for what everyone else has and values so highly, but this longing is mingled with self-contempt: not having it is one's own fault. Together these destructive feelings lead in a spiral down to unconquerable mistrust and hopeless isolation. Then there is not much to do but try to get out of the situation, get over it, find a new partner. Inevitably, however, past doubts weaken the confidence with which one approaches a new pairing. Certainly divorce is preferable to being tied to a husband or wife one hates and fears, living out a life of fury and frustration. But, overall, the result is to increase the individual's feeling of existing in a world of flux, a world of strangers, a world where the future is unpredictable, a world where one has had a chance at the prize and has missed. The treatment Masters and Johnson describe seems to work out less as emphasizing the pleasure of sex and more as deemphasizing the boundless depths of un-pleasure into which fear casts those who see themselves as failures. The result of their work is to return sex to a world of realistic pleasant experiences, to make it comfortable rather than passionate. One may feel that such an aim is in itself a bit unrealistic; but then, there is never any need to awaken passion. Sexual desire is perfectly able to do that without any help at all. What it can't do is make passion a viable sexual norm which everyone can expect to enjoy *ad lib.*

Even when things go well, there are special aspects to two-person relationships which make them rather tricky. In the first place, they invite testing. In larger groups, once a settled pecking order is established, challenging it means challenging the whole group. One may do that, of course, but not very often, and not without a powerful, driving reason. To challenge the domination of one other person is much easier. This is very often a healthy process which makes for a pleasant variety of responsibility and a satisfactory balance in which one partner is superior here and the other there, for the sort of reciprocity found in good marriages. But any balance at all, even the agreement to continue a contest, depends on mutual trust. Before one person can yield willingly to another, enough knowledge and enough faith must exist between them for the one who takes second place to believe that it is not a permanent or a degrading place, that his views will still be heard, that his turn will come around in other circumstances and give him another chance to see his wishes fulfilled.

The paradigm of such mutuality, the love relationship between mother and child, is built both on trust and on testing. The child who begins as a complete dependent grows by trying his strength, his newly learned skills and his increasing knowledge against the limits set by his mother. He is yielded to through love and learns to trust the love that yields and yet continues to ask more, always new, until he can stand alone. Out of this process grows not only love but mutual respect, the sense of the other person's needs and of his existence as an individual. Without the contest, the child would never learn autonomy. Without the trust learned through love, he would never dare use his autonomy to act in the world.

Adult two-person relationships, including sexual relationships, are bound to include an element of contest, but they must also include a minimum of trust, even if it is no more than a tacit agreement between the partners that their contests will not be mortal, that there will be some sort of limit and a certain enjoyment in the struggle, that an approach will receive a response. The battling couple in Albee's *Who's Afraid of Virginia Woolf?*, for instance, knew each other well enough to play their desperate game and trusted each other never quite to bring it to the horrid conclusion which the audience was invited to expect. One might take them as examples of a limiting situation, in which the largest possible amount of competitive hostility was just contained by the least possible amount of trust. At least we can say for our times that truly lethal marriages no longer exist. Those who stay together choose to do so, even if they seem to be bivouacking on a battlefield.

On the other hand, we must also say for our time that our social conditions make competitiveness more a part of pairing than ever before. Just because we live in a world of strangers, every casual encounter offers the chance of being something more. In village communities people were placed in a social scheme to begin with. Any individual found that there were some others who were close, while some were more distant, some hostile and some taboo. Later, when communities slackened into neighborhoods with their looser bonds, friendships were still apt to have a history of acquaintance-ship or of family knowledge. Now even this is disappearing. A couple that meets via computer-dating or as strangers in a singles' bar is in a very different situation from two people who have seen each other for years across a village schoolroom or a church, in the fields or the streets of a small community. One has to "present" oneself, come at the relationship being offered with a kind of "attack," in the musical sense. Meetings thus tend to become gambles, contests in which one fails or succeeds. Each participant competes to impress the other with his apparent command of the situation. The very lack of a social structure which would impose a form on such meetings makes them more, not less, demanding. And yet we cannot go back to the old communities with their complicated forms of acquaintanceship. We are known or not known, we know or don't know those we meet, in sharp definition. In such a world each of us needs a recognizable, clearly outlined and therefore simplified self to offer in such encounters. But a simplified self is a fake.

This difficulty exists in many other meetings besides those that may lead to sexual relationships, and it complicates them all. Even the best kind of simplified self never matches the truth and becomes, in time, a bore to maintain. But if one feels the need to find a partner to share in a terribly significant experience, and at the same time knows that one is holding something back and concealing a part of one's personality, once more one is being split and pulled two ways. It brings an extra feeling of doubt to already demanding circumstances.

And now women's new freedom to enjoy sex on the same terms as men has been added to the situation. On the face of it, it ought to make things easier and encounters more casual since they can be guaranteed not to produce unwanted consequences. If women really can be more like men, why shouldn't sex be friendly? Why are we not all relaxed, happy adults together, enjoying a shame-free, guilt-free earthly paradise, Eden before the fall? Why do obsessive ghosts still stalk Pornotopia, girls still imagine sex as a gift they make, men still pride themselves on the number of women they bring to climax? Isn't it all faintly, absurdly reminiscent of Prohibition Era boasts about the amount of liquor one could absorb? Why can't we achieve a condition of sensible comfort where what we call pleasure is only pleasant and not frightening?

Perhaps one day we shall, but hopes that such an easygoing state will be achieved quickly reckon without the world of mythology which surrounds and interprets the world of action. Our present attitudes are built, I have been arguing, on two myths: that of female weakness, and that of female power. The latter goes deeper, was born earlier and is universal. Male or female, we have all grown up in the shadow of the powerful mother. The myth of female weakness appears to be a reaction to this frightening figure; whether by origin or simply by present need, it holds the myth of female power at bay. But, once sex is detached from pregnancy, once women become as free to bed down where they choose as men are, the myth of female weakness is seriously challenged. With it are challenged the beliefs and behavior built up on its plausibility, and so is the psychosocial balance between the two myths.

Let us see how this challenge works out. The myth of female weakness declares that women must be protected because they bear and raise children. They need time to do this, and they need a special place, woman's place, where the contentious world does not intrude. A number of assumptions based on this fact then follow. If women are protected by being given a special place, they should stay there and not try to have it both ways, be free at one time and protected at another. In order to convince them of this, it is argued that child-bearing and -rearing are the central themes of woman's role, the overriding purpose of her life for which she is naturally gifted and (since myths don't mind being illogical) on which she must be continually encouraged to embark. She should look on the role of mother as her highest duty and her greatest fulfillment, and if she doesn't, sanctions will be applied. A woman who is contrary enough to prefer another role is odd. How odd depends on the surrounding culture. Traditionally, she became an outcast who could retain a place in society only if she embraced chastity and spinsterhood, thus giving up any hope of sexual pleasure for herself. Spinsterhood was an abnormal condition in the orthodox view, either piteous or sadly laughable. The only way that it could become acceptable or honored was by the sanctification of religious vows. But such vows are never entered into lightly. Now as in the past, they are the symbol of a very demanding role, dedicated and absorbing, which carries with it the obligation of close contact with sacred mysteries, a perilous and difficult way of life.

As we know, myths apply themselves universally because they declare that they are the repositories of truth. Now the myth of female weakness is being challenged by the fact that sex for women is no longer necessarily connected with childbearing: science, that highly respected authority, says so, and experience bears it out. Let us note that it is the universality of the mythic statement which is refuted, not the statement itself, for in all probability most women who do have children will continue to occupy a special and protected place for some period of time. Child-raising is a long-term proposition. Most children will be born in wedlock, and most of them will continue to be raised by their natural mothers, though (we may hope) with a bit more support from the community than they have been receiving lately. There is no reason to think that increased freedom for women to enjoy sex will have any direct effect on this customary and familiar procedure for raising children.

It's perfectly true, of course, that a woman doesn't have to be married to have a baby, but there's nothing new about *that*. The innovation lies in the fact that if she does want to, she can choose her own good time. But in our present social circumstances, raising a child alone isn't easy. Most of the problems young wives run into are due to their being too much alone, even with the help of their husbands. A single woman with a child is worse off, as any number of widows and divorcées can testify. Choosing to put oneself in this position isn't something that many women are going to do. Some who might like a child are aware that life without father is hard on the children as well as on the mother. Ideally, communal living of some kind offers a solution for it creates an acceptable substitute for the old, supportive extended family; but as yet, at any rate, it isn't easy to find such a setup, and many of those that exist are decidedly eccentric, or marginal, or shaky. Statistically, the woman who has, or who earns, enough to have a baby without having a husband and to be sure that the child will be properly looked after is so rare as to be unimportant, for until social change makes it possible for other women to follow her example, it may be publicized but it won't be plausible. The publicity may scare men, but it won't much influence other women.

In fact, I suspect that the weakening of the myth of female weakness is going to affect men's attitudes more dramatically than it is those of women. For one thing, a great many women are going to want to hang on to the myth. They were raised to believe that they had a special place in the world and that special characteristics fitted them for certain tasks and unfitted them for others. They want to be fulfilled by motherhood. They don't feel any need to storm the heights of power in a society as confused as ours. If they want jobs when the children are old enough to go to school, they assume that our economy will continue to be affluent enough for their work to be welcome. Woman's role has been widening fast enough for them, its restrictions have eased enough, and though they know that inequities remain, they don't feel them directly enough to want to take action. Out of habit and custom and because they believe in the myth themselves, they are content with the rate of change.

One can hardly fail to be aware that radical women are challenging this complacence very strongly. Women, they declare, have been conditioned into passivity and the acceptance of situations that can and ought to be changed. They are absolutely right, and no doubt some situations are going to be changed, but they are not going to be changed as fast, as easily or as directly as radical women want. Changing social situations is difficult and slow. Apparently simple circumstances ramify into others. What we want and what we can do are different things, and both are further complicated by the mythic assumptions we all make, radical and conservative alike, and take for granted. Even more important, our actions don't take place in a vacuum. We may think we are working in a straightforward way to a reasonable, clear goal—but do those around observing us understand the situation in the same way we do? All the things we do are judged by those who watch them in terms of what these actions seem to imply as connected behavior, as role-playing. Unfamiliar behavior is frightening to outsiders, it is difficult for the role-player who has to think it through and attack each step forcefully. A woman changing her familiar role has to be driven by her own ambitions and convictions and desires to gather the courage to make the change. Sometimes her own desires and ambitions act as blinders as well as spurs. Sometimes her pride in her own accomplishments cuts her off from others, to everyone's hurt.

Social change in the roles women play will of course continue to take place but, at the moment at any rate, Women's Liberation is operating less as active leadership in such change and more as an expressive demonstration that a good deal of change has already happened. How fast further steps that will affect more than a few women are going to be taken depends on how willing women are to tackle the unpleasant job of changing their image (including their self-image) and their behavior. They will do so only if they feel they have to. Many of them will continue to put up with treatment that radical women deplore (and deplore rightly) because they are used to putting up with things. The old tradition teaches them to get their own back deviously instead of through straightforward confrontation on issues, and this is a lesson that is hard to unlearn. Today's radicals have not yet made enough of an impact at mass level to begin to frighten people; but when they do, a lot of the people they frighten are going to be women—women who don't want to be thrust into a power struggle, who may sympathize with some of the goals of Women's Lib and envy their dash, but will nonetheless be ready to speak unkindly of them because, sad to say, they find that such remarks are pleasing to men and a policy of pleasing is still the better part of valor. The myth of female weakness is not only part of their conditioning: they cling to it because they know how to exploit it. For them, the fact that the pill relieves them of the burdens that the myth has helped them support in the past is no reason for abandoning it now. They will doubtless go on appealing to its protection as long as it remains plausible, and will try to keep it plausible in order to make this appeal.

For men the position is different. Not only is the decline of the myth frightening, but they can't control its acceptability to women. It is infuriating to men for women to take advantage of their special position at one moment and declare at another that they are men's equals—but, alas, this is exactly what the myth prescribes as women's behavior. *La donna è mobile;* women are fickle, unfair, unstable, and here they are demonstrating it while they declare their equality! Nor is this the whole story, for the argument that women have a special place and a special role is not based only on the myth of female weakness, but on the myth of female power too, on the pre-linguistic memory, buried beyond the reach of words, of the loving mother who gave and the threatening mother who withheld. The ancient powerful goddess stirs now in the new form of the woman who can choose sex as well as a man can and who cannot be confined to her special place by the threat of pregnancy. She claims equality, but is that really what she wants?

What men fear is, quite simply, that women will not stop at equality. Why should they not demand dominance? It doesn't matter that they deny this desire. The memory of the Mother Goddess recalls female power in action. Besides, women are role-changers, whether they admit it or not, because the mere existence of the pill undermines the power of the myth that enforced the old role. Role-changers can't be trusted to observe decent limits of action; no one knows where they will stop. I imagine, too, that a certain amount of unconscious guilt must get into men's fear that women won't be content with equality: were men content with it? No, they dominated women and enjoyed it. Why shouldn't they feel that deep, subliminal tremor which suggests that other people may like what they like and want it just as much as they do? As the myth of female weakness seems to crumble in their hands, they confront the myth of female power. What sacrifices will be demanded of them if women have their way? What do women want?

It's an interesting question. I mean that literally—it's more interesting than the answer, which is quite simple. Women want control over their own lives and authority or influence commensurate with their abilities in the external world. So does everyone else, i.e., men. Unfortunately very few people of either sex achieve as much of either compensation as they would like to have. That is the plain answer. The *question* is interesting because it implies, even asks for, quite different answers, and the implications tell us a good deal about what is going on in men's minds.

The first implication is that women won't be able to formulate an answer at all: that they don't know what they want, and are better off being given praise, presents and busywork by men. This is the nostalgic answer suggested by the fading myth of female weakness. The myth of female power, as we have seen, suggests the answer that women want to dominate men. This is so unlikely to happen that one can see it only as a projection of fear, the mythic fear that sees change as destruction. It arises because men do feel threatened—whether realistically or not doesn't matter— by women's new freedom. For if the female role is changing, at one pole of the relationship between men and women, man's role has got to take account of the change and adapt to it, so men feel the pressure to change, too, a pressure which they did not inaugurate and must consequently, predictably, resent. To change and reprogram the connections between feelings and actions is always difficult, but one puts up with it better if it suits one's own book instead of one's partner's. Nor can the change take place only in private, in the dark interior of the self. It must also be expressed publicly, in stance and behavior. Machismo, the exaggeration of virility, must surely often arise as an irritated reaction to the imposed need to change. "Women, you are asking too much!" it declares; at the same time it may serve as a shield for doubts, a gesture to save face when one knows the trend is really running the other way.

A third answer is offered, too, also revelatory and analytically useful. Edward Grossman's article, "In Pursuit of the American Woman," which appeared in *Harper's Magazine* for February 1970, supplies an example of this reply and brings us back to where we started; for Grossman believes that what women want is orgastic pleasure: "bigger and better orgasms." "Don't men?" one might ask in surprise. "Isn't that what Pornotopia is all about?" But Mr. Grossman has worked out a particular version of the myth of female power which persuades him that women are actually more capable of such pleasure than men. George P. Elliott contributes a story, "Femina Sapiens," on the theme of the woman who can't be satisfied by men, to the March 1970 issue of *Esquire,* so clearly the idea is in the air. In this new interpretation, we find old beliefs put forward: "Females are different from males," writes Grossman. But now this traditional idea is used to shore up a novel conclusion: "When at last unencumbered by tradition, unperverted by custom, their sexuality is stronger, more various and a good deal less comprehensible than male sexuality." [4] So once more the dark, mysterious goddess appears, bearing uncontrollable power. In Elliott's version, she has learned how to reproduce herself by parthenogenesis, and is considering doing away with the entire male sex.

The contributions of these intelligent gentlemen illustrate the fact that alterations in woman's role, activities and attitudes are more likely to arouse male fears and inhibitions than they are to encourage the cheerful sexual romps that one would suppose woman's new freedom to produce. Grossman, for instance, finds that "a universe ordered on the Pill, on the effective junking of marriage and the family, and on the homosexual contracting of liaisons right through an eventful middle age, is ugly, whereas a former universe ordered on the condom was less ugly, more hospitable to playfulness, to grand passions and small comforts." Clearly one likes what one knows, and equally clearly "logical" men are willing to throw grand passions and small comforts into the same basket and to assume that the Pill means the end of marriage. It is easy to disagree, easy to point out that the "former universe" was based not only on the use of condoms, but also on the diaphragm, which even then allowed women to decouple sex and pregnancy. But this is not a situation where winning an argument matters one way or another. It is more important to note that men feel very much threatened by women's advance toward sexual freedom, and blow it up to remarkable proportions, than to argue over whether or not they are right to do so. For myths, as we have seen, don't yield to logic.

What comes out of this investigation is that when women ask for equality, men take them to be demanding domination. We can trace this back to the myth of female power in more than one way. Grossman, we saw, was at pains to point out that females are different from males. Indeed they are, physiologically. But why does the conclusion based on this obvious fact always state that women are therefore unable to react sexually, psychologically and socially the way men do? Why is "anatomy destiny," whether destiny ordains that women are subordinate to men (the old view) or, in this new and frightening supposition, superior? The idea that race affects the brain is no longer intellectually acceptable; organized anthropologists have just voted to condemn officially the last attempt to put forward this thesis. But we seem to be inevitably and hopelessly involved with the view that sex does create an impassable barrier of feeling, character and mind.

One reason is that an enormous structure of meaning has been built on the physiological fact that men have a penis and women do not. Psychoanalysis has set up a complex system which explains differences of behavior and attitude between men and women as occurring because of penis envy and the castration complex. This hypothesis obviously ignores social and cultural forces and rests on the simple bodily difference of penis or not-penis. More interesting is that it also ignores what women have: a womb, and the capacity to bear children. This is because, in Freud's view, the little girl is afflicted with penis envy when she first discovers that her brother has something she lacks, and this occurs long before she is aware that she has sexual organs of her own. Jealous of the male endowment, she assumes somehow that she once had a penis, too, but lost it. This gives rise to the idea of castration: she was naughty, so her penis was cut off. And this, in turn, both convinces her of an ancient, buried guilt which turns her toward masochism, and awakens the wish to have a baby in order to replace the penis.

Now this extraordinary fable was not as odd at the time Freud formulated it as it appears now. The background of his patients was one of unyielding male domination and female inferiority. The step by which a girl-child is assumed to want to be a boy-child was taken so universally and inevitably (we might remember Gwen Raverat's remarks on this in Chapter 9) that it was never questioned. And the fact that awareness of bodily difference was taken to occur as a discovery and a shock implies that everyone, adults and children, was heavily, impenetrably clothed. But if we consider this idea objectively, we find it rather hard to credit as a picture of life in primitive societies, where a good deal of nakedness is common, where sexual connection is not as taboo and private as in the West, and where birth is not private either. Yet if the hypothesis is to hold, it ought to hold here too. Men and women are just as different physiologically, and we are supposed to ignore social differences.

It will not come as a surprise, I am sure, if I suggest that penis envy is a myth. One reason to think so is that it bears the marks of originating on the male, not the female, side. Of course all of us, male and female, have felt menaced by the world, by other people, by uncontrollable events, by ignorance which traps us in doing wrong when we don't know it and so can't stop. We all substitute one goal for another if we are convinced that the first is impossible. Such feelings are universal; but the locus of punishment in the hypothesis put forward by penis envy and fear of castration is male. Which sex is frightened by this threat? Surely the sex which has a penis to protect. Only in the mythic world has a penis been attached to a woman (including the mythic world of those pornographic works which bestow an outsize, erectile clitoris on the female). Women know perfectly well they never had the things and, never having had them, don't fear a loss which is physically impossible. Of course little girls are as curious about physical differences as their brothers, but it is surely little boys who experience a thrill of fear when they discover what their sisters lack, who imagine the lack as being a loss, and who then assume that the loss was inflicted, by the big people who must be feared because they are powerful, for wrongdoing. Little girls have got used to their bodies long before they are capable of wondering about the curious, rather useful, but not particularly attractive extra bits which belong to their brothers.

Fear of castration, in short, is a male reaction projected onto women with a perfectly sensible purpose: protect yourself and keep women inferior. Your penis, which she doesn't have, is the sign of your superiority. Its lack marks women as inferior, and if they accept this inferiority, they will feel guilty for having done something wrong and having been punished, which will make them easier to deal with. What myth does such a map of the inner world recall? That of female weakness? On the surface, perhaps, but not at the source. For it begins by telling women that once upon a time, a magical, mythical time, they did enjoy this wonderful gift of a penis, but they lost it—through their own fault. It is not a protective myth in any sense, but rather a threatening one. It insists that this famous difference between men and women, with all its consequences and the destiny it foretells, is due to woman's misbehavior and it warns her never, never to try to regain the power she once held, in mythic time, when men and women were equal. It is a defensive male reaction to the fear engendered by the myth of female power. Women, it declares, you are unworthy, and unable to challenge men. Nature forbids it! And the sign of this taboo is what you lack.

What we have got here is a fascinating mix-up of myth and reality. A further analysis will shed some new light on how myths work and why they persist. Let us agree that the penis is a symbol of superiority and especially of power, male power. A very good symbol it is for autonomous activity, growth, strength and defiance. Now this kind of power is exactly what women's traditional role denies them. Their lack of a penis symbolizes equally well the passivity, dependence and patience of the character assigned to them. The penis, then, stands for the power that men have and women lack. On this basis, penis envy should symbolize women's desire for autonomy and authority.

But that isn't the way the myth works. Suddenly the symbol switches to become the reality, and the reality becomes the symbol. The fable of penis envy operates to deflect women's goals from the world of reality to the world of myth, and so to contain them. What women want, it maintains, is not independence or freedom, not real control of things in the real world, but instead the mythic power they can't have, the symbolic penis—which is suddenly not symbolic at all. Instead, power has become the symbol, and the penis is the real, secret desire of those who lack it.

Can symbol and reality properly replace each other in this fashion? Not in any logical system of thought. Either power is a symbol for the penis, or the penis is a symbol of power. One simply can't accept a situation in which each can stand for the other—outside, that is, of the special situation of sexual intercourse, which we shall come to in a moment. But, in general, to say that reality and symbol *are the same thing* is inadmissible. The fallacy arises, I think, from a dangerous tendency in psycho- analytic thinking to bring symbol and reality so close together that they begin to coincide, that the phrase "This stands for that" is elided into "This *is* that," at which point the direction of sym- bolization is lost. Psychoanalysis has brilliantly explored and eluci- dated the importance of symbolic thinking, has learned a great deal and certainly was a spur to the study of language, dream and myth. But analysts will mislead themselves and confuse their thinking if they forget what artists, writers and musicians learn as the foundation of their craft: that the symbol *represents* reality, but is not real itself.

In the external world of event, it is misguided to think that women's ambitions for authority and control over their lives can be dealt with via the fable of penis envy. This kind of thinking not only inhibits sensible, pragmatic responses to women's efforts to achieve full citizenship, it is downright provocative. Tell an ambitious woman that she doesn't really want to become a bio- chemist, or conduct a symphony orchestra, or reach the presidency of an insurance company, that what she really wants is to possess the male sexual member though of course she doesn't know it, and you will find yourself face to face with a woman who is not simply resentful of this gambit, but contemptuous of the sort of mind that would offer it for serious consideration. And yet good minds continue to bring it forth on the general level, as the two recent magazine pieces I have cited indicate.

What brings such a thing about is the extension to the rest of the world of the relationship between men and women which occurs during coitus. For there the power to achieve the miracu- lous release of orgasm does reside in the penis, there symbol and reality become one. There properly (though not inevitably) wom- an's desire for sexual pleasure replaces her ambitions for autono- mous action in the world. There a man doesn't have to say, "You want what I have, but it is mine, not yours. I can give it or with- hold it," because this is the very basis of the encounter. Here there is either meeting and mutuality or a struggle.

A struggle in which penis and power are indeed the same thing. Here a couple in contest can frighten each other most. Here trust is most needed and, because of the need, mistrust rises most easily. Here the quality of affection is always being tested and renewed—or ground lost to hostile and fearful retreat. And this, in our time, is where that part of the revolutionary changes in living that has to do with sex brings a new weight to bear. No longer can men introduce into this encounter the myth of female weakness, no longer can they be certain that they are more free to enjoy pleasure than the woman who shares the act, no longer do such meetings involve a man who lends his power and leaves and a woman who waits and is submissive because she has been taught that she is the one who is supposed to suffer. Now both are equal.

Except that, with the myth of female power unrestrained by that of female weakness, men fear that they may find themselves not equal but dominated. Female sexuality has always made demands on men, but now the demands are felt as increased. "Can I satisfy her?" a man asks himself. Now he can no longer answer that it doesn't matter all that much whether he does or doesn't, because she is the weaker vessel, constrained by woman's role as bearer of children to stay in her place and submit to her husband. Now if he can't satisfy her, *she* may pick up and move on. No longer can he forbid her to do this by the unanswerable argument that if she acts promiscuously she will have a child and no husband to help her and support her, because now it isn't true. She will have a child only if she chooses to do so. Therefore she will stay only if she chooses to do so. Therefore she must be satisfied.

To say that such dark thoughts shadow all matings is, of course, absurd. But it is the nature of dark thoughts to appear in those situations which are least secure and most anxious, and anxiety and change often go together. Woman's new sexual freedom appears to be a Pandora's box which has let loose new fears and doubts and has so far failed to bring with it any luscious bonus of greater joy, easier pleasures and simpler happiness. So far it appears to be putting greater weight on sex and heightening the emotions surrounding it.

What can be done? Perhaps a reduction in the emotional weight we attach to sex is indeed in order. If there is a new tendency operating to reduce the intensity which we concentrate on sexual activity and to see it more in terms of a delightful game, this may be very healthy. Then, with the passing of our old romantic estimates, we might be able to begin again. Then the pleasure of orgasm will still be great and joyful, but it will take its place in a gradient of other delights and lose some of the terrifying emotional significance with which we have invested it. If it remains unique in the quality of pleasure it can bestow, it need not any longer be thought of as a measure of personal esteem or success.

Even so, our daily round is not quickly going to become that happy version of the earthly paradise where healthy polymorphous activity sweeps neuroses and anxieties away. For that, we would have to trust each other; and until we are able to construct new social supports for our emotions and new behavior patterns that express the feelings we aren't yet sure we have, we shall find it hard to arrive at trust. Not impossible—we have had to build worlds before—but hard.

CHAPTER 20

Mythological patterns have to an extreme degree the character of absolute objects which [would] neither lose their old elements nor acquire new ones if they were not affected by external influences. The result is that when the pattern undergoes some kind of transformation, all its aspects are affected at once.

Claude Lévi-Strauss
The Raw and the Cooked [1]

BAD TIMES DIFFER from good times not merely in being more interesting, but also because they challenge us to rethink our relationship to reality—to those "external influences" whose shifts affect the "mythological pattern" with which we are familiar. From the moment when each of us is born out of comfortable, even-temperatured darkness into a world that assaults us with demands to look and see and think and act, we search for defenses. Very early we find the myths that our ancestors have made and hung like a tapestry of dream between ourselves and the rattling, thumping, unexpected universe of phenomenal events. The assumptions embodied in this mythology channel our ways of thinking, of judging, of acting in and on the world around us, and of communicating with each other both in words and in the language of behavior, the roles we learn to play.

Such patterns of feeling and thought seem very old; and indeed they *are* old in the individual experience of each of us. We learn them so early, many of them before we learn language, that in our minds they antedate the logic which grows out of language. They feel like instincts; and whether or not we are justified in calling them by that name, the early imprints of pain and discomfort, like the first tides of joy to flood our spirits, color our deepest moral and ethical decisions. These impressions, these bursts of rage and tides of comfort, form the fundamental stratum of emotion against which we shall ever after test our judgments. But such fears and longings are not private, they are common to humanity. Therefore on them we base the structure of society. Over that structure rears the superstructure of culture and concepts, always part myth, which rationalizes our social forms, directs our desires toward accepted goals and helps to protect our "instinctive" actions and beliefs from disruptive doubt.

Bad times change all this patterned world and, as Lévi-Strauss warns, "all aspects are affected at once." In the humdrum days of continuity, the world might be hard, demanding and ungenerous, but it was permanent. The myths endured. The old rules worked, the old cosmologies were credible and one generation confirmed them to the next. Then not only were fathers right, grandfathers were even righter. Then the sum of actions over a lifetime seemed to add up comprehensibly and produce the expected result so often that the essence of the whole process could be called wisdom. Now this is over and we live in a time of change.

As we have seen, a time of change often appears like a maelstrom of destruction to those caught in it. Even though what is being destroyed is not everything, but simply our own particular myths, it is frightening. Through the gaps in the pattern we suddenly perceive the terrifying world of the way things "really work," a world that seems mysterious, disjointed, unpredictable and therefore infinitely menacing. How can we understand it with the framework of meaning gone, gone with the old patterns we knew? How can we hope to control it if we do not understand it? All around us the old positive values are beginning to seem questionable or false. What we had taken for proper patriotism is suddenly transmuted into aggressive imperialism, purity is seen as selfish withdrawal from action. Loving mothers are accused of stifling their children. Fathers find they are no longer leaders to be loved and followed but enemies to be attacked or fools to be ignored. Sex becomes a competitive struggle. Like the sorcerer's apprentice, science sets off forces it can't control. Violence, anger and suspicion shadow every encounter. Our truths have turned to lies and trapped us in error or enigma. There are no more happy endings, only the shadow of the Apocalypse.

Shall we sit down, then, by the waters of Babylon and hang up our harps? No, even though despair may be tempting. I say this

294   ELIZABETH JANEWAY

not out of wishful optimism, but for far more practical reasons. Unlike many other societies, ours is committed to activism. Change has been built into our lives for a very long time, and though it may upset us, we know that we cannot get rid of it. Whether we like it or not, we have become conditioned to dealing with an environment, both physical and social, which changes greatly within a man's lifetime, and generations of men and women have already experienced this. We may complain and groan over "culture shock" and "future shock," but we are not peasants sunk in the cake of custom, and changes that would have reduced other societies to catatonic apathy are things that we understand we have to put up with. We have evolved a habit of trying to deal with events and an apparatus—science and the scientific approach—that works at least part of the time, often enough, at any rate, for us to turn to it "instinctively" in the face of new challenges.

This activist attitude is the necessary foundation for accepting change as something that can be dealt with. Of course it is only a beginning, for there is no guarantee that we shall in fact deal *sensibly* with events. In addition, our scientific approach will have to be wrenched round from its traditional concentration on physical events to make it suitable for dealing with people and their emotions; an allowance for human dignity and diversity had better be programmed into computer planning. It is certainly over-optimistic to say we shall succeed in living with rapid change, but it is only realistic to note that a great deal of effort is going into the attempt. The social sciences are trying to deal with actual, ongoing processes. Our schools are bad; everyone knows it, and there is increasing interest in making them better. Universities, local governments, and many businesses have had revolutionary demands put down in their laps and some of them are struggling manfully to cope with them. Young people are not simply talking about experimental forms of living, they are practicing them. Ironically many people who cry loudest and most desperately that things are in terrible shape are trying hard to change them; they predict disaster and work like beavers to hold it off. It's perfectly possible that disaster will overtake us, but one thing is certain—it will not overtake us because we are sitting down fatalistically and waiting for it to arrive. And because we are working to prevent it, we are bound to develop a new structure of mythology to justify and implement the work we are doing. For us too, for us now, "Doing is being."

This book was written as an effort to understand how social mythology—*any* social mythology—evolves and operates, for not only our actions but even our perceptions are affected by the web of ideas in which we live. The myths that define woman's multiple role and that grow out of it to affect man's world were chosen for investigation because they are old, they are pervasive, and they seemed to me sufficiently well-defined to be easily followed. At the same time, they are analogous to other mythic formulations and can therefore be taken as examples of how the whole process works.

An attempt to define myth established that it is bound up with emotion, with what we fear may happen and what we hope will come true, and that it therefore prescribes behavior to ward off the worst and produce the best results, in terms of accepted beliefs. What myths tell us about the world is not a description of the way things are, couched in the indicative mood, but instructions for action, imperatives to be followed on pain of "disrupting the order of the universe." Myths therefore exist in a state of tension, a permanent present tense. Though the emotional drives they reveal feed the springs of art, they cannot be criticized or analyzed in the same way as can works of art, because they remain attached to those who believe in them, representing unfulfilled and unresolved desires. They cannot be dispelled logically by being disproved but must be evaluated by methods that allow for their emotional content. At the same time, the fact that myths attract many believers proves that they cannot be dismissed as mere fantasies. They are related to reality through shared feelings and as a response to actual situations which call forth common reactions.

This relation to reality works two ways. Myths are, first, an attempt to explain the world out there to ourselves so that we understand what is happening and how we are involved in events; but they are also an attempt to manipulate the world so that what is happening can be changed or held at bay. They strive to interpret, to justify or to rectify the way things are, sometimes—illogically—all at once. In the community at large they do this by enunciating beliefs and general assumptions: Women are passive, men are active, women intuitive, men rational—and so on and so on. In one's personal surroundings they prescribe roles and the proper behavior that goes with them: Woman's role is to nurture children, to please men, to support activity but not initiate it. Woman's traditional role bars her from the seats of power. So, by analogy, we find that equivalent roles are taken to justify cutting off other subordinated groups from power. Myth supports the status quo (from which it arises) by calling on sacred texts, ancient wisdom and "things we all know—instinctively." At the same time it tries to satisfy the emotional drives that the status quo leaves unfulfilled. It is deeply ambiguous, caught between what is and what we want to come to pass.

Today the old myths about women are being challenged, not just by verbal assaults and direct efforts to disprove them but, more important, by social change that is undermining the old patterns. Women, who had been cut off for the past century from doing work of economic value (at least in the middle-class area that the myth was tailored to fit), are moving out once more into the world of activity. The place they occupied at home, during the generations and in the regions that "homes" existed, has been shrinking, and more and more women have been finding it too narrow for living. Fewer children are being born to today's families, medical science assures that many more will live than in the old days, and the fraction of a woman's life that must be devoted to child care is declining. Moreover, science has now made it possible for women to choose when to have children. As a by-product, their sex relations can be as free from consequences as men's.

All these changes are bound up in and contribute to an enormous process of overall social change. An easy and obvious statement; but it is vital (and perhaps not so obvious) to consider how social change affects individuals. It does so, I have tried to show, not just by direct confrontation but also by bringing the usefulness of old roles into question. Social change demands psychological change: the macrocosm affects the microcosm immediately. But the shifts don't stop there, for a structure of relationships exists in between the individual and society as a whole, and it is a structure made up of roles and preserved or implemented by role behavior. Change shivers the world, then, both at the large, general social level and also within the psyche which must try to evaluate the new situation and adjust to it. In addition, it threatens the personal side of life, the precious, unthinking trust and affection and assurance that one has learned to count on within old, habitual role relationships. It creates loneliness.

Role-changing and role-breaking make heavy emotional demands both on the central figure, the role-player, and on the others who form part of the relationship which shaped the role. As we have seen, these breakdowns in role are often very frightening to all those involved, and fright creates anger and hostility. Old roles are shifting fast. Former "minorities" are refusing to play the old games. To the other players (who were often unconscious that any game existed because the pattern was so taken for granted), this kind of refusal appears as a threat. "Instinctively" men react to women's desires to move out into the world of work by imagining that what they want most to do there is to compete with men; whereas, in fact, women are thinking much less of this than of their need to find a separate connection of their own with the economic sphere which our society declares is so important. Women had such a connection in the past when much valuable work was done at home. They would like to regain the self-respect that the possession of genuinely useful skills once gave them. Again, "instinctively," men react to the discovery and use of birth-control pills by imagining that women who are free to have sex when they want it will use their freedom to subject men to their own desires.

What they are afraid of is that the change in a role will not bring about a mere shift in the relationship between man and woman that the role was geared to, but a complete destruction of any relationship or a total reversal of it. The two joined myths of female weakness and female power, which once justified the place assigned to women in man's world, live on. But their base has been jeopardized by the change in woman's place that is occurring today. Women are asserting that they are no longer weak, while the myth that declares them strong still retains its old power to frighten and menace. The "instinctive" reaction leaps the bounds of likelihood and common sense to suggest that doing away with Woman's Place in Man's World will mean that the world will become woman's entirely, with men lucky to have a place in it at all.

Such mythic thinking is dangerous because it freezes frightened people in old attitudes and inhibits their ability to think about social change in creative ways. As we look at our world, we activists who have become habituated to riding out social revolutions, let us take note that the pattern whose "aspects are all affected at once" includes, first, the large social structure; second, the individual who exists within it and must try to cope with it; and, third and not least important, the personal relationships with other individuals that have made up his experience and given warmth and meaning to his existence. The quality of these emotional ties affects the hope, the freshness and the dedication that any human being brings with him into his relations with a changing world.

To the extent that we can accept the universal, if uneven, alteration in personal and in public life which is taking place now and see it as presenting demands but not as threatening destruction, we shall be better able to deal with it. If there is any hopeful purpose in the writing of this book, it is to promote such a reaction; to suggest that when change confronts us, we refuse to shrink away, overwhelmed by mythic terror and convinced that we are caught in a dilemma of destruction or status quo. If we can think objectively about our myths, we won't be so compelled by them and we will be more able to see change as a chance to try out new approaches to problems. Extreme statements, from left and right alike, are inclined to declare that change will mean destruction; which means that such statements are adulterated with some degree of mythic thinking. Of course we must take them seriously (as we take all mythology seriously) for what they tell us about the drive, the determination, the world view and the ability to react with others of those who make them; and when they are made by the powerful, we must assume that the proponents of these views are somewhat more able to act as they wish than are the revolutionary aspirants to power. But I believe we can judge these threats and promises most rationally if we learn to sort out the difference between the emotional expression of mythic imperatives and the logical advancement of a thesis or plan. I hope I may have contributed to this ability.

And yet—let me repeat—we shall never get rid of the social mythology that shapes and explains our world and directs our actions and reactions, whether it is the mythology of the establishment or of a counterculture. Mythology is like gravity, inconvenient at times, but necessary for cohesion. It forms a ground of shared belief on the basis of which groups of people can act together; and we need to be able to act together. Undoubtedly new mythologies, incorporating a varying amount of old dogma, are in the making now. A generation ago the "left" thought only in terms of politics; but now a whole pattern of culture, with its special music and literature and dress and attitudes toward life, is growing up within the old order. Its radicalism is cultural and social, not simply political. Nascent revolutions begin by being negative because they react against old values which have lost their force and relevance. Today's radicalism is, tentatively, beginning to set up some positive goals of its own. These are still confined to a rather narrow range of experience. We can hardly see this counterculture as a viable alternative to the old one unless and until it applies itself to the mechanics—technological, scientific and economic—of running the social machinery. But in its emphasis on humanistic values and the need for closer communion in ways other than sexual and within groups other than those of the family, it has already had a healthy effect on the isolating patterns of the old way of life. To the extent that it deflates the almost lethal overemphasis on sex as the only meaningful close tie between human beings, it will increase the possibility of new kinds of relationships which may enrich our lives just as woman's move out into the world of work produces wider friendships and ties to others. Again, these are still uncertain experiments in living, but they point toward greater diversity.

How much we need diversity! And how much, particularly in bad times, we need the flexibility of mind that goes with it. A living social mythology which can connect authentically with a world of change can't be static. Can we build the possibility of change into our world view so that our superstructure of belief ceases to be a pattern that takes no account of time and becomes a process taking place in time? I don't know (obviously) and neither does anyone else, but it is worth thinking about as a goal. It would mean an effort to increase diversity, variety and pluralism in thinking and behavior, "doing your own thing" partly out of pleasure, partly because acceptance of differences conduces to flexible thinking and partly because some experiments may turn out to have continuing value.

At the very least, social experiments can be seen as unmistakable indications of where society-as-it-is has developed flaws or inadequacies. We might glance at a few examples of areas where the old mythology is facing challenge in order to see what an objective view of myth can tell us about them. Take the trend to communal living and the appearance of encounter groups as an instance. Clearly they represent determined, if marginal, efforts to supply substitutes for the kin and community groups of the past which used to offer shelter against a hostile world. The communes lack the stability and inner strength of clan groups, but they are evidently trying to reestablish intimacy and trust between lonely individuals.

Suppose, to go a step further, this way of life did one day become more general and lose the air of defiant opposition which sets it off from the normal course of life today. In itself, as a variant sort of domesticity, it has positive values to offer. It could substitute for the extended family as a locus for child-raising. That would solve the problems of the lonely, overworked young mother; small children would find natural playmates close around, and they would grow up with a number of adults to learn from and to take as models. Obviously, domestic and sexual arrangements within such a group would have to be worked out by the group, but there's no reason to equate communal living with promiscuity, for half a dozen couples living close together in utter monogamous fidelity could profit by communal housekeeping, cooking and child-raising. The very fact that ties between commune dwellers would be looser than family ties might be a good thing in a society, like ours, that demands a great deal of social and geographical mobility.

Existing communes have been founded, like their nineteenth-century predecessors, as retreats from the usual pattern of single-family life. But suppose that our change-habituated, flexible society accepted them as simply another mode of living suitable for some like-minded people, handy as temporary habitation for others, while those who preferred privacy and independence continued to live in nuclear families or as couples. Widening the choice of ways to live could solve social as well as psychological problems, not only for the young, but for the lonely old. Obviously any change like this won't happen quickly, but it could happen, and if it did, our social mythology might not find it too difficult to accept: religious groups have lived in communities for centuries, extended families have done so for millenniums. A society, in short, that is willing to think of itself as changing can find useful, tested patterns of living in the past which can be adapted to new needs. Those who are hit hardest by change are those who imagine that it has never happened before.

In the same way, the changes that women are demanding indicate another area where social strains have become uncomfortably great. Women want to get out of a place that has become isolated from the mainstream of life and too narrow for them to use their abilities—that's very clear. The debate over how they can get out and how far they should come rages on; but let us, for the moment, ignore the terms of the debate and consider the larger meaning of woman's demands to have greater freedom. It seems to me quite remarkably hopeful; for in a time of disruption and uncertainty, women are refusing to sit passively by in their old protected place. Man's world is in trouble, and in spite of this, women are hell-bent to get out into it and go to work on its problems! One can, of course, see this as simply silly, as a badly timed and slightly hysterical decision to join the rat race. Or one can see it, more encouragingly, as a hardheaded refusal to put up any longer with vicarious living, a determination to find out what's going on out in the world even if the experience is not all rewarding.

Whatever the motive, foolish or admirable, unless women do move out and take action in the world they won't know how to act at all. Assume that social, economic and political processes need changing. It's impossible to change them with any hope of success unless one has some idea of how they work. How are women to find that out unless they make contact with the great machine for living that we have invented over the centuries? Just for their own sakes women are better off getting their hands dirty and their minds adjusted to technical processes than living in a world that shields them from things they need to know. And if our world needs mending, all of us, male and female, conservatives and revolutionaries, will be better off acting in terms of real political processes and economic events bound up in the troubled situation than in arguing about the fantasies of myth. What's more, social change that doesn't allow for its effect on women may have unforeseen results and produce unexpected difficulties.

Thus, it was only after the great move to the suburbs had lasted for some time that anyone stopped to wonder about possible negative effects on the family. Overcrowding in the cities drove people out, of course, but many went in the grip of a rather unrealistic dream of achieving the good life and natural freedom in the country. What they achieved instead (and, ironically, at a time when the gospel of family togetherness was being fervently preached) was a greater split in the family than that which had already existed. I noted, in Chapter 13, that the end of work of economic value done within the household cut children as well as women off from knowing much about the way things happen in the external world. Suburban living intensified this. The day-long absence of the husband and father and the isolation of children and mother in a purely residential area raised the barrier between generations higher because the world of work became utterly invisible and its imperatives incomprehensible.

The Moynihan report, *The Negro Family,* dealing with life in the black ghettos, reported a situation there of fatherless families cut off from the mainstream of economic life and different in structure from social norms.[2] In Moynihan's opinion, they tended to reproduce themselves in a continuing process which ensured that deprivation and abnormal living patterns would be handed on from generation to generation. The universal applicability of this finding has been challenged and its conclusions disputed, but the endemic breakdown in what is taken to be the orthodox family pattern remains clear. If we now look at Suburbia with the Moynihan report in our heads, we can see that middle-class "normative" families, fleeing the city and its threats, have converted themselves unwittingly into the same sort of family-with-an-absent-father that was reckoned as highly disruptive of social structure when it occurred in the slums.

No doubt the women who made the move to the suburbs concurred in it, or most of them did; but in fact it was a move based on a view of woman's role as being pretty well nonexistent outside the family. It accepted a picture of the world as divided between man, the breadwinner, and woman, the homemaker. As we know, this puts the children outside the world of work, on the woman's side of the line. Should we, then, be quite so surprised as we are that some middle-class young people don't take work seriously and find that an expressive, emotional way of life, seen in our social

mythology as typically feminine, is the one they prefer? Should
we be quite so astonished at their willingness to substitute a private, seemingly controllable drug-world where one can find satisfaction and relief at will for an unknown, external world of event
and striving whose laws are strange to them, whose demands seem
threatening and whose rewards have no attraction?

The drug business is perhaps the strongest indication of all that
social problems are affecting private lives in ways that disturb and
baffle us because they are unresponsive to traditional approaches.
Our first attempt to deal with the problem is to see it as a crime
and punish those who use drugs. This doesn't work very well. Our
next effort is to convince drug users, rationally, that the use of
these substances is an illness that can be cured. That doesn't seem
to work either. The dangers of drug-taking (including punishment)
are perfectly clear, probably clearer to those who take drugs than
to those who don't: the former know they risk arrest and they see
the unpleasant effects of addiction both in themselves and in those
who share the habit. But the dangers don't put them off.[3]

May I suggest that since neither the mythic, "This is a crime"
approach nor the rational, "This is an illness" approach seems to
help, we try to use a knowledge of social mythology in looking at
the drug problem? If we drop our foregone conclusions and simply
regard the situation as it exists, we observe that an increasing
number of people, and particularly an increasing number of young
people, find that the pleasures and satisfactions provided by drugs
offset the dangers and the physical distress that drugs subject
them to. Those who lose themselves in this fantasyland are telling
us, even at a considerable price, that fantasy is preferable to the
reality they have contact with. And this suggests, as does our
present intense concentration on sexual pleasure, that our ordinary
life is distinctly lacking in immediate emotional rewards and joyful goals, that the world as it is today is hard to find a place in and
very stingy with the pleasures that it offers. This is the emotional
message that drug use carries.

No attempt to deal with the problem without seeing it in this
context is going to produce lasting or widespread results. Unless
we understand that drug use has a social aspect and is a response
to the inadequate and indeed crippling kind of life offered to
many people today and, at the same time, is evidence of a dy-

304   ELIZABETH JANEWAY

namic psychological urge to find the emotional reward denied by
that life, our approach to it will be inadequate. I believe that the
concept of "social mythology" shows us how to put these two
aspects together, so that we give full weight to both the real need
and the inappropriate response. It doesn't offer a solution, but it
tells us something about the kind of solution that's needed. Drug
use is very old in the history of the world and very widespread.
Sometimes the enhancement of life it offers has been made part of
religious practice, as with the soma of the gods in ancient India,
or with peyote among the Navajos today. Sometimes, like coca in
Peru, drugs have been used to make backbreaking labor bearable.

Today's suddenly stepped-up drug use, consequently, doesn't
just indicate an area of social strain, it points to a profound lack
in our culture of other sources of joy. The old pattern is failing us
here in a general way. The intensity of the rewards offered people
is growing less, the significance of life as a whole is losing its
weight. I think we must conclude that the drive toward a new
mythology is more than a negative reaction against what exists.
It is also a demand for new ways for feeling happiness through
bodily action, new access to the extension and interpretation of
life which art offers, new depths of shared experience in work
toward new goals, new connections with a reality that reaches
beyond the personal. Certainly drug use is a bad way to arrive at
these aims (though our old social patterns have long included
alcohol as a drug-of-choice to blur pain and salve discontent) because it is a method that changes nothing except the temporary
reactions of the user. But the acceptance of new drugs and the
increase in their use offers a direct warning that our patterns of
life are losing their ability to explain and justify the world and,
therefore, to attract loyalty. Our mythology neither gives nor even
promises enough to hold its constituency.

The fact that our lives need refreshment doesn't mean that it is
going to come about quickly or easily. Only mythic thinking
expects quick solutions. In the area of life with which we have
been particularly concerned, Yin and Yang still divide the world
between them and the old myths still justify the barrier between
man's world and woman's place. Neither logic nor compulsion
will get rid of that barrier for it is based on feelings that are un-
reachable by either approach. This is especially true today when

the old masculine virtues of strength, daring, physical courage and the ability to act quickly and decisively are failing to bring the rewards and the success they used to. "Men," wrote David McClelland of Harvard, expressing the traditional view, "are interested in things and women in people." [4] If so, men are in trouble, for command over things by physical skills has largely been made over to machines. Dealing with people, contrariwise, is becoming increasingly vital. Not only is it needed to manage the social strains apparent today, but if we are to win a new sort of command over things by commanding and correcting our deteriorating environment, we have to begin by dealing with people, for we must persuade groups within our society to sacrifice their immediate needs to general, long-term goals.

One might describe these changes as the tendency for woman's place and role to expand and take over man's world: to feminize it, as the first women's movement aimed to do. When we look at the situation this way, we see that men are being pressured from within by women's increased freedom in personal relations and particularly by the control over their lives which the Pill has given them. In addition, men are being confronted by external situations that demand shifts in the way they look at themselves, shifts that seem to threaten their masculinity. The more they prize their maleness (and if that is all they have to cling to, they will prize it highly—just as women in the same position prize their mother role highly and cling to their children), the more such changes appear to threaten degradation and humiliation, the more they are seen as destructive.

Angry reactions grow out of this internal malaise, this fear of the growing strength of women unchecked by the traditional limits placed on them in the past. It is almost too easy to find examples of aggressive male fantasies in recent fiction (as Kate Millett and Mary Ellmann have done) and equally easy to find masochistic female fantasies which are quite as disconcerting: Joan Didion and Lois Gould, for instance, call for analysis as much as does Norman Mailer. But in all such cases, the emotions which power these fantasies of male attacks on women, of sexual rage and sexual submission, should not be dismissed as nonsensical illogic. Exposing them will disprove or discredit them only to those who don't feel the emotions described in such works. The writers whom Ellmann and Millett attack are neither stupid nor inept. If D. H. Lawrence,

Henry Miller and Norman Mailer tell us that men feel anger and
fear for women we'd better believe them. These are mythic emotions, but that should warn us not to think that they can be argued
down. To imagine that they can is also an example of mythic thinking, this time the sort that angry women fall into.

It is more illuminating all around to take, once more, Erik Erikson's advice on exploring myth: "It is useless to try to show that it
has no basis in fact; nor to claim that its fiction is fake and nonsense. . . . To study a myth critically . . . means to analyze its images and themes." If we do that, we find that Mailer himself gives
us a fine and perceptive delineation of exactly that source of male
fear which I have called the myth of female power. He is replying
(in the March 1971 issue of *Harper's Magazine*) to Kate Millett's
dissection of Henry Miller's work in her *Sexual Politics* [5]:

Miller (he writes) "captured something in the sexuality of men
as it had never been seen before, precisely that it was man's sense
of awe before women, his dread of her position one step closer to
eternity (for in that step were her powers) which made men
detest women, revile them, humiliate them, defecate symbolically
upon them, do everything to reduce them so one might dare to
enter them and take pleasure of them. . . . So do men look to destroy every quality in a woman which will give her the powers of a
male, for she is in their eyes already armed with the power that she
brought them forth, and that is a power beyond measure—the
earliest etchings of memory go back to that woman between whose
legs they were conceived, nurtured, and near-strangled in the
hours of birth. . . . It is not unnatural that men, perhaps a majority
of men, go through the years of their sex with women in some com-
pound detachment of lust which will enable them to be as fierce
as any female awash in the great ocean of the fuck, for as it can
appear to the man, great forces beyond his measure seem to be calling to the woman then." [6] It seems to me that we will deal with
these fears and fantasies best if we accept the fact that they are not
peculiar to either sex, but a human disability in which we all share:
the tendency to invest our emotions in stubborn belief in those
things we know that aren't so, and to cling to the mythic metaphors
of early childhood as substitutes for realistic action and the acceptance of change.

I hope that by isolating and examining the idea of social mythology as a field of force operating within and upon human events I have offered some clues to comprehending the world around us, in which the emotional drive that sustains beliefs must be taken seriously even if the beliefs themselves cannot be. Our mythology is a map of feeling which dates back, for each of us, to the earliest, most impressionable stages of life. No social structure will stand if it simply ignores the stresses shown by that map. This does not mean that we must accept the map as right, but rather that, if we seek to change it, we'll do so best if we recognize that we are contending not with disprovable facts, but with treasured emotions, with pride and desire and "age-old" dogma that seems to carry the force of instinct.

What can prevail against these myths? Not logic alone, and not compulsion, but instead an answer *in reality* to those needs which the myth answers in fantasy. Social mythology links up emotions and events in an inappropriate way, but this doesn't invalidate the drive behind it: the need, today, to find a depth of experience which illuminates the passing moment with joy and to discover, in the pattern of life itself, some convincing expression of meaning. No doubt such discoveries are in part illusory, for the superstructure of culture is always part myth; but the yearning for satisfaction, comfort and joy remains at the root of all desires, and the effort to meet its demands in reality will be able to call on powerful motivations.

We might recall that when our ancestors projected a revolution here in America, they stated its aims to be not only life and liberty, but something beyond those two, something without which they are meaningless: the pursuit of happiness. When bad times frighten us, that goal may well come to seem childishly absurd, the daydream of a halcyon golden age. It isn't though, and the proof lies in the stubborn desires that sustain our myths. They stand as evidence of our determined pursuit of happiness. Can we detach this drive from the brittle and ineffective structure of fantasy and turn it outward toward the multiplex crisis we face?

NOTES

Epigraph. Langer, Susanne K., "The Growing Center of Knowledge," in *Philosophical Sketches*. Baltimore: Johns Hopkins Press, 1962. Page 147.

CHAPTER 1

1. Erik Erikson discusses this experiment most fully in *Childhood and Society*, 2nd edition, New York: W. W. Norton, 1963, pages 97–108. But is is also drawn on in later books. See *Identity, Youth and Crisis*, New York: W. W. Norton, 1968, pages 268–274, for particular reference to feminine roles.
2. For a presentation of psychological tests and conclusions drawn from them, see David McClelland, "Wanted: A New Self-Image for Women," in *The Woman in America*, Lifton, Robert Jay, ed. Boston: Houghton Mifflin Company, 1965. Pages 174–184.
3. Advertisement, *The New York Times Magazine*, June 8, 1969.
4. McClelland, *op. cit.*, page 187.
5. Ariès, Philippe, *Centuries of Childhood*. New York: Vintage Books (Random House), 1965. Page 10.
6. Bridenbaugh, Carl, *Vexed and Troubled Englishmen*. New York: Oxford University Press, 1968. Page 70.
7. *Ibid.*, page 72.
8. *Ibid.*, page 135.
9. Saalman, Howard, *Medieval Cities*. New York: George Braziller, 1968. Page 39.
10. Cornelisen, Ann, *Torregreca*. Boston: Little, Brown and Company, 1969. An Atlantic Monthly Press Book. Pages 196, 194.
11. Lewis, Oscar, *La Vida*. New York: Random House, 1966. Page 5.
12. Bridenbaugh, *op. cit.*, page 51.
13. Dick, Oliver Lawson, ed., *Aubrey's Brief Lives*. Ann Arbor: University of Michigan Press, 1957. Pages 144–145.
14. Tawney, R. H., *The Agrarian Problem in the 16th Century*. London, 1912. Page 233. (Quoted in Bridenbaugh, *op. cit.*, page 86.)
15. Tudor life at Barton's End is described in Ordish, George, *The Living House*. Philadelphia: J. B. Lippincott, 1960. Chapters 1 and 2.
16. For Alice de Bryene's house management, see Bennett, H. S., *Six Medieval Men and Women*. Cambridge, England: Cambridge University Press, 1955. Page 111.
17. *Ibid.*, p 113.
18. Notestein, Wallace, "The English Woman, 1580–1650," in *Studies in Social History*, Plumb, J. H., ed. London: Longmans Green and Company, 1955. Page 94. For merchant life in medieval cties, see also Saalman, *op. cit.*; Origo, Iris, *The Merchant of Prato*. New York: Alfred A. Knopf, 1957; and Kraus, Henry, *The Living Theatre of Medieval Art*. Bloomington: Indiana University Press, 1967. Much material exists, but these are vivid and readable accounts.

19. The Geneva Bible and Hooker, *The Laws of Ecclesiastical Polity*, are quoted in Bridenbaugh, *op. cit.*, page 32.
20: Ariès, *op. cit.*, pages 398–399.
21. Figures on working women from *Bulletin of the Bureau of Labor Statistics*, Report 120. Figures for March 1969.
22. Keniston, Kenneth, *The Uncommitted*. New York: Harcourt, Brace and World, 1965. Pages 276, 278.
23. Laing, Ronald D., *The Politics of Experience*. New York: Ballantine Books, Inc., 1968. Pages 88, 87.
24. *Bulletin of the Bureau of Labor Statistics, op. cit.*

CHAPTER 2

1. Erikson, *Childhood and Society, op. cit.*, page 45.
2. *Ibid.*, pages 327–328.
3. Nabokov, Vladimir, *Speak, Memory*. New York: G. P. Putnam's Sons, 1966. Page 275.

CHAPTER 3

1. Ginzberg, Eli, *Life Styles of Educated Women*. New York: Columbia University Press, 1966. Page 7.
2. Miller, Merle, "Marriage à la Mode," in *Women Today*, Bragdon, Elizabeth, ed. Indianapolis: The Bobbs Merrill Company, 1953.
3. Quotes from The Inquiring Fotographer (sic), *The New York Daily News*, November 12, 1969, and December 28, 1969.
4. The government survey of the Aid to Dependent Children Program was cited in *The New York Times*, April 12, 1970.
5. McGinley, Phyllis, *Sixpence in Her Shoe*. New York: The Macmillan Company, 1964. Page 47.
6. Malinowski, Bronislaw, *Myth in Primitive Psychology*, 1926, quoted in Eliade, Mircea, *Myth and Reality*. New York: Harper & Row, 1963. Page 20.
7. Thomas, Dylan, "Fern Hill," in *Dylan Thomas*. New York: New Directions, 1946. Page 80.
8. Bettelheim, Bruno, *The Empty Fortress*. New York: The Free Press, 1967. Page 14.
9. Cohn, Norman, *The Pursuit of the Millennium*. London: Secker and Warburg, 1957. Page 255. The quotation is from Thomas Müntzer, the German Anabaptist and millenary preacher, 1489–1525.
10. The report on the Cornerstone Project meeting appeared in *The New York Times*, July 30, 1967.

CHAPTER 4

1. Nin, Anais, *Diary, 1931–1934*. New York: The Swallow Press, Harcourt, Brace and World, Inc., 1966. Page 53.
2. Campbell, Joseph, *The Masks of God: Primitive Mythology*. New York: The Viking Press, 1959. Page 315.
3. *Ibid.*, page 325.
4. Graziosi, Paolo, *Paleolithic Art*. New York: McGraw-Hill, 1960. Page 60.
5. Sandford, Mrs. E., *Woman in Her Social and Domestic Character*. London,

1831. Page 13. Quoted in Taylor, Gordon Rattray, *The Angel-Makers*. London: Heinemann, 1958. Page 97.

6. Lundberg, Ferdinand, and Farnham, Marynia, *Modern Woman: The Lost Sex*. New York: Harper Brothers, 1947. Pages 237 ff.

7. Canetti, Elias, *Crowds and Power*. New York: The Viking Press, 1966. Pages 221, 222.

8. Lundberg and Farnham, *op. cit.*, page 127.

9. McGinley, *op. cit.*, page 14.

10. Lifton, Robert Jay, "Woman as Knower," in Lifton, ed., *op. cit.*, page 44.

CHAPTER 5

1. St. Augustine's sermon to a Council of Bishops in Carthage, May 5, 418, is quoted in Auerbach, Erich, *Literary Language and Its Public in Late Latin Antiquity and in the Middle Ages*. Bollingen Series LXXIV. New York: Pantheon Books, 1965. Page 29.

2. For the meaning of the hunt to primitive man, illuminating discussions of cave art will be found in Giedion, S., *The Eternal Present: The Beginnings of Art*. Bollingen Series XXXV. 6. 1. New York: Pantheon Books, 1962; and La Barre, Weston, *The Ghost Dance*. New York: Doubleday and Company, 1970. Chapter XIII.

3. For discussion and representations of the Great Goddess at Catal Hüyük, see Mellart, James, *Catal Hüyük*. New York: McGraw-Hill, 1967.

4. Eliade, Mircea, *op. cit.*, page 188.

5. Reage, Pauline, *The Story of O*. New York: Grove Press, 1966.

6. Marcus, Steven, *The Other Victorians*. New York: Basic Books, 1966. Pages 273–274.

7. *Ibid.*, page 272.

CHAPTER 6

1. Parsons, Talcott, "The Superego and the Theory of Social Systems," in Parsons, Talcott, Bales, Robert F., and Shils, Edward, *Working Papers in The Theory of Action*. New York: The Free Press, 1953. Page 18.

2. Parsons, Talcott, *The Social System*. New York: The Free Press, 1951. Page 25.

3. On the role of the shaman, see Giedion, *op. cit.*, and La Barre, *op. cit.*

4. Goffman, Erving, *Encounters*. Indianapolis: The Bobbs Merrill Company, Inc., 1961. Page 87.

5. *Ibid.*, pages 87–88.

6. Friedan, Betty, *The Feminine Mystique*. New York: W. W. Norton, 1963.

7. For feminine role as advantageous, see Goodman, Paul, *Growing Up Absurd*. New York: Random House, 1960. Page 13.

8. Laslett, Peter, *The World We Have Lost*. London: Methuen and Co. Ltd., 1965. Page 21.

9. For figures on households in Goodnestone, Kent, April 1676, see *Ibid.*, page 64.

10. Goffman, *op. cit.*, note, page 102.

CHAPTER 7

1. Pehrson, Robert N., *The Social Organization of the Marri Baluch*. Chicago: Aldine Publishing Company, 1966. Page 59.

2. McClelland, *op. cit.*, pages 187–188.

3. Parsons, *Superego,* in Parsons, Bales and Shils, *op. cit.,* page 21.
4. Erikson, Erik, *Identity, Youth and Crisis, op. cit.,* pages 270–271, 273.
5. *Ibid.,* page 290.
6. Benz, Margaret G., "United States," in *Women in the Modern World,* Patai, Raphael, ed. New York: The Free Press, 1967. Page 509.
7. Ahmed, Shereen Aziz, "Pakistan," in Patai, ed., *op. cit.,* page 58.

CHAPTER 8

1. Bard, Bernard, Column, "The Blackboard," in *New York Post,* August 17, 1968.
2. Freedman, Richard, "Lines from a Ladies' Seminary," in *Book World, The Washington Post,* August 18, 1968.
3. Erikson, *Childhood and Society, op. cit.,* page 286.
4. Watson, James, *The Double Helix.* New York: Atheneum, 1968. Page 20.
5. *Ibid.,* pages 89–90.

CHAPTER 9

1. Friedenberg, Edgar Z., *Coming of Age in America.* New York: Random House, 1965. Pages 47–48.
2. De Beauvoir, Simone, *The Second Sex.* New York: Alfred A. Knopf, 1953.
3. Podhoretz, Norman, *Making It.* New York: Random House, 1967. Page 98. For isolation of the poor and inability to act for themselves, see Willie, Charles V., "Two Men and Their Families," and Haggstrom, Warren C., "Can the Poor Transform the World?" Both are included in *Among the People,* edited by Irwin Deutscher and Elizabeth J. Thompson. New York: Basic Books, 1968. For differential incidence of mental disease among the poor and the well-to-do, see Hollingshead, August B., and Redlich, Frederick C., *Social Class and Mental Illness.* New York: John Wiley and Sons, Inc., 1958. Pages 173, 174, 176, 241 ff.
4. Raverat, Gwen, *Period Piece.* New York: W. W. Norton, 1953. Page 129.
5. Reisman, David, "Two Generations," in Lifton, ed., *op. cit.,* pages 91–92.
6. McClelland, *op. cit.,* page 187.
7. Anderson, Patrick, *The Presidents' Men.* New York: Doubleday and Company, 1968. Page 154.
8. For a perceptive discussion of shame as a psychological force, see Lynd, Helen Merrill, *On Shame and the Search for Identity.* New York: Harcourt Brace and Company, 1958.
9. Acton, William, *The Functions and Disorders of the Reproductive Organs.* London, 1857. Quoted in Marcus, *op. cit.,* page 31.
10. Letter to *The New York Times Magazine* (Mrs. P. J. Hagerstrom), March 24, 1968.

CHAPTER 10

1. Field, M. J., *Search for Security.* London: Faber and Faber, 1960. Pages 36, 39.
2. Lifton, *op. cit.,* page 41.
3. Huizinga, Johan, *The Waning of the Middle Ages.* London: Edward Arnold, 1924.
4. For a discussion of the play factor in culture, see Huizinga, Johan, *Homo Ludens.* Boston: The Beacon Press, 1955.
5. Bettelheim, *op. cit.,* page 71.

6. Trevor-Roper, Hugh, "The Witch Craze," *Encounter*, London, May and June 1967.
7. Epstein, Scarlett, "A Sociological Analysis of Witch Beliefs," in *Magic, Witchcraft and Curing*, Middleton, John, ed. New York: The Natural History Press, Page 144.
8. Laing, Ronald D., *Self and Others*. New York: Pantheon Books, 1969. Page 122.
9. *Ibid.*, pages 124–125.

CHAPTER 11

1. Langer, *op. cit.*, pages 145–146.
2. For a brief presentation of Eliade's views on myth, see Eliade, *op. cit.*
3. Kinsey, Alfred C., Pomeroy, Wardell B., and Martin, Clyde E., *Sexual Behavior in the Human Male*. Philadelphia: W. B. Saunders Co., 1948; Kinsey, Alfred C., *et al*, *Sexual Behavior in the Human Female*. Philadelphia: W. B. Saunders Co., 1953.
4. Masters, William H., and Johnson, Virginia E., *Human Sexual Response*. Boston: Little, Brown and Co., 1966.
5. Parsons, Talcott, "The American Family," in Parsons, Talcott, and Bales, Robert F., *Family, Socialization and Interaction Process*. New York: The Free Press, 1955. Page 16.

CHAPTER 12

1. Keniston, *op. cit.*, pages 294–295.
2. For an objective history and assessment of the feminist movement, see O'Neill, William L., *Everyone Was Brave*. Chicago: Quadrangle Books, 1969. Also, Smith, Page, *Daughters of the Promised Land*. Boston: Little, Brown and Co., 1970. Chapters 7, 11 and 18.
3. Minturn, Leigh, and Lambert, William W., ed., *Mothers of Six Cultures*. New York: John Wiley and Sons, Inc. Pages 189–190.
4. *Ibid.*, pages 191 and 193.
5. Bettelheim, Bruno, *The Children of the Dream*. New York: Macmillan, 1969.
6. Keniston, *op. cit.*, page 113.
7. *Ibid.*, page 294.
8. Minturn and Lambert, *op. cit.*, page 198.

CHAPTER 13

1. Orden, Susan R., and Bradburn, Norman M., "Working Wives and Marriage Happiness," *The American Journal of Sociology*, January 1969, page 395.
2. Wylie, Laurence, *Chanzeaux, A Village in Anjou*. Cambridge, Massachusetts: Harvard University Press, 1966. Page 100.
3. Orden and Bradburn, *op. cit.*, page 395.
4. Levenson, Edgar A. Quoted in the *New York Post*, November 11, 1967, page 59.

CHAPTER 14

1. Sexton, Patricia Cayo, "Speaking for the Working-Class Wife," *Harper's Magazine*, October 1962, page 130.
2. *Ibid.*, page 130.

3. The condition of working women in Victorian England is most vividly documented in Henry Mayhew's *London Labor and the London Poor*. Accessible is an excerpted edition, edited by Peter Quennell, *Mayhew's London*. London: Spring Books, no date. For the period of the nineties, see also *Charles Booth's London*, Fried, Albert, and Elman, Richard M., eds. New York: Pantheon, 1968. For the Edwardian period, an excellent brief study of working-class conditions and homes can be found in *Edwardian England*, edited by Simon Nowell-Smith. London, Oxford University Press, 1964.

4. Parsons, *The American Family, op. cit.*, page 19.

CHAPTER 15

1. Joyce, James, *Ulysses*. New York: Random House, Modern Library, 1946. Page 764.

2. Ecklestein, quoted from *The New York Times*, July 30, 1967.

3. Amis, Kingsley, *I Want It Now*. New York: Harcourt, Brace and World, 1969.

4. Pehrson, *op. cit.*, page 59.

5. *Ibid.*, page 60.

6. *Ibid.*, pages 61, 65, 63.

7. *Ibid.*, pages 64, 69.

CHAPTER 16

1. Auden, W. H., *For the Time Being*. New York: Random House, 1944. Page 110.

2. Parsons, Talcott, "Age and Sex in the Social Structure," in *The Family: Its Structure and Function*, Coser, Rose Lamb, ed. New York: St. Martin's Press, 1964. Page 261.

3. *Ibid.*, page 261.

4. *Ibid.*

5. Gagnon, John H., and Simon, William, "Perspectives on the Sexual Scene," in *The Sexual Scene*, Gagnon and Simon, ed. Chicago: Aldine, 1970. Pages 10, 11.

6. Gavron, Hannah, *The Captive Wife*. London: Routledge and Kegan Paul, 1966. Pages 114, 119.

CHAPTER 17

1. Bohannon, Paul, and Middleton, John, ed., *Marriage, Family and Residence*. New York: The Natural History Press, 1968. Page IX.

2. Orden and Bradburn, *op. cit.*, page 398.

3. *Ibid.*, page 400.

4. *Ibid.*, page 407.

5. Quotations are from personal communications to the author or notes taken from an anonymous survey. All are in the author's possession. They appeared in the *Atlantic Monthly* for February 1970, which printed an earlier version of this chapter. Copyright is held by the author.

6. The Fitzgerald material is copious, but new insight is offered into the relationship between Scott and Zelda by Nancy Milford's biography, *Zelda*. New York: Harper and Row, 1970.

7. Personal communication to author. See footnote 5 above.

8. *Ibid.*

9. London, *The Sunday Times*, December 7, 1969.

CHAPTER 18

1. Langer, *op. cit.*, page 178.
2. For West African "progressive marriages," see Jean-Claude Muller, "Preferential Marriage among the Rukuba of Benue-Plateau State, Nigeria," *American Anthropologist*, December 1969.
3. Gagnon and Simon, *op. cit.*, page 12.
4. For Effie Ruskin's marriage, see the two volumes of Ruskin letters edited by Mary Lutyens, *Young Mrs. Ruskin in Venice*, New York: Vanguard Press, 1965, and *Millais and the Ruskins*, London: Murray, 1967.
5. Bohannon and Middleton, *op. cit.*, page IX.
6. Langer, *op. cit.*, page 178.
7. For an interesting discussion of attitudes among pilots in the Second World War, see Douglas D. Bond, *The Love and Fear of Flying*. New York: International Universities Press, 1952. Dr. Bond was Director of Psychiatry, 1st. C.M.E., 8th Air Force, 1943–1945, and, later, Consultant in Psychiatry, Headquarters, Army Air Forces.
8. Blythe, Ronald, *Akenfield*. New York: Pantheon Books, 1969.
9. Wylie, Laurance, *op. cit.*, and *Village in the Vaucluse*. Cambridge, Massachusetts: Harvard University Press, 1960.
10. Fel, Edit, and Hofer, Tamas, *Proper Peasants*. Chicago: Aldine Publishing Company, 1969.

CHAPTER 19

1. Minturn and Lambert, *op. cit.*, pages 189–190.
2. Keniston, *op. cit.*, pages 294–295.
3. Masters, William H., and Johnson, Virginia E., *Human Sexual Inadequacy*. Boston: Little, Brown and Co., 1970. Pages 12, 10.
4. Grossman, Edward, "In Pursuit of the American Woman," *Harper's Magazine*, February 1970, pages 68, 69.

CHAPTER 20

1. Lévi-Strauss, Claude, *The Raw and the Cooked*. New York: Harper and Row, 1969. Page 13.
2. Moynihan, Daniel P., *The Negro Family*. Washington: U.S. Dept. of Labor, Office of Policy Planning and Research, 1965.
3. An interesting study of the sociology of marijuana use (at a time when it was less frequent than at present and therefore a better guide to patterns of deviant behavior) can be found in Becker, Howard S., *Outsiders*. Glencoe: The Free Press, 1963.
4. McClelland, *op. cit.*, pages 177–178.
5. Millett, Kate, *Sexual Politics*. New York: Doubleday, 1970.
6. Mailer, Norman, "The Prisoner of Sex," *Harper's Magazine*, March 1971, page 66.

INDEX

Acton, Lord, 106, 107
Acton, William, 116, 311
Adams, Sherman, 113–114
Adultery, 210, 221–222
Ahmed, Shereen Aziz, 311
Akenfield (Blythe), 267, 314
Albee, Edward, 277
American Family, The (Parsons), 189, 312, 313
Amis, Kingsley, 204, 313
Anaximander, 36
Anderson, Patrick, 113, 311
Ariès, Philippe, 13–14, 21, 23, 25, 76, 308, 309
Art, myth and, 29–31
Aubrey, John, 18
Auden, W. H., 137, 209, 210, 313
Auerbach, Eric, 310
Augustine, St., 59, 310

Bales, Robert F., 310, 311, 312
Bar mitzvah ceremony, 51
Bard, Bernard, 97, 311
Barton, John, 18, 19
Barton, Mary, 18, 19, 20
Barton, Richard, 18, 19
Bear, The (Faulkner), 263
Beauvoir, Simone de, 108, 311
Becker, Howard S., 314
Bennett, H. S., 19, 308
Benz, Margaret G., 311
Bettelheim, Bruno, 43, 127, 156–159, 309, 311, 312
Bewick, Thomas, 109
Bierce, Ambrose, 233
Billings, Josh, 10
Bitch, role of, 199–200, 205
Blythe, Ronald, 267, 314
Bohannon, Paul, 227, 228, 255, 313, 314
Bond, Douglas D., 314
Bradburn, Norman M., 163, 169, 235, 236, 312, 313
Bragdon, Elizabeth, 309
Bridenbaugh, Carl, 16, 308, 309
Bryene, Alice de, 18–19, 308
Burke, Kenneth, 73, 87, 90
Burns, Robert, 22
Byron, Lord, 199

Campbell, Joseph, 48–49, 309
Campbell, Mrs. Patrick, 258
Canetti, Elias, 54, 57, 310
Career women, 256
Castration, fear of, 286, 287
Catal Hüyük, 61, 310
Catherine the Great, Queen (Russia), 123
Ceres, 61
Change, acceptance of, 138–146
Chaucer, Geoffrey, 16, 17
Chiang Kai-shek, 137
Childhood and Society (Erikson), 28, 99, 308, 309, 311
Children of the Dream, The (Bettelheim), 156, 312
Children of working mothers, 187–190
Christianity, 57, 59
Christina, Queen (Sweden), 123
Cohn, Norman, 309
Coitus, 289–290
Communal living, 300
Copernicus, 261
Corn Mother, 61
Cornelisen, Ann, 16–17, 308
Cornerstone Project, 45, 46, 309
Coser, Rose Lamb, 313
Courtship, 202
Cowper, William, 23
Crick, Francis, 102–103
Crick, Odile, 102–103
Crowds and Power (Canetti), 54, 310
Curie, Madame, 123

Darwin, Charles, 40
Darwin, Gwen, *see* Raverat, Gwen
Daydreams, 223
Decision-making, 88
Demeter, 61
Deutscher, Irwin, 311
Dick, Oliver Lawson, 308
Didactic formula, 35, 36
Dilke, Sir Charles, 222
Divorce, 200, 222–223, 228, 248, 276
Dostoevski, Feodor, 195
Double Helix, The (Watson), 102, 311
Drugs, use of, 46, 62, 273, 303–304
Dryden, John, 230
Du Bellay, Joachim, 22